BY THE RIVERS OF BABYLON

BY THE RIVERS OF BABYLON

BLUEPRINT FOR A CHURCH IN EXILE

ROBERT P. HOCH

Fortress Press
Minneapolis

BY THE RIVERS OF BABYLON

Blueprint for a Church in Exile

Cover image: Illegal immigrants waiting for dark to cross the border into the U.S. © LYNN JOHNSON/National Geographic Stock

Cover design: Laurie Ingram

Library of Congress Cataloging-in-Publication Data is available

Print ISBN 978-0-8006-9853-9

eBook ISBN 978-1-4514-3850-5

The paper used in this publication meets the minimum requirements of American National Standard for Information Sciences — Permanence of Paper for Printed Library Materials, ANSI Z329.48-1984.

Manufactured in the U.S.A.

This book was produced using PressBooks.com, and PDF rendering was done by PrinceXML.

CONTENTS

Acknowledgments

It is fitting that a book on communities living in exilic conditions would only be possible through frequent and generous expressions of hospitality. Dr. Jeffery Bullock, president; Dr. Bradley Longfield, dean; and the Board of Trustees of the University of Dubuque Theological Seminary gave me a semester-long sabbatical for research and writing. My colleagues at UDTS provided stimulating conversation as the book moved through its different stages. Across the street, Wartburg Theological Seminary offered me office space as well as a forum to talk about my work as it was in progress. Each of these communities offered me gifts of hospitality in the form of sabbatical, physical space, intellectual collegiality, and sympathetic hearings, all of which helped to bring the work to completion.

Seminary students, too, played their part, particularly in worship classes, where they listened patiently as their sometimes-scattered professor knit together ideas, images, and implications for the life of the church in the twenty-first century. Their questions and open minds provided fertile and playful space for me as I spoke out loud what eventually would find its way into print. Significantly, I began writing this book around the same time I began a DMin cohort, serving alongside Dr. Jin S. Kim, pastor of the Church of All Nations in the Minneapolis/St. Paul area. The cohort included Revs. Enna Antunez, Maggie Hayward, Matthew Reeves, Ryan Mills, Tracy Edwards, Harlan Gillespie, Joo Kim, and Jennifer Jennings. The cohort not only read early drafts of the manuscript but also helped me to continue to digest themes represented in this book within a larger field of pastoral concern and scholarly labor. While many despair of the life and witness of the church in North America, this small but gifted community of pastors gives me ample reason to feel hope for our future life together.

Unlike many books, this one does not primarily depend on citing published works (although it does) but instead partakes of the cup and fellowship of living communities, communities that graciously opened their "chapters and seasons" to my reading eye and listening ear. They were also unfailingly generous as they, in turn, read and responded to what my "listening ear" had tried, imperfectly, to share as a story for others.

As a writer, I felt on the one hand deeply blessed to be a guest in such communities but also on the other a deep burden to represent the wisdom and richness of their respective vocations. These communities included the pastor of Church of the Indian Fellowship in Puyallup, Washington, Rev. Irvin Porter, and the Talmaks Nez Perce Presbyterian Camp Fellowship near Craigmont, Idaho; the community of Frontera de Cristo in Douglas and Agua Prieta, along the border between the United States and Mexico, especially Rev. Mark Adams and Miriam Adams, two people for whom the night is always young; Rev. John Fife, pastor emeritus of Southside Presbyterian Church in Tucson, Arizona, who introduced me to the spirituality of the Altar Valley and the migrant path; and the community at Cherith Brook Catholic Worker, Kansas City, Missouri, particularly Eric and Jodi Garbison, their children, Henri and Diana, and Nick Pickrell, Josh Armfield, Jeffrey New, Elisabeth Rutschman, Paul Newman, and Allison Rozga. I often felt like an infant among giants in the faith as each one gave witness to God's shalom with joy, courage, humility, and zest. I feel honored to be able to say that I was a student in these classrooms and that they, as well as many others I don't have space to name, were my teachers. With a student's heart, I say to each of them, named and unnamed, "Thank you."

I would be remiss if I did not mention David Lott, a good friend and fine editor, who shepherded the early stages of this book. I am also grateful to the careful editing of the team at Fortress Press. There is nothing quite like having one's work considered and mentored by a group of very smart and exceptionally well-read people. Their patience with my questions as well as the sometimes slow progress of writing is something for which I will continue to give thanks.

Finally, and not least, I give thanks to Rebecca, my best friend in life. You bore two babies during the time that it took me to write this book. You listened as I returned home frustrated with my writing or, alternatively, exulting in a good day. You read many, many versions of the manuscript and listened patiently, talking with me about the ideas and the experiences represented in its pages. You often did all this while nursing. Thank you for your love, patience, generosity, and grace.

I dedicate this book to you.

Salvaging Exile

*Why did Christ heal the sick and suffering
if he didn't consider such external
conditions important? Why is the kingdom
of God equated with the deaf hear, the
blind see? . . . And where do we get the
incredible presumption to spiritualize these
things that Christ saw and did very
concretely?*
*We must end this audacious, sanctimonious
spiritualization of the gospel. Take it as it
is, or hate it honestly!*

–Dietrich Bonhoeffer[1]

Exile, as we often hear it in the church, refers to a "spiritual" experience, our
sense of being "strangers in a strange land" but not *actually* strangers in a strange
land. In this book, I argue the theological language of exile is inescapably bound
up with the fleshy language of being an exile. Theologically, exile is flesh *and* it
is spirit. Exile, indeed, may signify a disruptive paradigm shift, or a felt anxiety,
or the modern sense of "homelessness," the idea that, as George Steiner puts
it, we are "monads haunted by communion."[2] While not denying the power
of those understandings, when exile comes to signify such broad and diffuse
notions of experience, it can happen that we lose sight of the actual exile. Exile
may refer to more than the exile of the body, but we must always remember
that it will never be less than the exile of the body: the body deported, the body
put into shackles, the body bruised, the body profiled, the body tortured, the
body crucified. This book takes the body, the flesh experience of exile, seriously,
which is to say, this book takes it theologically. The phenomenon of exile poses
not only a sociopolitical and economic crisis, but a contemporary ecclesiological
crisis. This book takes that crisis seriously by joining communities that live,

1. Dietrich Bonhoeffer, "Lazarus and the Rich Man," in The Collected Sermons of Dietrich
Bonhoeffer, ed. Isabel Best and trans. Douglas W. Stott, Anne Schmidt-Lange, et al. (Minneapolis:
Fortress Press, 2012), 37.

2. George Steiner, *Real Presences* (Chicago: The University of Chicago Press, 1989), 140.

worship, and witness in the borderlands of the twenty-first century, exploring their missiological and ecclesiological responses to exilic realities. But it also takes exile seriously as a societal crisis. We need to take the flesh of exile seriously, as flesh, as a problem of the economic and political body, as it is, and not as a "window" to see something else.

By and large, we do not hear the language of exile this way, as flesh and blood reality, at least not often in church on Sunday morning. This is odd. When the church speaks of exile it often speaks of exile as if it were a spiritual phenomenon primarily, as if exiles today did not exist, this despite the fact that, according to the United Nation's International Migration Report (2005), the number of people living outside the country of their natal birth (the official definition of a migrant) increased from 120 million in 1990 to 191 million in 2005;[3] despite the fact that nearly 11 million undocumented people live in the United States;[4] despite the U.S. Department of Homeland Security's official mandate to deport undocumented peoples in the United States;[5] despite the claim that, according to legal scholar and activist Michelle Alexander, the U.S. judicial and criminal justice system is growing the ranks of African Americans who cannot get jobs, escape poverty, find affordable housing, or contribute to their communities through democratic processes;[6] and despite

---

3. See "Global Migrants Reach 191 Million," BBC News, June 7, 2006, http://news.bbc.co.uk/2/hi/ americas/5054214.stm, cited by Gemma Tulud Cruz, "Expanding the Boundaries: Turning Borders into Spaces" in *Mission after Christendom: Emergent Themes in Contemporary Mission*, ed. Ogbu U. Kalu, Peter Vethanayagamony, and Edmund Kee-Fook Chia (Louisville, KY: Westminster John Knox Press, 2010).

4. Michael Hoefer, Nancy Rytina, and Bryan C. Baker, "Population Estimates: Estimates of the Unauthorized Immigrant Population Residing in the United States: January 2010," Department of Homeland Security, Office of Immigration Statistics, http://www.dhs.gov/xlibrary/assets/statistics/ publications/ois_ill_pe_2010.pdf.

5. The Immigration, Control, and Enforcement (ICE) website states the following as its mission: "To identify, arrest, and remove aliens who present a danger to national security or are a risk to public safety, as well as those who enter the United States illegally or otherwise undermine the integrity of our immigration laws and our border control efforts. ERO [Enforcement and Removal Operations] upholds America's immigration laws at, within and beyond our borders through efficient enforcement and removal operations." See ICE website at http://www.ice.gov/about/offices/enforcement-removal-operations/. At the time of my writing, the Department of Homeland Security enforces its right to deport selectively, for example targeting persons who have criminal records. Additionally, under the present administration, deportation is being delayed by two years for individuals (who meet certain criteria) who come forward. While selective deportation may be a positive development, especially if it signals progress toward legalization, by itself "selective" enforcement of deportation orders operates as an ever-present threat, the guillotine always just about to be dropped. See also Nicholas de Genova and Nathalie Peutz, "Introduction," in *The Deportation Regime: Sovereignty, Space, and the Freedom of Movement*, ed. Nicholas de Genova and Nathalie Peutz (Durham, NC: Duke University Press, 2010), 4.

the displacement of indigenous peoples within national boundaries and the exploitation of indigenous peoples and their natural resources by transnational corporations.[7]

Often, despite the long list of instances of actual exile, it exists outside the ecclesiological imagination. Churches may offer charity to exiles but do not forge their identity as an expression of the church's solidarity with the alien. As a consequence, the church may be therapeutic but not prophetic; it may bemoan its loss of institutional privilege but does not actively contribute to the formation of theologically and ecclesiologically meaningful alternatives to contemporary patterns of political, ethnic, and cultural displacement; it does not foster the new community of Christ. When churches fail to see the phenomenon of displacement as a formal feature of the global financial system, their members come to view contemporary experiences of exile as routine rather than tragic and unjust. As a result, the witness of the church falls silent and its worship, no matter how progressive or orthodox, rings false against the rising tide of multiple assaults on human dignity.

Of course, congregations often hear pastors invoke the figure of exilic experience. This, in itself, is no surprise: the sociopolitical experience of exile supplies the "signature" historical problem within much of the Old Testament whereas colonization (a form of displacement) appears in the context of the New Testament. Interpreters are confronted on either side of the biblical spine with some refraction of that theme. Beyond the text itself, in the past twenty years or so pastors have been shaped by scholarship dedicated to the exploration of the language and theology of exile. Theological titles abound with some reference to the church's experience of displacement in the twentieth and twenty-first centuries. Additionally, perhaps as a response to the Great Recession, pastors and congregations are talking more about the disenfranchised. LifeWay Research shows a significant increase among pastors who are willing to speak about the needs of the poor and who report that the congregations they serve had "mobilized its members to directly engage and care for the poor in their communities." According to the study, which was based on a survey of 1000 pastors, in 2009, just 76 percent of the pastors affirmed this statement; in 2010 that percentage increased to 85 percent; and in 2012, it increased to 90 percent.[8] This seems promising especially if those statistical

---

6. See Michelle Alexander, *The New Jim Crow: Mass Incarceration in the Age of Colorblindness* (New York: New Press, 2010).

7. See for example the chapter entitled, "Robbing the Poor to Feed the Rich," in Charles Clover, *The End of the Line: How Overfishing Is Changing the World and What We Eat* (New York: New Press, 2006), 41–53.

numbers get translated into more holistic expressions of mission, worship, and witness. Nevertheless, even with these promising developments, the language of exile often shows up in ways that are either skewed or, worse, falsifying of core identities that nurture the life of the church with authentic foretastes of the new creation inaugurated in Christ's resurrection.

Sometimes, for example, we hear the language of exile when pastors remind their flocks, "You had options today; you could have gone to the beach or spent your Sunday morning with a hot cup of coffee and the *New York Times*. But instead you came to church." This might mean, among other things, that the people of the church enjoy the luxury of options, and participating in worship is one of those options. Perhaps it means we function primarily as consumers and the church is, likewise, one product among other products on offer on a Sunday morning. It may also be a compliment to the gathered community: while they had a multitude of options, they nevertheless chose church. They are, in other words, discerning consumers. Going a little further with this message, perhaps the pastor would argue that, no, we are not consumers after all but instead the called, baptized people of God. Nevertheless, the consumerist figure for exile would be about as close to exilic reality as the congregation would ever get. Never mind that in order to be a consumer one needs an ample number of easily exploited, mostly invisible people—namely, migrants and the working poor.

This example is not far-fetched. Student preachers, not unlike their ordained counterparts, frequently invoke the language of exile as a figure for the consumer, in psychological or spiritual ways, or, quite often, to underscore the institutional church's loss of privilege or its minority status in a secular world. Preaching from Mark 1:21-28 (the story of Jesus healing the demoniac in the synagogue), one student relates an "outdoor" worship event in which someone (not a member of the church) yells aspersions during the sermon, as if to "drown out" the witness of the church. The "stage lights" were so bright that, according to the student, the voice seemed to come out of the darkness itself. In this sermon, the world and the church exist in separate and opposed universes. One community, the church, is washed in light while the other, captive to the powers of chaos and secularism, remains buried in darkness. The preacher seems to draw a clear line of demarcation between the holy and the unholy, between those who belong to God and those who clearly do not. This proves an ironic interpretation given Mark's juxtaposition of the demoniac *in* the synagogue, to

8. Ed Stetzer, "The World as God Intends" in *Sojourners* (September–October 2013): 31.

say nothing of the paradox of the reign of God drawing near to the synagogue by way of Christ's interaction with a demoniac, the very expression of exile.

A more complicated representation of exile shows up in a Lord's Day sermon based on Isa. 60:1-7, the Lord's promise to gather those who had been dispersed. Introducing the message, the preacher, a student, compares the experience of displaced people in the developing world as analogous to what the people of Israel experienced: crushed, without a national identity, longing to return home but perhaps too lost to know or remember the way. The preacher also qualifies the analogy, saying that many in the church do not have this experience. They do not "identify" with the experience of exile. Nevertheless, they do know something like exile: the experience of losing a job (fully anticipating regaining equal or even better employment), a diagnosis of cancer (adequate health care almost always assumed), or depression (usually solved with a good mixture of corporately produced medication). The experience of the majority culture frequently eclipses the actual experiences of a growing minority.

As it happens, the sermon on Isaiah 60 was shared in an urban, mostly White congregation, where a significant number of the members live outside the downtown area.[9] They "commute" to church on Sunday. They would not claim to know exile concretely, but they may identify with it figuratively, as the preacher guessed. However, this is also a church where First Nations[10] peoples worship; where first-generation immigrants, living in subsidized apartments a

9. Throughout this book, I use the term *White* to refer to Caucasian peoples in the United States. I will sometimes use "majority culture" as a loose synonym. Neither term is perfect. The term *White* points to the sense that whiteness in the United States is not simply an "ethnic" identity but also a cultural construct that introduces systemic forms of racism. More positively, in ordinary speech, it is common for minority ethnic groups to refer to Caucasians as "White people" rather than using "Anglo-Saxon" or "Euro-American"; in the context of this work I wanted to privilege the space and speech of exilic communities. When people of color casually invoke the term *White*, it refers not only to an ethnic group but also to a historical and political relationship. Among Native peoples, European colonialists were first White and then, secondarily, English or German or French. Colonialism and missions were "colored" White from the start. Nevertheless, as a term, it does have drawbacks: many Whites, especially the poor, are excluded as well as manipulated by middle-class assumptions built into whiteness. Moreover, those who self-identify as "mixed blood" (as I do) can never be completely comfortable with the determinism that frequently accompanies language about ethnicity in America. And not insignificantly, the skin of poverty—and its different hues—is an abased "ethnicity" in the United States. For this reason, I will sometimes use the term *majority culture* as I try to name the plight of those who "slip" through the cracks of ethnic determinisms.

10. In the United States, indigenous peoples are either Native Americans or Alaska Natives. The indigenous peoples of Canada use the term *First Nations*. I will use that latter term inclusively for all indigenous peoples in North America.

few blocks away, offer their tithes, pray, and sing; where a middle-aged woman shares her battle with meth addiction during congregational prayers; where a man with a felony sometimes worships; and where others work two and three jobs, at shifts throughout the day and night and at different sites across town, just so they can afford to pay for health care. It is also a place where undocumented persons (their legal status mostly unknown to the congregation) have sometimes shared their gifts and, at other times, sought out sanctuary and help in times of crisis (also mostly unknown to the congregation).

Additionally, like many congregations and their pastoral leaders, the question of how to "mobilize" and "care" for the disenfranchised in the surrounding community is a very real one for this congregation. Perhaps, however, the congregation views the concrete reality of the exile as mostly external to its primary identity, where the exile receives "help" but whose life and gifts remain separate and distinct from the church's self-understanding. I witnessed in an all too personal way how this division in the body gets reflected in ways that tear at the deepest fabric of being a human community. Each summer this same church hosts an "ice cream social" at an adjacent neighborhood park. Ostensibly, the "social" was designed to introduce the neighborhood to the church and the church members to the neighborhood. But in fact, the spirit of the social seemed more like a missional flash, without deeper purpose, to the surrounding neighborhood, a predominantly low-income and African American community.

I had come to help alongside other volunteers, but our children, like the children from the apartments, began to line up, one after another, for the ice cream. Soon, the children were coming back for seconds or perhaps thirds. Maybe the small group of volunteers was beginning to feel overwhelmed as the crowd of children grew. Whatever the reason, it wasn't long before a volunteer announced that if a child had already been through the line once, she, the volunteer, would mark the back of their hands with a marks-a-lot pen. In this way, she explained, we, the hosts, could exert some "crowd control" over the growing numbers of children. I guess it seemed reasonable enough at the time. What happened next was not intended to hurt anyone, of that I am sure. But as the children crowded around her, my heart began to sink. One after another, she swiped the pen across the backs of their hands. And then my daughter, too, offered her hand, just as the others had done. And when she did, the volunteer laughed, tousling her hair, saying, "I don't need to mark your hand. We know you!"

Was it just an accident that the volunteer marked only the hands of poor, African American children? Was it an insignificant thing, a minor mistake at most? Or was it a microcosm of a certain mentality, the predictable outcome of a congregational mindset that "helps" the poor but does not ultimately understand its life as arising from the communion Christ keeps with the crucified, the outcast, and the deported? A congregation that would recognize its own reflection but does not recognize the thirsty Christ, the welfare Christ, the profiled Christ, the drug addled Christ, the mentally ill Christ, the Christ forlorn?

When experiences of actually displaced communities shape neither the sermon nor the imagination of the congregation, the whole body, its actual and natural body, suffers diminishment. If these examples of preaching and mission are indicative of a larger pattern of interpretation, churches may imagine exile as a biblical category but it does not exist as a real, material phenomenon in twenty-first-century communities. And to that extent, congregations show an underdeveloped knowledge of theologically robust expressions of community amid exilic realities. Congregations may well invest themselves in activities designed to "help" the disenfranchised, but in so doing they risk masking how they themselves play a part and are stakeholders in the perpetuation of such dehumanizing realities.

Bonhoeffer reminds us that we misconstrue the gospel if we spiritualize the things that Jesus himself took as concrete realities. Of course, the reign of God proclaimed gives a mad man his right mind; a crowd oppressed by hunger a feast; a captive freedom. God's reign, inaugurated in Christ's resurrection, is more real than these concrete things. Nevertheless, Bonhoeffer would have us remember these things, their reality. Perhaps he spoke as strongly as he did because he understood that in spiritualizing such things we risk losing the gracious and earthy character of the community formed by Jesus Christ. Jean Vanier, founder of the L'Arche (the Ark) communities, houses in which persons with disabilities share a common life with able-bodied sisters and brothers, provides a glimpse of what the church might look like were it to take the body of the displaced as basic to its expression of faithful Christian community:

> The point of fidelity which distinguishes [the church] from institutions and hospitals is the call to live with marginal, wounded, and handicapped people. This living together involves much more than coexisting under the same roof and eating at the same table. We discover that we are members one of another, that we share a mutual commitment and mutual concern.[11]

11. Jean Vanier, "Reflections on Christian Community" in *Sojourners* 6 (1 December 1977): 10.

Someone might say, well, this is true, this is something we should try to remember, but in fact the biblical text does not exclude a "spiritual" reading of this term. It is not always and everywhere a literal term. After all, the text asks its readers to listen for the Word of the Lord. In this sense, the interpretation of exile that is more symbolic than sociological or political is a legitimate interpretative move. The text invites listeners to be addressed by something more abiding than the world of politics, economics, and ethnicity; to view the present suffering as not worth comparing to the future promise of glory (Rom. 8:18); to recall that "for now we see in a mirror, dimly, but then we will see face to face" (1 Cor. 13:12a). However, while it is true that the text is never reducible to actual exilic experiences as such, the text never introduces the promise of God without a vital connection to human history. Always the two interact, with the actions of God framing every other reaction (economic, political, and historical) as a response to God's first activity.

Jeremiah, for instance, speaks of historical exile: "the priests, the prophets, and all the people, whom Nebuchadnezzar had taken into exile" (29:1b). The historicity of the exile is, in Jeremiah's account, not in dispute. Yet, with Jeremiah, the overarching assertion remains ultimately and decisively that the exile is the work of God: "Thus says the Lord of hosts, the God of Israel, to all the exiles whom *I have sent into exile* from Jerusalem to Babylon" (4), and "But seek the welfare of the city where *I have sent you into exile*, and pray to the Lord on its behalf, for in its welfare you will find your welfare" (7). The historical experience of exile within the text may be easy to detect, but the more radical and sustaining witness of Scripture is that God is the *agent of exile* and, amid its reality, the one who will effect the promised return. Thus, when Paul, in Acts 13:17-41, introduces his sermon in Antioch, he uses the memory of Israel's captivity in Egypt and the Mosaic law to set the context for Jesus Christ's gift of the forgiveness of sins (38, 39). The gift of salvation far outweighs the narrative of captivity. That gift reframes every exile, whether personal or political. Another example appears in the salutation of 1 Peter: "To the exiles of the Dispersion in Pontus, Galatia, Cappadocia, Asia, and Bithynia" (1:1). In a similar way, exilic identity, no matter how significant in terms of trials (6), is framed by the assurance that they have been "chosen and destined by God the Father and sanctified by the Spirit to be obedient to Jesus Christ and to be sprinkled with his blood" (2). The sanctification and election they know through the triune God operates as a surpassing antidote to the exilic condition. The condition of exile itself will not define the community, but instead the community "live[s] in reverent fear [of God] during the time of your exile" (17).

Exile is real enough, but the promise and electing activity of God frames the exilic narrative with a theological rather than merely political and economic narrative. These texts practically invite a "spiritual" or at least analogical hearing of the history of exile and displacement. At the same time, if exilic spirituality and symbolic relationship is all we hear in these texts, then we have not heard nearly enough—these texts provide a language for twenty-first-century experiences of exile. *Crucially, these texts upend the notion that the church is swept up by exile: it is, in fact, sent by God into exile.* With that theological agency within and throughout the church's political and historical context, the church gains a profound and subtle narrative for its interpretation and embodiment of its vocation in the world. If it is God's exile and only penultimately Babylon's, then the exile we experience now is not merely exile but promise, not merely displacement but the intimation of promised return, not merely the loss of coherence but the drama of our own humanization.

If we fail to detect the catalytic potential of theologically framed exilic narratives in our own historical context, we cut away the transformative dynamic of the worship and witness of the church in the twenty-first century. The uncritical spiritualization of exile contributes to the shape of the church, to the sense that the church is more of a chaplaincy than a mission, a club of likenesses rather than an unlikely community forged by God's reconciling love. Members of the church increasingly believe that the church is a zone for spiritual nurture but not necessarily a space for alternative politics and economies. The tendency to imagine exile primarily through the lens of a middle-class experience contributes to the sense that exile as actual reality is more likely to be found on the news or in a refugee camp in the Sudan or on a short-term mission trip, rather than in the next pew. Yet, more and more often, that is precisely where the exile is to be found. When this happens, not surprisingly, congregations often don't know what to do or how to be the church.

Rev. Eric Garbison, a member of the Cherith Brook Catholic Worker House in Kansas City, Missouri, tells me that he sometimes gets phone calls from churches looking for help with a homeless person who has started worshipping in their church. The homeless often have needs, one of them being a place to stay, but even more they need a community of hospitality. Church leaders often call to ask if Cherith Brook, a community situated in an impoverished area of Kansas City, will provide shelter (and community) for their homeless visitor.

"Sure," Eric answers, "but there's a problem. If you send this person to us, he won't be able to worship in your community anymore since your church is on 119th Street and we're on 12th Street and that's about a thirty-minute drive."

Instead of sending him across town or "deporting" him to another part of town, depriving the congregation as well as their newfound friend of a meaningful communal life, Garbison suggests that someone in the church open up a room in his or her home or, alternatively, the church convert one of its spaces into a temporary room, what the Catholic Worker House calls a "Christ Room."

"Do you ever hear back from these churches?" I ask.

"No," he answers, "no one has ever called back."

What if that conversation were to continue, not only to meet the particular needs of the homeless, but also to probe for the image of the church as exile, among exiles, and as antidote to exile? What might happen if the church attempted to think and theologize alongside the bodies of the displaced, not only the figuratively "deported" but the *actually* deported? Many of the deported are, after all, baptized people, shaped in the church where "spiritually nomadic" people worship. What if the church were to attempt to do theology with the accent of the mulatto, the real hungers and longings of a person eking out a life in the narrow, often highly exposed places of the borderlands, charting a migrant's trail of mixed ancestries, lost tongues, and multiple allegiances? What if liturgies, instead of being read in sanctuaries of symbolic churchliness, were performed alongside and among the drifting populations of the poor in America's streets? What kind of church might be born out of a conversation like that? What might all of us, those who experience deportation as "playfully inexact" metaphor[12] and those who know it as bodily displacement, discover about the Christ who dwells with us, about our lives in communities that simultaneously gather and send?

I am writing to continue that conversation on behalf of pastors and students who ache for a church that lives, worships, and witnesses on the sidewalks and underpasses of American society. I am writing for those who, in one way or another, met God on the margins. They looked and they caught a glimpse of God, a figure more like shadow than light, moving with the hungry and the restive. They looked and they saw God as God should never have been seen: as flesh, meat on a cross; asleep on a sidewalk; with skin blistered by exposure; a refugee on the run from bloodthirsty powers.

---

12. Walter Brueggemann coins this phrase, defining exile as "not primarily geographical but liturgic and symbolic" (15). See Walter Brueggemann, *Cadences of Home: Preaching among Exiles* (Louisville: Westminster John Knox, 1997).

They looked and they saw not only God, but the church God created, growing in the place where, by all rights, it should never have grown: among the sick, the broken, the lost, those without hope.

Many of us, maybe all of us, were formed this way, sometimes without knowing it or without knowing it deeply, in the community of those who were once numbered among the lost, in the fellowship of those who were once numbered among the dead; many of us were sanctified by their prayers; many were blessed by those the world cursed, healed by those the world wounded; many became wise through the folly and scandal of the saints.

Maybe we wonder if this church still exists, or if it does exist, we imagine it only in the spirit but not in the flesh; perhaps we ache to imagine its shape, its body in the world of principalities and powers. Many of us long to see this thing, not only in theory but in spirit and flesh, just as the people who listened to Jesus yearned for the fullness of his appearing. This book shares in that longing but also attempts to evoke that appearing with glimpses of God in the spirit and flesh of Christ's body, the church.

This book has another purpose: I am writing so that what I believe I have seen may find some friends—friends who will not only read the stories of this book but also take them as invitations to create new stories, new ways of being the church in the borderlands of the twenty-first century.

I am writing so that the church may grow with Christ and in the pattern of Christ, flourishing where, according to worldly criteria, it ought not flourish: outside the gates of the city, among the downcast, the wounded, and the crucified.

I am writing for the church that gathers to worship as exile, among exiles, and as antidote to exile.

1

An Exilic Landscape
Postville, Iowa

*To be a diaspora church means that there is
no longer any discernible difference between
missiology and ecclesiology.*
—DANIEL L. SMITH-CHRISTOPHER[1]

In June 2010, on the way home from a denominational meeting in Minneapolis, I decided to make a short detour to Postville, Iowa, about an hour or so north of our home in Dubuque. I wanted a firsthand look at this otherwise unremarkable town that had become the epicenter of a national debate on the issue of illegal immigration.

Almost two years before, on 12 May 2008, Immigration, Control, and Enforcement (ICE) agents descended on Agriprocessors, Inc., in Postville, which at one time served as the nation's largest supplier of kosher beef. On that day, while black helicopters circled above, ICE used several dozen agents from sixteen local, state, and federal agencies to arrest nearly four hundred undocumented workers, sending the small town into a tailspin from which it has yet to recover.[2] The dynamics leading up to this raid go back at least as far as 1987, when Aaron Rubashkin and about two hundred Hasidic Jews moved to Postville from New York, reopening a defunct meatpacking plant with the help of cheap labor imported from all over the globe. Agriprocessors

---

1. DANIEL L. SMITH-CHRISTOPHER, *A BIBLICAL THEOLOGY OF EXILE* (MINNEAPOLIS: FORTRESS PRESS, 2002), 202.

2. Nigel Duara, William Petroski, and Grant Schulte, "Claims of Fraud Lead to Largest Raid in State History," *Des Moines Register*, 12 May 2008, http://www.desmoinesregister.com/print/article/20080512/NEWS/80512012/Claims-ID-fraud-lead-largest-raid-state-history.

and its workers helped turn Postville into a veritable Midwestern boomtown, effectively reversing decades-long trends of decline. But like other "boom" economies, this one was also deeply flawed, as later court proceedings would demonstrate.[3] At the same time, according to the *Des Moines Register*, the arrival of Agriprocessors turned this community of just over two thousand people into one of Iowa's most diverse cities.[4] Diversity wasn't the only thing Agriprocessors brought to Postville: it also thrust Postville into the eye of the national debate about illegal immigration, a debate that reached a dramatic climax with the ICE raid of 2008.

The U.S. attorney for the Northern District of Iowa, Matt M. Dumeroth, declared the 2008 raid "the largest operation of its type ever in Iowa."[5] The Postville school superintendent, David Strudthoff, likened the arrest of more than 10 percent of the town's population of 2,300 to a "natural disaster—only this one [was] manmade."[6] Others, like Antonio Escobedo and his wife, went into hiding, taking refuge inside St. Bridget's Catholic Church of Postville along with hundreds of other Guatemalan and Mexican families hoping to avoid arrest.[7] On the day of the arrests, then mayor Robert Penrod repeated ICE assurances that "kids [of undocumented workers] were going to be taken care of." Penrod believed that most people in town understood the economic value of Agriprocessors. But, he added, "there's people who hate the Hispanics, and there's people who don't like the Jews and would like to run them out of town."[8]

---

3. Workers alleged a variety of abuses at the plant. At the time of the raid, the Department of Labor was conducting an investigation of labor abuses at the plant. Most of the witnesses for that investigation were arrested and many deported, thus subordinating human rights to legal status (see note note 12 below). One of these abuses included a charge that a supervisor blindfolded a Guatemalan worker with duct tape and hit him with a meat hook. Duara, Petroski, and Schulte, "Claims of Fraud." See for other examples of exploitation, Julia Preston, "Life Sentence Is Debated for Meat Plant Ex-Chief," *New York Times*, 28 April 2010, http://www.nytimes.com/2010/04/29/us/29postville.html?_r=0. A follow-up story by Liz Goodwin notes that fifty-seven minors were employed there, one as young as thirteen years of age and "many . . . said they had been physically or sexually abused at the plant." See Liz Goodwin, "Years after Immigration Raid, Iowa Town Feels Poorer and Less Stable," *Lookout*, 7 December 2011, http://news.yahoo.com/blogs/lookout/years-immigration-raid-iowa-town-feels-poorer-less-133035414.html.

4. Duara, Petroski, and Schulte, "Claims of ID Fraud."

5. Ibid.

6. Spencer S. Hsu, "Immigration Raid Jars a Small Town," *Washington Post*, 18 May 2008, http://www.washingtonpost.com/wp-dyn/content/article/2008/05/17/AR2008051702474.html.

7. Hsu, "Immigration Raid Jars a Small Town."

8. Duara, Petroski, and Schulte, "Claims of ID Fraud."

Churches in the area seemed likewise conflicted by the raid, maybe even more so than the general public. Rev. Lloyd Paul Ouderkirk, the parish priest of St. Bridget's Catholic Church, the church where many sought sanctuary during the raids, expressed outrage in October of the same year, saying, "I think every elected politician—no exceptions—should bow their heads in shame." As he was speaking to a reporter, about two dozen women, along with two men, began arriving at St. Bridget's. They were among those released by ICE on humanitarian grounds because they were parents to American citizens. But their release hardly meant liberation, the electronic ankle bracelets they wore bearing mute testimony to their captivity. "They walk the streets here monitored wherever they go," said Ouderkirk. "They can't leave, they can't work, they all have children. So effectively, they are prisoners in our town and in this parish."[9]

St. Paul's Lutheran Church in downtown Postville had this plaintive account of the raids on their website almost four years after the event:

> On May 12, 2008, an immigration raid executed against the Agriprocessors meatpacking plant in Postville led to the arrest of 389 members of our community. The impact of the raid continues to be felt to this day. Families were torn apart, the majority of those arrested were given criminal identity theft charges and forced to serve five month jail terms. Dozens of women were released with GPS tracking devises [sic] affixed to their ankles. One year after the raid many were still wearing those devices as they waited for their cases to be dealt with by the judicial system. Some family members who were arrested had lived in Postville for 15 years. The raid has done little to curb illegal immigration at an enormous cost to taxpayers. The raid has done much to destroy the economic viability of Postville. The removal of so many workers at one time made it impossible for Agriprocessors to recover. The owners declared bankruptcy within five months of the raid. While our town has been devastated by the raid, the residents of Postville and its civic and religious organizations continue to work together to build a future for our town.[10]

9. Wayne Drash, "Priest: 'Nobody Can Tell Me to Shut Up,'" CNN U.S., 15 October 2008, http://articles.cnn.com/2008-10-15/us/postville.priest_1_meatpacking-plant-illegal-immigrants-postville?_s=PM:US.

10. St. Paul's Lutheran Church (Postville, IA), "Our Ministries: Immigration Reform," http://stpaulpostville.org/immigration.html.

The confusion and outrage of churches is understandable, especially when people are being turned into meat, officially processed for deportation. But in truth, the undocumented were treated that way to begin with, as human supplements to a hungry financial system. The raid only turned that raw flesh out into the street, dumping it into the public square where no one could ignore it.

In what Allison L. McCarthy, a legal scholar, calls a "sad irony," the people ICE arrested in the slaughterhouse of Postville were delivered by police-escorted tour buses to the National Cattle Congress in Waterloo, a place normally used to show livestock. This would serve as temporary detention center and makeshift courthouse.[11] The detainees were then thrust into a process of "expedited justice" or "fast tracking," a legal procedure criticized by Professor Erik Camayd-Freixas for treating immigrant workers "like the livestock prepared for slaughter at Agriprocessors . . . efficiently packaged, convicted, and ordered deported."[12]

Driving into Postville two years later, I saw just one stoplight on the main street and hardly any traffic. The apocalyptic raid, black helicopters, and swarms of police of two years ago seemed remote, something out of Hollywood. The town almost seemed abandoned; I wondered whether I would see or hear anything at all. I parked the car and walked into the Taste of Mexico restaurant on Lawler Street. From the looks of the 1950s-style booths and tables, it was probably once a typical diner, a greasy spoon, hole-in-the-wall café.On that day, true to its name if not to its decor, I sat down to chorizo tacos, black beans, and a cilantro-rich salsa. My booth faced out onto the street, and in the space of forty-five minutes, I watched as a Latina pushed a baby carriage through the crosswalk, a toddler clinging to the hem of her dress; noted a Somali Muslim stroll down the sidewalk; observed a White family packed into the cab of a beat-up truck, waiting at the intersection; and saw two Hasidic Jews, dressed in traditional black garb, walking along the same street, all of them betraying familiarity with those streets, spaces they seemed to inhabit with confidence.

As I took this in, I also struck up a conversation with a middle-aged White male, shoulder-length hair, unshaven, his shirt (a work uniform) open to his

---

11. Allison L. McCarthy, "The May 12, 2008 Postville, Iowa Immigration Raid: A Human Rights Perspective," *Transnational Law and Contemporary Problems* 19 (Winter 2010): 295, http://www.uiowa.edu/~tlcp/TLCP Articles/19-1/mccarthy.finalfinal.mlb.022710.pdf.

12. The focus on immigration status rather than human rights led to the deportation of nearly three hundred potential witnesses to an ongoing U.S. Department of Labor investigation into labor violations, including the violation of child labor laws, by Agriprocessors. See McCarthy, "Immigration Raid: A Human Rights Perspective," 299.

waist, who came in a few minutes after I did. The only two people in the restaurant, separated by one table, we began a halting conversation. At first we talked about the food but eventually the conversation moved toward how he had come to live and work in Postville. He explained that he had taken one of the jobs at Agri Star Meat and Poultry, the company that eventually took ownership of the plant after Agriprocessors declared bankruptcy. Now, when he wasn't working at Agri Star, he stayed in a rented apartment nearby. And he was lonely, in some ways the most displaced person in that whole town. He wondered out loud whether he should join his sister in Wyoming, and how long he might stay in Postville. Like a piece of driftwood, he was stranded on a nameless beach, only waiting for the tide of happenstance to pull his narrative into its currents once more, to let this place and this story disappear, swallowed up by the waters. His story resembles the stories of the terminally poor, who take up temporary residence in church-supported homeless shelters as they drift from one low-paying job to the next, dulling the absence of roots with alcohol, often traveling on bus tickets purchased on their behalf by employee-starved businesses, but never finding a home, never a land to grow.

Exiles: Lost in Translation

While Postville may be unique in some respects, in many others it looks like a lot of other "typical" towns and cities across North America along with their "typical" constellations of churches and church-supported charities. The raid only made Postville into the most obvious display of the commodification and consumption of peoples, both at home and abroad. The churches that were confronted by this experience offered mixed responses. On the one hand, at least one church, St. Bridget's, served as political sanctuary of last resort as people fled persecution. One wonders how the church embodied political sanctuary before the raids. At a minimum it served as belated political sanctuary, but where was the witness of the church when Agriprocessors violated child labor laws, among others? Given the way the undocumented employees identified the church as sanctuary, it might have been aware of ongoing exploitative practices by the company itself. Even if it was not aware of exploitation by Agriprocessors, those who took refuge in St. Bridget's clearly viewed the church as political sanctuary. This is a good sign. But it only begs the question: what of the church's relationship to the financial system? To what extent was the church an agent of resistance and transformation in this regard? Positively, the outcry of the churches, ranging from the almost startled outrage of St. Bridget's to the conflicted response of the St. Paul's congregation, suggests their sensitivity to narratives of socioeconomic displacement and deportation.

Whether consciously or unconsciously, their communities are inextricably linked to that of the exile. At the same time, their belated outrage and transparently conflicted response to actual exiles suggest a struggle to respond to those narratives in a coherent manner. A mixed response to narratives of exile in itself is hardly unusual; in one sense that is the definition of exile, the unmaking of coherence.[13] But that loss of coherent *theological response* to exile by churches does suggest that congregations are struggling to link their life as "spiritual" exiles to those who are actually exiled.

This loss becomes all the more difficult to reconcile when we take into account the burgeoning literature on the theology of exile. These days, few can pass through seminary without being reminded of the church's decline, its disestablishment, its cultural irrelevance, its peculiar narrative, and so on. Few, if any, entertain notions that the church still enjoys the cultural privileges of Christendom. We talk about exile as if it were second nature, and yet, when confronted by actual exilic experience, the church seems, at best, startled and confused, uncertain about the way it ought to respond or, at worst, unresponsive, as if it didn't exist at all. One would think that, having been exposed to at least two decades' worth of exilic scholarship, there would be some sense of coherent response. But, if Postville is any indication, that coherency is in short supply.

How did this come about? When did we start thinking of exile almost exclusively in terms of its symbolic quality rather than in its concrete substance? How did the church come to segregate its "spiritual" reflections on exile from those who actually experience exile? What are some of the tacit sociological assumptions behind prominent spiritualties and ecclesiologies of exile? And what are the consequences?

Perhaps one clue to the exile of exile appears in Gary Eberle's book *The Geography of Nowhere: Finding One's Self in the Postmodern World.*[14] Eberle uses the metaphor of a map as a way of charting the "spiritual geography of the modern and post-modern world." The map, he claims, represents the way world religions, myths, and rituals organizes a chaos of experience into a field of meaning. As metaphor, it is not, in itself, constitutive: "You must know that highways are not blue and red lines, that bridges are not inverted parentheses. .

13. Elaine Scarry, in *The Body in Pain* (New York: Oxford University Press, Inc., 1985), speaks of how, when the body is systematically tortured, it unmakes the human being. Torture, she argues, is a systematic act of unmaking the creation. Likewise, exile as a political, ethnic, and economic construction "unmakes" human wholeness, human community.

14. Gary Eberle, *The Geography of Nowhere: Finding One's Self in the Postmodern World* (Kansas City, MO: Sheed and Ward, 1994).

. ." His point is straightforward: "There is always a danger in this business that one can begin to confuse the metaphor with what it describes, to take the map for the landscape it represents." However, when he wants to help his readers see this spiritual exile, he draws from socially and politically located analogies, in effect constituting our experience of displacement in the rhetoric of colonialism: "Spiritually, I believe, we are in the position of those early cartographers, the first to reach what they called The New World. . . . We, too, stand at the edge of a brave new continent. After past centuries of 'progress' we seem to have found ourselves in the middle of a dark forest with no stars, no discernible landmarks to guide us or locate us in space or time with any accuracy."[15]

The problem with this metaphor is twofold. First, it uses the colonialist rhetoric that was the ideological basis for the dehumanization of indigenous peoples in the Americas. The characterization of the "new world" as "a dark forest, with no stars, no discernible landmarks" is based largely on the assumed ignorance of the "native" population, that they have no culture, or at least no culture capable of slowing or rivaling the expansion of a "new" empire. The inhabitants of the "new world" have no intrinsic worth. This in itself should be a troubling move, since it evokes the memory of a massive cultural and ethnic genocide, one that arguably continues to this day.

Second, when Eberle warns us not to confuse the "map" for the reality, he makes the mistake of believing that metaphors do not contribute to the formation of reality. Metaphors invariably contribute to the formation of reality just as they contribute to the formation of meaning. A striking example of this appears when we think of what is commonly taken as the "metaphor" of the U.S. citizen: mostly White, probably male. That this contributes to the formation of reality was suggested when, some years ago, a newspaper reported that U.S. immigration officials rejected the applications of Asian-African-American descendants of African American soldiers in Vietnam and Korea. The reason? They did not "look" American. In this instance, immigration officials screened out those whose physiognomy did not fit the metaphor of the U.S. citizen, a metaphor that was, at heart, a political construction designed to preserve and perpetuate the myth of American whiteness. The point: metaphors are never politically innocent, never merely decorative, but always contribute to the formation of meaning that, in turn, shapes (or prescribes) our understanding of what it means to be human and in community.

---

15. Eberle, *Geography of Nowhere*, 144.

Diana Butler Bass, who has written extensively on what she claims is a resurgence among mainline, left-of-center congregations, shows similar problems. One of Bass's favorite metaphors for the exilic experience is that of the tourist being transformed into the pilgrim.[16] Churches that innovate will be in the business of turning tourists into pilgrims: "In an age of fragmentation, it may well be the case that the vocation of congregations is to turn tourists into pilgrims—those who no longer journey aimlessly, but, rather, those who journey in God and whose lives are mapped by the grace of Christian practices."[17]

A tourist, in this context, counts as a metaphor for exile, but, as metaphor, it draws from actual political and economic assumptions about life: "Being a tourist takes us outside of daily life, and when we are at the beach, we know that we experience the place in an entirely different way than do the year-round locals."[18] But a tourist, as William Cavanaugh points out, depends on the figure of the migrant, its countersign: "Tourism is the aesthetic of globalism in both its economic and political forms."[19] Tourism, as a form of consumerism, is impossible without systems in place to perpetuate the migrant's poverty and captivity.[20]

Sometimes Bass pairs the word "tourist" with its socially marginalized counterparts, "vagrant" or "nomads," but even here she speaks of people whose lives, in terms of socioeconomic class and educational background, remain at some remove from actual poverty. At one point, she uses the tourist metaphor anachronistically (a tourist is a quintessentially modern figure) and confusingly: "Ancient and medieval church history is rife with accounts of vagrants and tourists, mostly people [including "tourists"?] uprooted by social turmoil and war, who find their way to monasteries for temporary shelter or safety and wind up as novices, later to become brothers and sisters"[21] She compares the spiritual nomad's pilgrimage to commercial air travel: "The plane [tourists take in order to be transformed into a pilgrim identity] lands to be refueled or, perhaps, to tinker with the mechanics. These pilgrims understand that, in the contemporary

---

16. Diana Butler Bass, *The Practicing Congregation: Imagining a New Old Church* (Herndon, VA: Alban Institute, 2004), 59–63, 102. See also Diana Butler Bass and Joseph Stewart-Sticking, eds., *From Nomads to Pilgrims: Stories from Practicing Congregations* (Herndon, VA: Alban Institute, 2006), xi–xiii, 176.

17. Bass, *Practicing Congregation*, 60.

18. Bass, *From Nomads to Pilgrims*, xii.

19. William Cavanaugh, *Migrations of the Holy: God, State, and the Political Meaning of the Church* (Grand Rapids, MI: William B. Eerdmans, 2011), 77.

20. Cavanaugh, *Migrations of the Holy*, 72–79.

21. Bass, *Practicing Congregations*, 61.

world, the gospel means that one never finally arrives"—or perhaps ever actually "lands" in anything remotely like exilic reality.[22]

It is not as if Bass is unsympathetic to justice concerns. She points to experiences of not only spiritual nomads but also "nomads [who] were strangers—children, the unchurched, gay and lesbian members, the homeless, artist, or social justice activists—seeking to connect with God."[23] More promisingly, she has this to say about actual homelessness and those who experience themselves as only figuratively homeless: "It intrigued us to see how many of the congregations had ministries serving the homeless. Many people mentioned how, despite the fact that they live in houses, that they, too, 'felt homeless' and experienced a surprising kinship to the actual homeless people they befriended."[24] Some of the contributors to *From Nomads to Pilgrims* allowed the exilic experience to shape ecclesiological identity. J. Mari Luti of First Church, Cambridge, for instance, chronicles the way the church acknowledged and then sought to address the absence of children in how they imagined the church: "We began to realize," she writes, "that a new focus on kids would not be just for the kids' sake, but for everybody's. We felt called to reshape our community to ensure *everyone* an honored place."[25] And yet, with Bass, this seems mostly like a one way street, the experiences of the poor enriching the figuratively poor: ". . . Homeless people had taught them [spiritual nomads] about the spiritual life, trust, stewardship, healing, and commitment."[26] When Bass announces that in each of the congregational case studies, "the pastor and people sought to create or renew a congregation that would touch the lives of spiritual nomads—serving as spiritual bridges from the nomadic life to a life of faithful discipleship," one gets the distinct sense that these bridges, at least in her own mind, were being built predominantly for the spiritual benefit of one socioeconomic class.[27]

22. Ibid., 101-2.

23. Diana Butler Bass, "Conclusion," in *Nomads to Pilgrims*, 168.

24. Ibid., 172.

25. J. Mary Luti, "Enlarging Hospitality: Where Are the Children," in *Nomads to Pilgrims*, 37 (emphasis in original).

26. Bass, "Conclusion," 172.

27. Ibid., 168 (my italics). While not all the communities represented in Nomads to Pilgrims were affluent, many of the contributors ministered in places of significant economic privilege. They bear names like Cornerstone United Methodist Church in Naples, Florida (median income in the City of Naples, according to the U.S. Census Bureau, $71,322); First Church Congregational in Cambridge, Massachusetts (median income in the city of Cambridge, $64,420); Scottsdale Congregational United Church of Christ in Scottsdale, Arizona (median income the city of Scottsdale, $70,040). Another contributor served a church in Xenia, Ohio, where the Census Bureau reports a median income of

While a critical reading of the language of exile is important in order to name the problem that makes a book like the present one necessary, the purpose here is not primarily critical but rather, in the best sense of the word, imaginative. Imagination, true, betrays a critical element, just as parables of Jesus evoke critical reflection. But the lasting and revelatory quality of Jesus' parables is not so much found in the *world they criticize* as in the *world they imagine*. The heart of this work is not primarily to critique the church or churches, but to imagine a church in the borderlands by joining communities that forge their worship and witness amid actual exilic realities. These communities, the interactions between the church and the world they imagine, supply something like a "parabolic" expression of being the church in America's borderlands. They do offer criticism, but even more they offer communally dynamic and contemporary evocations of God becoming human in our time and place.

METHOD, COMMUNITIES, AND ORGANIZATION

The following chapters entangle the theological imagination with the realities of exile in order to energize a deeper knowledge of what it means to be the church in the twenty-first century. Each chapter includes metaphors that evoke the character of being the church at worship in exile. Through metaphor, they probe the boundaries and borders of our ecclesiological, political, and economic imaginations. I offer them as personal narrations that remain open rather than conclusive, invitational rather than decisive, creative rather than exhaustive. In this way, I hope they feel a bit like the reflective life of the local church even though they are exposed or disclosed in settings of exilic experience. They reflect interaction between the realities of exile and theologically laden activities—namely, worship, and witness in the borderlands. They do not replace theological thought but make theological thought possible. Soundings of sociological and political exile will be made, but these will be undertaken in the framework of a pastoral theology.

A word about the method of research: interviews were digitally recorded wherever indicated. Otherwise, the quotes were written down, again as indicated in the notes. In some cases, interviewees requested that they not be identified. In those instances where interviewees might experience reprisals,

$40,741 (see http://quickfacts.census.gov/qfd/index.html). The Census Bureau reports considerably lower percentages of non-White peoples residing in the wealthier cities as compared to outlying regions. See for example the statistics for Scottsdale, Arizona, at http://quickfacts.census.gov/qfd/states/04/0465000.html.

I have also changed identifying details. Members of the communities also reviewed the chapters that dealt with them.

My main point of contact with the communities that make up the bulk of this book was through their leaders or the visionaries behind the communities. They, however, were not my primary or exclusive concern. Although the background of these visionaries figured as part of my research, my main focus was on the communities themselves and how they gained expression through metaphor, symbol, and practice.

THE COMMUNITIES

The communities that supply the narratives of this book were formed out of a theological promise to exiles and as practical antidotes to different exilic realities: among Latina and Latino peoples in the borderlands of the Southwest, among the histories of the Nez Perce people in North America, and with the urban poor of the upper Midwest. Though different in contexts and challenges, they share at least two distinguishing characteristics: they are each innovative in worship and striking in the act of witness. Witness and worship, sending and gathering are mutually interdependent within these communities. As each of these communities gathers to worship, one witnesses its distinctive sending; and as each of these communities sends, one anticipates its imminent act of gathering. The dynamic relationship between the gathering and sending evidenced in these communities tests not only the boundaries of the principalities and powers but, crucially, the boundaries we have come to inhabit as normative for the life of the local church. They suggest the diaphanous nature of boundaries, the porous relationship between sending and gathering, witness and worship, the permeability of spirit and skin. They offer tantalizing glimpses into one part of what is being called the missional church, a broad movement in scope and diversity. Because these communities arise out of specific contexts of exile, they represent particular expressions of the missional church. These communities live and thrive on the sidewalks, reservations, and underpasses of North American society by inscribing cultures of deportation with the witness of God's sending and gathering activity.

THEOLOGICAL ORIENTATION

The image of the indigenous person, the way they appeared or were portrayed around the period that historical anthropologists call the era of "first contact," best captures my theological orientation. This was a period that "clothed" the bodies of Native peoples with a "mixture" of indigenous and Western textiles and implements. Posing to be photographed by a missionary or an anthropologist, Native peoples would combine Western jackets and boots, a conspicuous timepiece on a chain, perhaps a book resting on one knee, together with beadwork and headdresses, flowing hair, body tattoos and piercings, a center-fire rifle, and perhaps, just visible, the handle of a knife for closer, more intimate contact. The juxtaposition and violence of those symbols suggest the conflict of cultures and, more ominously, the colonization and disfigurement of Native peoples by White North America.[28] Another way of thinking about this odd jumble of symbols emerges when we think of these images as glimpses of exilic personhood. The exilic person, denied the privilege of purity, chooses instead the language of adoption, innovation, and boundary crossing. At the same time, exilic personhood practices a form of cultural salvage, recovering what still can be recovered and letting go, at least for the time being, what cannot be retained. This kind of activity reflects a decision to survive but to do so with dignity.

Theologically, the political and ethnic exile chooses something analogous, though not on the same order, to what Paul chooses when he invokes the body of a lactating woman in order to evoke the nature of his body in relation to the church as an apostle of the crucified God. Paul tells the churches that compared to the surpassing richness of knowing Christ Jesus, everything he knew and valued before—class, education, ethnicity, labors, gender—was as good as nothing and worse (Phil. 3:4-8). At this point, Paul sounds like an exile. In fact, he speaks as an exile, yet he does so with none of the despair or loss of coherence characteristic of exile. This is not the nakedness of exploitation but the nakedness with which one receives the sacrament of Baptism. And yet, at the same time, his new identity strains for a more fitting garment, a garment of celebration, a robe of honor, but a robe of unusual honor.

Beverly Gaventa's provocatively titled book, *Our Mother St. Paul*, asks us to reconsider the metaphors Paul employs to explain his relationship to the churches as well as his experience of a new humanity in Christ. For example, in 1 Thess. 2:7, Paul speaks metaphorically of his embodied relationship to the church as a lactating woman, the apostle's breasts ripe and swollen, nipples dripping with the milk of the gospel. Writing on Paul's use of this metaphor in 1 Cor. 3:1-2, Gaventa makes the following connection: "Paul compromises

28. Arguing from the standpoint of cultural-ethnic agency, these photos reflect culturally significant practices of adoption by Native peoples. When "adopting" Western clothing and technology, Native peoples were acting as Native people, doing what they had done for thousands of years: adopting new technologies, befriending new trading partners, and so on. When confronted with the threat of Babylonian deportation, some become martyrs; others plant gardens, marry, raise children. Either way you go, it remains a tragic and moral decision.

his own standing as a 'real man.' . . . [not unlike] the crucified Jesus, who is no more a 'real man' by the world's standards than is a nursing Paul."[29] The very incongruity of the apostolic metaphor, according to Gaventa, seems oddly fitting to one who serves in the name of Jesus Christ, the crucified God.

Paul's metaphoric self-description also supplies a hint as to the character of the witness and worship of the faith community created by Christ, the way church acts as an antidote to exile amid exilic conditions. The church, constituted as it is by Christ, acts as a sojourner in this world, a stranger in a far country. Who or what can compare to the surpassing knowledge of God's love in Jesus Christ? Thus, without any creaturely standard adequate to its Lord, the church seems, in one sense, to be naked, like the exile. However, unlike the destitution of the stranger, the sojourning body of Christ nurtures the drama of our humanization, clothing our naked humanity with joyful foretastes of the new creation amid the world's ruins. Those "foretastes" of the new creation find evocation through alternative liturgy, politics, and economy. The beloved community may struggle, but it struggles in the knowledge that its victory is already won. The anthropology that ultimately counts in the economy of God's salvation is the anthropology of the crucified God.

ORGANIZATION

Each chapter builds on biblical and sociopolitical contexts of exile, exploring how worshipping communities interact with those settings, creating spaces amid the narrow places of the borderlands. These thick evocations of place and witness serve as catalysts for theological reflection on the nature of the church today. Chapter 2, "House of the Butterfly," introduces the contemporary problem of exile through a reading of the book of Ruth as a narrative of migration and, theologically, as a narrative of unlikely return. Chapter 3, "Desert Shrines," builds on the theology of return in the book of Ruth as it looks at different constellations of the act of returning, both north and south of the U.S. border with Mexico, as represented by the activities of No More Deaths and Frontera de Cristo, the latter being a bi-national mission of the Presbyterian Church (USA) and the Presbytery of Chihuahua, Mexico. Chapter 4, "A Broken Benediction," critiques Christendom models of Christian community through an alternative reading of Matthew's Gospel, especially focusing on Matthew's community as an alternative to the violence and exclusivity of the Roman Empire. Chapter 5, "A Labyrinth of the Streets,"

---

29. Beverly Roberts Gaventa, *Our Mother Saint Paul* (Louisville, KY: Westminster John Knox Press, 2007), 50.

focuses on concrete expressions of exilic spirituality, especially as they are embodied in the peacemaking and alternative economics represented in the Cherith Brook Catholic Worker House in Kansas City, Missouri. Chapter 6, "Changing Clothes," introduces a theology of clothing and nakedness. Employing narratives of Native American assimilation as a form of coerced "stripping" or "skinning," this chapter taps into biblical metaphors of nakedness and adornment, especially in the way God, electing nakedness in Christ, clothes the human condition with the compassion and mercy of Christ. With this pattern of Christ's self-emptying, the community is both "externalized" in its "naked" or unapologetic relation to the crucified God and "clothed" through the companionship of Christ and cross. Rev. Irvin Porter (Pima, T'hono O'dham, Nez Perce), pastor of the Church of the Indian Fellowship, situated on a reservation in Puyallup, Washington, supplies a firsthand account of First Nations worship, holding together the painful history of missions, the particular struggles of Native Christians in North America, and symbols that evoke Christ becoming human for, among, and as indigenous peoples. This chapter points to the dangerous proximity between Baptism and Babylon, lament and doxology, in order to show the never-quite-finished work of mending the torn fabric of identity through the textiles of words. Chapter 7, "Setting Waters on Fire," invites congregational leaders to reflect on ways the church is claiming its exilic condition as a theological and worldly reality.

Perspective

Each journey within this book was significant for me, taking me along paths I was unaccustomed to walking and into communities unlike the ones I live in on a day-to-day basis. None were exotic, however. To begin with, as a teaching elder in the Presbyterian Church (USA), I was, predictably, predisposed toward Presbyterian-related communities. Two of the communities are part of the Presbyterian Church (USA), one as an organized congregation and the other as a binational mission of the Presbyterian Church (USA) and the Presbytery of Chihuahua, Mexico. My connection to Cherith Brook Catholic Worker House was, in significant part, formed through overlapping relationships within the PC(USA).

Many of these journeys found their beginning literally just down the hall or up the street, outside of the denominational connections. A homeless shelter here in Dubuque, about a fifteen minutes' walk from our house, provided some of the basic questions that led to the writing of this book. Over a two-year period I led a Bible reflection group with residents at the shelter and shared in its regular worship services. Those experiences eventually led me to ask a number of questions: How does one form faith communities among the poor? What sorts of challenges does one encounter? How does one offer shelter but also more than mere shelter? How do people explain these communities, and their part in them, in terms of their faith? Those sorts of questions led me to visit the Cherith Brook Catholic Worker in Kansas City, Missouri, in January 2012.

Likewise, my journey to the Southwest borderlands began in Dubuque about five years ago when I attended an immigration reform rally where a Latina spoke about her experience as an immigrant to the United States. Not incidentally, when she spoke at the rally, she was flanked by members of the Catholic sisterhood. Later, I would learn that she, along with some members of her family, were undocumented. Over time, our families formed a friendship. Eventually, in the summer of 2011, I spent about three weeks in the Southwest talking with people who live every day on the border, listening to their experiences, their faith, and their sense of the shape of the church in the often-volatile world of the borderlands.

In the same way, the connection with the Nez Perce at Talmaks grew out of Dubuque Theological Seminary's historic relationship with First Nations peoples. I stayed in Talmaks for about ten days in 2006, and that experience proved significant beyond my guessing, especially as it gave me a firsthand glimpse of how First Nations peoples today continue to respond to an exile that has been ongoing for the last five hundred years.

Although I am not related tribally to the Nez Perce, going to Talmaks was somehow like visiting a distant cousin, providing a window into how my narrative might have been had things been different. As it is, I am the son of three generations of Athabascan (Alaska Native) women who married White men. My great-grandmother's marriage was "arranged" as a trade, and that is important to understanding what came after. But it doesn't explain everything, certainly not the motives of my grandmother and mother. I have a better sense of the politics, the vulnerabilities of gender and poverty, the power of racial inequality, the way assimilation (a polite word for cultural genocide) was held out as a "promise" to Native people. My mother, like other First Nations peoples, must have believed the story of assimilation, too, but maybe not completely. My mother told me once that White men were mostly "drifters" in Alaska, unhinged from the land of their ancestors. In a sense, that's not too far removed from the way my mother must have felt herself, a mixed blood caught in a "neither nor" world. It's in this way that my life reflects one strand of the broad and systematic act of racial and cultural deportation in the United States.

So, perhaps ironically, Talmaks played a part in the most deeply personal and impossibly long journey of all, one that spans generations, continents, and skins. My own journey began a long time ago, but my first memory of that journey came about on the day my mother took my siblings and me to the graveyard in Cordova, Alaska. Cordova is a small, landlocked fishing town, and it holds the remains of one part of my story. On the day we went to the graveyard, my mother told us we were looking for her mother's grave, the grave of my grandmother. I was a boy, probably six years old, and my younger brother and sister were in tow. I remember following my mother as she went from grave marker to grave marker, looking for her mother's burial place. Although I didn't have words for it then, I still remember the feeling of searching for something or someone that one should never have to search for, not even in death. But still searching.

We eventually found her, my mother's mother and my grandmother, an Athabascan woman. My first and closest encounter with her was her plot overgrown with weeds, a spindly aluminum stand holding an index-card-sized piece of paper inside a plastic sheath, with my grandmother's name typed on it. Over the decades, I would only get parts of her life, mostly tragic, including the story of her death. One picture of her came to us, however. In the photo, she's an adolescent, perhaps fourteen or sixteen years old. She's wearing a checkered dress, sitting luxuriously atop a bench. I recognize the landscape around her as the subarctic landscape of the region around Fairbanks, flat and quiet. It looks like summer. She's smiling.

In 1989, I returned to Alaska, my ancestral home, to visit with family. While there, my maternal uncle underwent surgery so I went to visit him at the Native hospital in Anchorage. While at the hospital, I visited its gift shop, full of baskets and carvings by Alaska Native artists. Among these I saw a yellow cedar face mask, its features smooth, unblemished, and circular, its eyes vacant. That was the "dominant" image, the whole face, so to speak. As an image, it speaks to First Nations' belief in reciprocity, balance, and the presence of the Spirit that gives things shape. However, as artists do, the artist who crafted this mask introduced something that did not seem to quite fit: pressing through the left temple, pulling away from the dominant skin as if it were a tumor or a captive, was another face, this one smaller, but fierce and determined, or in terror.

As an Alaska Native descendant, I am bound to be intrigued by this image, this face or faces, especially since, at least on first glance, I only appear to have one face, the face of the dominant skin. Being born to the third generation of First Nations women who married White men, some might say I am one face, assimilated, smooth, without "blemish" of color. As a children's book puts it,

"Two eyes, a nose, and a mouth make a face." Assimilation was conceived as a way of "erasing" the color and language, land, culture, and religion from the faces and skins of indigenous peoples.

For the descendants of assimilation, some of us lost not only language (the more subtle expression of human skin) but also our physical skins. Now the dominant face, the face the world sees and expects, the face we sometimes represent as primary, is the face of the Western world. And yet, still the other face, smaller but all the more determined because of its displacement, cries out. Our ancestors cry out, like Abel continued to cry out from the face of the earth. Cain had become the "face of the human being" through an act of fratricide, and yet, though Abel's life was gone, his blood cried out all the more, so that neither God nor the human being could ignore the absence of Abel's voice, his detectable expression.

The poet Eleanor Wilner writes, "There are always in each of us these two: the one who stays, the one who goes away."[30]

Maybe that explains why, sometimes, I dream my skin is red, my hair black, and sometimes I feel an ancestor against the inside of my temple, so real it seems like others might see it too, and their fingers touch its expression, their ears hear its voice.

And yet, mostly, they do not.

I am trying to find a place for this one I apparently am not, these faces sharing one body, one a citizen, the other a fugitive, a remnant of what was left and what still remains, though not the same, still here, reconciled in one body, Jew and gentile, slave and free, male and female, Christ's body, fully God and fully human, without confusion, diminishment, terror, or disfigurement.

One body, a multitude of faces. . . .

30. Eleanor Wilner, "Emigration," in *Vital Signs: Contemporary American Poetry from the University Presses*, ed. Ronald Wallace (Madison: University of Wisconsin Press, 1989), 91.

2

House of the Butterfly

The Witness of Ruth and Casa Mariposa, Tucson, Arizona

But you shall live in tents all your days,
that you may live many days in the land
where you reside.

−Jeremiah 35:7

Casa Mariposa ("Butterfly House"), a purple stuccoed house, was only about a block away from the hostel where I was staying in Tucson. I had been told to visit because this was one of the nerve centers for immigration reform, advocacy, as well as sanctuary, providing beds and table and clean clothing for pilgrims on the way. The house was easy to find: outside someone posted a sign, "Humanitarian Aid is NOT a Crime." Symbols of the migrant trail littered the property. Inside the house, in the middle of the central hallway, stood a shrine, salvaged from the things left behind on the migrant trail. The building itself was a salvage: at one time, Casa Mariposa served as a railroad house, the back of the property butting up against an alley, formerly a railroad track. Today, its rooms (arranged on either side of the hallway) serve as temporary sanctuary for people who need a safe place to rest. On the far end of the hallway, a central dining area welcomes guests to a simple meal and table fellowship. In a sense, it continues as a railroad house, but today it does so in the spirit of the Underground Railroad communities that helped to "smuggle" African American peoples out of slavery in the period leading up to the Civil War.

In one of Casa Mariposa's side rooms I met and talked with Lucia (not her real name) after her second and, according to her, last undocumented migration across the border between the United States and Mexico.[1] As we talked, Lucia, a soft-spoken woman in her late forties with long black hair, sat on a couch, her legs curled up beneath her, wearing a faded orange T-shirt. She was married (but separated), her adopted home being in Colorado, where she earned a living as an agricultural worker on an onion farm. She had been living in Colorado for decades where, in addition to working, she had extended family. Lucia came to the United States as a child, when she was just eleven years old. She said her parents were disabled and poor. They told her to go to the United States to live with family that had already migrated into the United States to work. She crossed, she said, with another boy. They were met on the other side of the border, in Phoenix, and then were driven the rest of the way to Colorado.

The first time she crossed, the border was more fluid and open than it is now. Today, the border between Mexico and the United States is both militarized and violent. To cross the same border now is to undertake a harrowing journey, and I asked why she would return understanding the risks. She explained that she went back to her home state of Nayarit (on the west coast of Mexico) to see her mother who, she said, was ill and probably dying. She stayed for about a year. In August 2011, when I met her, she was on the last leg of her return to the United States. She almost didn't make it. The day before she was found lying down, unconscious, in a convenience store on the U.S. side of the border. Somehow she was placed in the care of a nurse who was affiliated with a church committed to justice ministries for undocumented peoples. It was that connection that led to her receiving temporary sanctuary at Casa Mariposa.

"Would you cross again?" I asked.

"No," she replied flatly, "never again." While the first time she crossed was uneventful (as migrations go), this journey was terrifying but, at another level, chillingly familiar. She told how the human smuggler acted wildly, apparently taking her group in circles, as if he were on drugs; of being physically assaulted by another migrant; of being spotted by U.S. Border Patrol agents in the distance and then hiding in the scrub brush as border patrol helicopters flew overhead, looking for them. Later, she and another migrant would be hunted by border patrol dogs as she hid in an underground culvert and her companion hid somewhere else. What ultimately became of her companion, she didn't know—she never saw him again.

As she spoke, she mimed what it was like as she hid in the culvert or under the cover of the bushes, her body bending, her hands lifted slightly as if to protect her face, her eyes looking up as if to see her pursuers and yet, at the same time, to remain unseen. She also spoke with an eerie sense of detachment. There

1. Lucia, interview by author, audiovisual recording, trans. by Gabriela Vega, Tucson, AZ, 5 August 2011.

were no tears, barely any trace of emotion in her voice, as if being physically assaulted as a woman were "normal" or "expected" on the road to the United States, as if, in order to survive these multiple assaults, she detached herself from them, psychological detachment permitting her to see and not be seen, to disclose something yet to do so without being revealed.

EXILE: A GLOBAL PERSPECTIVE

Gemma Tulud Cruz, a scholar who studies the phenomenon of migration from a theologian's perspective, might say that Lucia's story shows the unique marks of migration in the twenty-first century: a woman, poor, terrorized by agents of the state, vulnerable to sexual and physical predation, and almost invisible. At the same time, she would probably also say that Lucia's story fits into the larger patterns of human history: "Journeys," according to Cruz, "are, indeed, part of humanity's story."[2] People have moved from the land and country of their birth for a variety of reasons, including fear of invasion, as refugees escaping political or religious persecution, for economic reasons (the grass is greener on the other side), for purposes of trade, or to experiment with new models of societal organization. To that extent, migration is of a piece with broad themes of human history.[3]

Yet Cruz, along with other scholars, believes that globalization represents a unique period in the history of migration. Beginning in the sixteenth century, the era of colonialism "laid down the routes for globalization."[4] Global communications, the free movement of capital, and the captivity of labor within the boundaries of the nation-state only compounds and intensifies the colonialist imagination.

Migration in the era of globalization is also distinct from previous historical periods. First, the scope and intensity of migrations is global in reach rather than limited by regional circumstances or causes. Cruz cites a United Nations report on migration as evidence of the particular character of worldwide migration in a globalized financial system. According to the UN, there were 120 million people living outside the country of their birth (the formal definition of a migrant) in 1990. By 2005, that number increased to 191 million people. It estimates that one in thirty-five people today is a migrant. A 2008 report by

2. Gemma Tulud Cruz, "Expanding the Boundaries, Turning Borders into Spaces" in *Mission after Christendom: Emergent Themes in Contemporary Mission*, ed. Ogbu U. Kalu, Peter Vethanayagamony, and Edmund Kee-Fook Chia (Louisville, KY: Westminster John Knox Press, 2010), 71.

3. Ibid.

4. Gemma Tulud Cruz, "Between Identity and Security: Theological Implications of Migration in the Context of Globalization," *Theological Studies* 69, no. 2 (June 2008): 358.

the *Economist* estimates that the global stock of migrants, legal and illegal, rests at about 200 million people. If migrants were to constitute a country, theirs would be the sixth most populous in the world. Citing the same UN report, she notes that 60 percent of migrants worldwide live in developed countries, accounting for as much as two-thirds of population growth in these countries. Symptomatic of the asymmetrical quality of migration, about 75 percent of all migrants live in just twenty-eight countries.[5]

More interesting, according to Cruz, is that the UN report challenges the way migration has traditionally been understood—namely, with Western Europe and North America being the primary receiving nations. Trending against that perception, in 2005 North America received 23 percent of migrants while Asia received 28 percent. Even so, the United States received about one million legal immigrants between 2002 and 2006—more than all other nations combined. Ethnic minorities will make up half the U.S. population by 2050. While the phenomenon of migration in the twenty-first century is enormously complex, these numbers do lend support to the theory that migration, as we see it today, has taken on a quality that marks it off as historically distinct in the modern era. In part, this sort of "hypermobility" can be attributed to the advent of the culture of "trains, planes, and automobiles"—simple mobility plays a part in the rapidity of population movement but it doesn't explain the depth of social and cultural upheaval evident within migratory populations or their host countries.[6]

A second difference appears in the profile of the migrant: historically, migrations tended to progress in more widely spaced waves, beginning with young males, then afterward, only gradually, women and children. Women today make up nearly half of all migrants, a sharp departure from the conventional pattern of young men making up the majority.[7] Cruz reports that, among "exporting" countries, the percentage of women is often far higher, with nations like the Philippines reporting that a whopping 67 percent of their overseas workers in 2007 were women. Unskilled migrant women take what are called the "3D jobs" (dirty, dangerous, and disdained) and "SALEP jobs" (shunned by all the citizens except the poor). The denigration of this kind of labor often turns migrant women into invisible laborers, easily exploited and largely unprotected by labor laws. "Poverty," according to Cruz, "has always had a woman's face, and if globalization has changed anything, it is to underscore this fact of poverty."[8]

5. Cruz, "Expanding Boundaries," 72.

6. Ibid., 71–74.

7. Ibid., 72.

Reflecting a similar change in the migratory profile, children account for a growing part of the migrant pool, but their presence accents another dimension of modern migration: their migrations are often coerced, resembling the "migrations" of Africans to the Americas as part of the slave trade. The numbers of children migrants is staggering. UNICEF estimates that out of the thirty-three million international migrants under twenty years of age, eleven million are between fifteen and nineteen years of age; nine million are between ten and fourteen; seven million are five to nine; and another six million are from birth to four years of age.[9] The U.S. Committee for Refugees and Immigrants, an advocacy organization, reports that an average of seven thousand children cross the U.S. border each year, illegally, without a parent or guardian.[10]

Children and women, in particular, are vulnerable to exploitation as commodities used in the sex trade or as slave laborers. According to a State Department report, the trafficking of women and children around the world claims some 20.9 million victims at any one time.[11] One of those victims is Maria Elena. Like many children who migrate, she was encouraged by a family acquaintance to go to the United States. She was told that she would make ten times more money waiting tables in the United States than she could make in her village, an all-too-common story with an all-too-tragic outcome:

> She and several other girls were driven across the border, and then continued the rest of the way on foot. They traveled four days and nights through the desert, making their way into Texas, then crossing east toward Florida. Finally, Maria Elena and the other girls arrived at their destination, a rundown trailer where they were forced into prostitution. Maria Elena was gang-raped and locked in the trailer until she agreed to do what she was told. She lived under 24-hour watch and was forced to have sex with up to 30 men a day. When she got pregnant, she was forced to have an abortion and sent back to work the next day. Maria Elena finally made her escape only to be arrested along with her traffickers.[12]

8. Cruz, "Between Identity and Security," 366–67.

9. UNICEF, "Global Estimates of Migrant Children and Adolescents," http://www.unicef.org/socialpolicy/files/Handout_Children_Adolescents_and_Migration_Nov_2010.pdf.

10. U.S. Committee for Refugees and Immigrants, "USCRI's Immigrant Services Division," http://www.refugees.org/our-work/child-migrants/about-ncric.html.

11. U.S. Department of State, "Trafficking in Persons Report," June 2012, 45.

12. Ibid., 8.

She was thirteen years old at the time. The International Labor Organization "estimates that 55 percent of forced labor victims are women and girls, as are 98 percent of sex trafficking victims."[13] "In the global ontological capital," Cruz writes, "women [and children] are both consumer and consumed, properties and commodities."[14]

Third, the complex and interrelated roles of the modern nation–state, financial system, and underground markets (e.g., drug and sex trades) also shape the narrative of migration in especially pernicious ways. William Cavanaugh connects the ironic relationship between "the mobility of capital" and the "immobility of labor." Paying workers just south of the border a tenth of what you would pay them north of the border (a border that is locked for everyone but the most privileged, the White, and the most wealthy) contributes to the formation of a captive population—namely, the poor—that has virtually no power to negotiate wages or working conditions with employers. As people crowd into border cities (e.g., Ciudad Juarez) for factory jobs that are here today and "disappeared" tomorrow, they provide an ample labor pool for cartels and other forms of illegal economic activity. Cavanaugh believes that the "impermeability of borders for laborers accounts for much of what we call 'globalization.'"[15] Cruz echoes this sentiment but points to its deleterious effects on women who are ingested by the financial system as "'hot commodities' [to be had] at 'cheap prices' as part of the 'circulating resources' or 'disposable capital' in the world.'"[16] The growth in prostitution worldwide reflects the way the commodification of women bleeds into the wholesale consumption of human bodies.

While globalization enriches some, it devours many more, especially women and children of color. It does not depend on the uplift of the many, but rather on the captivity of the many as passive commodities for consumption by the elite few. It requires that women like Lucia remain invisible, ready to receive blows or to hide amid the threat of force. It insists on their silence in the public square, their captivity in their apartments, fields, and slaughterhouses. It insists that they cannot return, either to their home or to their whole humanity. Indeed, the financial and political system that consumes the sweat and skin of the exile's body acts as if her humanity never existed to begin with. It would seem that there is no such thing as a return for Lucia, or anyone like her.

13. Ibid., 45.

14. Cruz, "Between Identity and Security," 367.

15. William Cavanaugh, *Migrations of the Holy: God, State, and the Political Meaning of the Church* (Grand Rapids, MI: William B. Eerdmans, 2011), 73.

16. Cruz, "Between Identity and Security," 367.

A STORY OF RETURN

The book of Ruth begins with an almost formulaic introduction, but an introduction many economic migrants would recognize: "In the days when the judges ruled, there was a famine in the land, and a certain man of Bethlehem in Judah went to live in the country of Moab, he and his wife and two sons" (1:1). Famine drove the family to another country, a far country with which they had little to do, except as enemies. It must have been a terrible famine to drive them away from their home, to Moab, one of Israel's historic enemies. The narrator emphasizes the identity of the country, Moab, repeating it five times in the space of six verses (1b, 2b, 4a, 6a, and 6b). Perhaps we can imagine the shock of the small village on the day they announced their departure: "Did you hear where they're going? Moab!? I never imagined this day would ever come." For contemporary readers, maybe it calls to mind another unlikely story of "escape"—Matthew's account of Joseph and Mary "fleeing" to Egypt, a slave nation (Matt. 2:13). If Matthew tells the story of a refugee family fleeing political persecution, Ruth tells the story of economic migration. Theirs is a journey begun with a profound hunger in the belly, so profound that it could drive an entire family into the bosom of a historic enemy, the geographic antithesis of promise and hope and home.

Ruth focuses on migration as an act of survival, a story of survival in which the narrator pulls away the skin of culture, human dignity, and even hope itself. Indeed, the exposure of the migrant community, its vulnerability to predation and diminishment, seems to be implied by the text, both through the compression of time (i.e., Naomi's desolation comes quickly in the narrative) and through the layered and compounded losses that would be experienced by the migrant family. Among these losses are the loss of the nation of Judah, the loss of economic and cultural security, the loss of Naomi's identity as wife following the death of Elimelech, the tacit renunciation of Torah evident in Naomi's sons taking Moabite wives, the death of Naomi's sons, the loss of Naomi's youth, and, profoundly, the death of hope.[17]

---

17. According to Ellen F. Davis, "Intermarriage with foreigners was expressly forbidden in Torah (Exod. 34:16; Deut. 7:3), and the prohibition on Moabite alliances was the most stringent of all. In Moses' farewell address, the teaching is explicitly given: 'No Ammonite or Moabite shall come into the congregation of YHWH, even to the tenth generation. . . .' Centuries after 'the days of the judges' judging' . . . that prohibition would not be wholly forgotten. Nehemiah . . . wields it like a weapon against Jews who had married 'women—Ashdodites, Ammonites, Moabites' (Neh. 13:1-3, 23-27) and raised children who could not even speak Hebrew." Ellen F. Davis, trans. and notes, and Margaret Adams Parker, illustrator, *Who Are You, My Daughter: Reading Ruth through Image and Text* (Louisville, KY: Westminster John Knox Press, 2003), 9.

WHY STAY?

Before going further in the narrative, one other question might occur to us: why didn't Naomi just return to Judah sooner, perhaps after her husband died? First, we can infer that the decision to go to Moab was a profound one, not easily undone or taken back. For the poor, then as now, to cross a border means to make a decisive and, in some instances, irrevocable decision. While the narrator does not explicitly say that Elimelech was poor, he was evidently sufficiently vulnerable to the force of famine to contemplate economic migration. Crossing borders remains difficult, even for the wealthy. For the poor, however, crossing borders often entails a lifetime, and in some instances a life-threatening, decision.

Second, the narrator says Elimelech and Naomi and their two sons "remained" in Moab (2); the Hebrew word suggests a sense of permanency, as if they had "settled" there. According to Davis's translation, they put down roots.[18] It was a decisive move, not a temporary one. The narrator does not give us a clear indication of the time they spent in Moab. The narrator reports that "when they had lived there about ten years," the two sons died (4b). This could mean, according to Davis, that Naomi and her sons had lived in Moab for an undisclosed number of years before her sons married Ruth and Orpah and then, after those marriages, lived for an additional ten years before the sons died. Or the ten years could refer to the total time they spent in Moab. While specifying just how long they were in Moab is probably impossible, the exact time is not important. The narrator would have us understand that they had been there long enough to feel as if this place were home, albeit a home full of misfortune, a home but not quite, and maybe even a profound antithesis to the deepest sense of home.[19]

COMING HOME EMPTY

Naomi was in Moab long enough to bury her husband (1:3) and, afterwards, to marry her two sons off to Moabite wives (4), only to see her sons Mahlon and Chilion die (5) as well. The narrator announces the grim results of this migration: "The woman was left without her two sons and her husband" (5). With regard to the death of Naomi's sons, Davis notes that the Hebrew refers to her dead sons as "her boys" (5b), a word not ordinarily applied to mature adults. She explains that, in Near Eastern culture, her sons "died, in effect, as children, leaving no children of their own to give them [or Naomi] enduring memory."[20]

18. Ibid., 8.
19. Ibid., 10–11.
20. Ibid., 13.

Something similar can be said of Naomi herself. When the narrator first introduced the reader to Naomi, she represented a whole person, a person within a community, deeply embedded in a network of relationships, spanning time and space. She enjoyed security and stability: "The name of the man was Elimelech and the name of his wife Naomi, and the names of his two sons were Mahlon and Chilion; they were Ephrathites from Bethlehem in Judah" (1:2). Within the culture of ancient world, she wore the clothing of conventional economic security, even amid conditions of famine. But when she goes to the land of Moab, a far country in the ancient world of Israel, she begins a journey that bares her skin to exposure. It also tests assumptions about her own culture. Over the course of the story, the narrator bares the skin of Naomi, layer by excruciating layer: finally, only the woman was left (5).

Perhaps one hears echoes of the second creation story, where we read of the beginning of the story of human community, of woman and man (Genesis 2:5-25). The second story of the creation includes a story of a fall, but it loads the narrative toward God's merciful interaction, where the nakedness and shame of exilic flesh receive the tender sacraments of God's steadfast love: "And the Lord God made garments of skin for the man and for his wife, and clothed them" (3:21). But in the case of the first chapter of Ruth, we witness the unraveling of the creation story, the story powering in reverse, until only the woman was left and, in the view of Near Eastern cultures, less than a woman was left, since she is without a husband or sons. We might hear other resonances within the larger biblical narrative, especially having to do with themes of fertility. Namely, Naomi's reaction to Orpah and Ruth's determination to remain with her as she returned to Judah brings to mind Sarah's reaction to God's promise that she would bear a child. Sarah laughs or snorts in disbelief. Naomi's reaction is similarly disbelieving, but it is laced with bitter sarcasm: "Do I still have sons in my womb that they may become your husbands?'" (1:11b).

Readers, by now, are alert to the problem of return: how can Naomi return? And what future is there for Ruth? According to Davis, the Hebrew verb *to return* occurs twelve times in the first chapter alone (1:6, 7, 8, 10, 11, 12, 15, 16, 21, 22). The repetition of this word points to its thematic significance in the story of Ruth, but it also signifies the peculiar way Ruth will comes to embody the act of return. What kind of return? Will this be a spiritual transformation or a societal one, or perhaps both?

The Hebrew word for return, according to Davis, frequently signifies turning away from false worship in order to worship the true God.[21] In Ruth the act of return does not exclude spiritual reorientation, but it doesn't accent it either. Rather, its narrative primarily revolves around questions of stability, identity, and security. Naomi's plea, that Orpah and Ruth turn back "that you may find security, each of you in the house of your husband" (1:9a), could indicate both a patriarchal system and a theological framework. According to the Old Testament scholars Danna Nolan Fewell and David Miller Gunn, Naomi's understanding of security depends on "male-centered" values.[22] In contrast, Davis translates the Hebrew word for security as "rest" with this explanation: "[I]t conveys a sense of deep belonging, of security. . . . 'Rest' is the unshakeable assurance that a person or a people feels in the presence of God, even when enemies threaten (Ps. 23:2; Isa. 32:18)."[23] Which of the two ranks highest for Naomi is difficult to guess. Perhaps it is best to say that these two worldviews are rivals, with Ruth expressing a deeper rest than Naomi could possibly imagine alone.

The book of Ruth depicts the economy as inextricably linked to identity: the unmaking of Naomi's identity, not questions of false or true worship, remains her most distinguishing characteristic in this story. While we can speculate on whether she remained faithful to the God of Israel, this, while not absent, seems less important to the story. At minimum, Naomi blames God for her circumstances, but it also seems that, in her theology, the determination of Ruth to remain with her embodies the calamity that has befallen her, her harsh treatment by the Lord (1:21). She does not see God acting redemptively through Ruth, but actually the opposite, as we will see in a moment. But God's activity, as such, seems more like commentary than direct agency. The narrator stresses the problem of Naomi's return in language representing the migrant's experience: she left Judah because of famine; she returned to Judah still firmly in the grip of famine; she returned, her womb empty. She does not enjoy the security of sons or the protection of a husband. Her journey as well as her faith is shaped primarily through the lens of actual famine. She began the return to Judah in order to coincide with the beginning of the harvest season, when cheap, disposable labor would be in demand. She returned to Judah along with a wave of other migrant laborers—and without hope or youth.

A CLINGY RELATIONSHIP

If we read this text as a pilgrimage, where one foot stands on the promise and the other foot slips on the reality of exilic experience, the narrator's

21. Ibid., 13.

22. Danna Nolan Fewell and David Miller Gunn, *Compromising Redemption: Relating Characters in the Book of Ruth* (Lousiville, KY: Westminster John Knox Press, 1990), 82.

23. Davis, *Who Are You My Daughter*, 19.

juxtaposition of the two speeches of Ruth and Naomi between 1:16-17 and 1:20-21 proves fascinating. Ruth's testimony stands out for its covenantal themes and prefigures everything that follows in the story. The narrator would have us not only hear the words that Ruth speaks, but how she speaks them, her body clinging to her mother-in-law (14). Her posture mimes the pathos of the words she speaks—to use a theological term: we get a glimpse of the incarnational significance of her testimony. But it is not an incarnation of an individual as much as it is the incarnation of a family.

Ruth in effect "marries" her destiny to Naomi's poverty. It is a voluntary attachment, which, according to Davis, may deliberately recall the biblical description of marriage: "Therefore a man leaves his father and his mother and *clings* to his wife, and they become one flesh" (Gen. 2:24). Davis believes that no indication of a sexual bond exists between the two. Nevertheless, Ruth's vow of fidelity births a radically new expression of family. With or without sexual overtones, the "marriage" of Ruth and Naomi marks a dramatic departure from the formation of a family between male and female partners: "[Ruth] creates the foundation of love on which a new family structure will eventually be erected."[24]

We see, coupled with her testimony, the entanglement of the lives of two very different women, two persons who come from rival nations, and two people with very different ideas about the way to achieve security. Phyllis Trible, Old Testament scholar, concludes that "Ruth's commitment to Naomi is Naomi's withdrawal from Ruth."[25] Ironically, though the two women walk together, they remain profoundly separate, given that Naomi still clings to conventional understandings of stability and gender roles (which Orpah tacitly confirmed in her departure) whereas Ruth, inexplicably and to her own seeming ruin, clings to Naomi.[26]

An inexplicable bond holds them together despite all that would pull them apart: Ruth's youth, her reasonably bright future in Moab, their religious differences, Naomi's age, poverty, bitterness, and the burden that Ruth would pose to Naomi in Judah. Against societal standards and conventional solutions, which both Orpah and Naomi affirm, the writer shows an image of delicate, fierce words of affection entangled with raw, bitterly sore flesh. Ruth's unapologetic testimony gets bound up with Naomi's silent resignation: "When Naomi saw that she was determined to go with her, she said no more to her" (18). Nevertheless, Naomi will have her say but not before the narrator

24. Davis, *Who Are You My Daughter*, 23.

25. Phyllis Trible, *God and the Rhetoric of Sexuality* (Philadelphia: Fortress Press, 1978), 173.

26. Ibid., 172–73.

implies her changed appearance, stressing her *un*making: "and the women [of the village] said, 'Is this Naomi?'" (19b). If we see Ruth's faithfulness cling to Naomi in her testimony, we see Naomi's identity falling away into the dishevelment characteristic of her loss. She returns but not really—she returns as a shell of what she was when she left: "[Naomi] said to them 'Call me no longer Naomi [Pleasant], call me Mara [Bitter], for the Almighty has dealt bitterly with me. I went away full, but the Lord has brought me back empty; why call me Naomi when the Lord has dealt harshly with me, and the Almighty has brought calamity upon me?'" (20-21).

Naomi changes her name to "bitter" upon her "return"—she no longer recognizes herself. This is no private, secret loss: upon seeing her, the townsfolk seem to withdraw in shock, not speaking to her but rather about her. The problem of return is not only the physical journey, the geographic obstacles to going back to Judah. Borders of loss, the seemingly irretrievable loss of youth and identity also figure into the problem of a meaningful return. But Ruth's presence in this episode poses another kind of problem: "Ruth is nothing," according to Fewell and Gunn. "Naomi speaks as though the loyal companion at her side were invisible."[27] Not only does Ruth's faithfulness receive no reply from Naomi on the road back, but upon her return, when Naomi has, in the geographical sense at least, arrived, she speaks as if Ruth were nothing, and less than nothing, perhaps the embarrassing "baggage" that comes when one intermixes with foreigners.

As it is, the first chapter closes with a lament, not the jubilation one might anticipate upon arriving back home. It ends with a lament because the return hoped for in the story is one of deepest restoration, not merely leaving Moab or even escaping famine. Paradoxically, the intimation of Naomi's wholeness comes by way of a stranger, a stranger she, for all practical purposes, blames for her condition. The symbolic center of antihome supplies the DNA of Naomi's, and perhaps Israel's, deepest expression of return to home. The remainder of Ruth turns to this restoration, the most profound and subtle expression appearing at the end of Ruth: "Then Naomi took the child [born of Ruth and Boaz] and laid him in her bosom, and became his nurse. The women of the neighborhood gave him a name, saying, 'A son has been born to Naomi'" (4:16-17b).

---

27. Fewell and Gunn, *Compromising Redemption*, 75.

A THEOLOGY OF RETURN: SECURITY AND SURVIVAL

The story of Ruth's faithfulness supplies the reader with an unusual analogy of God's faithfulness. First, the story of God's faithfulness comes by way of a Moabite and a woman, Ruth. Second, Ruth's pledge of faithfulness radicalizes God's faithfulness to provide security beyond the conventional standards of society, even those standards that would seem to prejudice God against the solidarity between Ruth and Naomi, such as the prohibition against forming alliances with the Moabites.[28] God will also subvert the ordinary patterns of male and female relations in order to secure the peace of Ruth and Naomi. Third, the story of reconciliation unfolds, on the one hand, through Naomi's determination to gain security for Ruth (and also for herself) but, even more dramatically, through Ruth's boldness with regard to Boaz, an assertiveness that conjoins both her sexuality and her claim to the covenantal rule of God.

This, of course, draws out the theological implications of the text and not the explicit statements of the text regarding the character of God. The text itself speaks very little about God, except in the testimony of Naomi who believes that God has been unkind to her. Ruth's pledge of faithfulness to God seems ambiguous: how much does she really know of Yahweh? When she says that her Moabite god will be exchanged for Naomi's Hebrew God, is she simply changing national loyalties? Applying, in effect, for citizenship status? As for Naomi, she clings to a nationalistic and theistic religion, a god of patriarchy, but, to her chagrin, her salvation will come by way of a stranger.[29] Mostly, the theology of Ruth comes by way of indirection, through the human, fleshly actions of Ruth. We are to see the way God is in the shadows of her actions, through her peculiarly assertive sexuality. Perhaps this informs the narrator's decision to couch the act and difficulty of return in concrete, fleshly rather than primarily religious terms.

Ruth does not sniff at stratagems that lead to security but confers on these the dignity they deserve. That dignity surfaces in several recurring themes. First, as an expression of return, we witness an act of migration as a legitimate response to famine, whether in Judah or in Moab, or throughout the world. It was in hope of relief from famine that Elimelech went to Moab. And it was again a response to famine that led the three women, Orpah (initially), Ruth, and Naomi, to return to Bethlehem as they sought economic security and probably, if possible, prosperity. Ruth confers narrative legitimacy on the problem of survival. This will not be a book about theology six feet above

28. Davis, *Who Are You, My Daughter*, 9. See note 17 above.
29. Fewell and Gunn, *Compromising Redemption*, 82.

contradiction, but rather a theology worked out in the fields and threshing floor of God's providence. It will not be written in the stars or on the stone tablets of Moses, or even in the "still small voice" of Elijah, but rather in the actions of Ruth, which are almost but not quite hidden from the reader's perception. Instead, according to Trible, the radicalism of this text arises from within "the darkness of night, at the corner of a grain heap, in whispers between female and male."[30]

Second, in the patriarchal society of the time, Naomi, like Ruth, was to remain passive. Against this cultural expectation, the narrator of this text foregrounds the testimony of women, a testimony that is only more pronounced because of the "silence" of Naomi at the beginning. For the first part of the story, Naomi fulfilled her part. Naomi followed, a silent partner in the migration to Moab. She remains passive even when her sons take Moabite wives. Stability and security come by way of patriarchy in the world of Naomi. However, that worldview suffers a devastating blow with the loss of her husband and sons. Promised stability vanishes and thus she flees famine once again, only this time asserting her own will, though she subordinates her identity to the ravaged worldview she still apparently believed in.

In other words, she flees a famine but clings to a social construction of reality that had previously held her world together. Though she clings to that social construction of reality, she can no longer assume its integrity. Whether she is prepared to accept it or not, the crisis of famine and exile has thrown the entire edifice of patriarchy, sexuality, and security into question. As the text progresses, women speak, and often, amid the rupture. The first indication of this rupture appears in Naomi's speech as she counsels Orpah and Ruth to leave, to essentially continue in the traditions to which she and her daughters, as women, must comply. At first this does not seem like much of a revolution: she simply asserts the status quo. But to articulate it, to feel the compulsion put it into words as your own, to say it this way represents an unspoken question that prompts a crisis, a decision. Naomi, the one who only a few verses before was a woman bereft, with neither a name nor a husband nor sons, now speaks. She does not merely follow. Her words do not suggest a passive cooperation with the status quo, but a pronounced one, as the repeated phrases "Go back" and "Turn back" suggest. The more she implores, the more doubt is cast upon the whole system. It can no longer be taken for granted. Ironically, Naomi implores Ruth and Orpah to choose a system that denies their power to choose.

---

30. "Does [Ruth] prefer to leave the details of her radical behavior where they occurred—in the darkness of night, at the corner of a grain heap, in whispers between female and male?" Trible, *God and the Rhetoric of Sexuality*, 187.

Orpah, who reluctantly agrees with Naomi, chooses to return or "turn back," and she disappears from the story. By contrast, Ruth introduces radical fidelity, inexplicable by any social standard or economic model, and "clings" to Naomi who would shun her with her sarcasm and silence. Though the narrator shows the image of Ruth clinging to Naomi, the two effectively "part ways" even as they are joined together in a narrative of survival.

Even in the sexually suggestive scene of the threshing floor, we hear Ruth's voice, an especially unusual event given that Ruth's sexuality would presumably be more requisite to the needs of the hour than her speech, or so one would expect from Naomi's instructions to Ruth: "When he lies down, observe the place where he lies; then, go and uncover his feet and lie down; and he will tell you what to do" (3:4). And Ruth seems to agree to the plan, to *do* rather than to *speak*, to *be instructed* rather than to *provide instructions*, seemingly "turning back" to a patriarchal and sexist system. And yet, parting ways again with Naomi, she paradoxically clings to her. Ruth speaks amid the "whispers between female and male" calling Boaz to a covenantal obligation he himself did not volunteer.[31]

Third, the story does not eschew human sexuality, and, in particular, women's sexuality, which makes them vulnerable but also powerful agents in the working out of the narrative of return. Naomi's relationship to Elimelech and Ruth's to Boaz are more background to the real story of two women who, by virtue of their gender and sexuality, are "marked out" as other, even when they are at home in the nation of Judah. The narrator does not blush in the face of issues related to gender and sexuality, providing its readers an unalloyed picture of the conditions facing immigrant women, including their vulnerability to rape, the difficulties of socio-economic instability, the routine way in which the labor of immigrants is exploited, and the way patterns of human sexuality forge (or potentially undermine) just community. The economic construction of gender, too, plays a role in the kind of work that is available to Ruth and the kind of labor that seems to be expected from her: "[Ruth] has been on her feet from early this morning until now, without resting even for a moment" (2:7b).

Fourth, despite the anti-return of Naomi, her role as a cultural insider within Judah puts her in a position to broker Ruth's security: "My daughter, I need to seek some security for you, so that it may be well with you" (3:1). But this is a dangerous form of brokerage, as Fewell and Gunn point out, since it entails exposing Ruth to the whims of Boaz and potential scandal.[32] After all,

---

31. Ibid., 186.
32. Fewell and Gunn, *Compromising Redemption*, 77–78.

Naomi views sexuality as the only power a woman possesses, but it is sexuality at the disposal of a man: "He will tell you what to do" (3:4b). To be fair to Naomi, the obstacles to not only her security but Ruth's are considerable, as the narrator continues to repeat Ruth's status as a Moabite (e.g., 2:2, 6, 21; 4:5, 10). Paradoxically, Ruth's peculiar sexuality comes to play a crucial part in Naomi's understanding of the acquisition of security (3:1). Security will not come primarily by the whim of a male-dominated universe but through a sexuality that is neither passive nor seen apart from a broad ethical network of covenantal relationships.

In the well-known account of Ruth's visit to the threshing floor, Boaz rolls over and is startled: "At midnight the man was startled, and turned over, and there, lying at his feet, was a woman!" (3:8). Boaz, the man, asks, "Who are you?" (9a). It's a loaded question, both given the sexual connotations of the text and the narrative memory of Naomi's condition when, after her multiple losses in Moab, we see her, Naomi, as something less than a woman ("so that the woman was left without her two sons and her husband" (1:5b)). But on this occasion, covenant language and its obligations surface both in the question that Boaz asks and in Ruth's reply: "'I am Ruth, your servant; spread your cloak over your servant, for you are next-of-kin'" (9b). Ruth's sexuality is in service of her humanity and not the other way around, as Naomi conceived it. Ruth's human dignity within community plays a central part in the theology of covenant within the narrative as a whole, intersecting with a complex web of relationships, something Boaz himself acknowledges in his subsequent actions.

There is a sense in which the entire story gathers its dramatic force as the theologically dense language of Ruth and the devastating lament of Naomi are juxtaposed in 1:16-21 and reconciled in the gritty stratagems of fleshly survival and eventual prosperity. While none of these strategies, singly or together, matches the sum total of theological return, each is dignified in the sweep of the testimony of God's faithfulness. Indeed, God's faithfulness in restoration and renewal shapes the narrative, since Naomi's declaration of loss would seem complete. While the loss experienced by Naomi is not minimized, it is not the last word. The narrator shows that these two characters, both human and both vulnerable in concrete ways, are swept in the even-more-real promises of God. As such, the journey charts a peculiar path between a spirituality of exile and a gendered and ethnically complex narrative of displacement and the almost worldly tactics of achieving security.

"Ruth's Church"

To foreground this narrative as an expression of the church, especially in its gritty connection to human life, leads to an analogy of the church that locates the bedrock of its theology not primarily within abstract doctrines of covenant but in the actual labor of relationships laden (or riven) with sexuality, politics, and economic currents. To ask Ruth to set aside her sexuality (or the church its politics) is like asking her to cease to be or asking her to flatly deny both her vulnerability and her legitimate and peculiar power. Ruth's church evokes sexuality and it does so within a robust web of covenantal living. The way society constructs gender exposes her sexuality to risk and exploitation. Ruth's church cannot hide from these realities because, in a profound way, she lives and breathes them, even as something else, something more pervasive and profound than these, remains the dynamic and ultimate agent of the story.

Ruth also raises the questions regarding the church's peculiar visibility to the larger world. Many would, for example, recognize the "tall steeple" as a reasonably adequate metaphor for the church. But if Ruth were to supply the parabolic substance of the church's witness, would we see anything different? We might begin to answer that question by asking, Why do we care about the story of Ruth? Clearly, calling it a "romance" or "love story"—the way those terms are used today—fails to do it justice. In truth, Boaz looks more like a foil used to demonstrate the radical expression of love between Ruth and Naomi, a love that overcomes considerable odds to form a new family. This is part of its uniqueness: it breaks out of the boundaries of "conventional" love stories—but it does so subtly, using our attachment to a poor girl being "noticed" by a wealthy male to reorient our thinking to the improbable and liberating love of God through the assertive and ethically powerful sexuality of a young woman. The story startles us as well, in part, because it is visible in the all the wrong ways: a Jewish family leaving Judah, migrating "out of the promised land" and then remaining in the land of Moab, "assimilating" into Moab so completely that their sons marry Moabite women; and then, as if to confirm that God judges the sorts of people who do these sorts of things, Naomi returns to Judah, empty. She returns empty biologically, politically, and economically, perhaps even theologically. And with baggage. The peculiar expression of Ruth's love for Naomi does not escape the notice of the women of Judah: "for your daughter-in-law who loves you, who is more to you than seven sons, has borne him" (4:16). From the spectacle of love on the road back to Judah—"Ruth clung to [Naomi]" (1:14b)—the reader witness a story that is uniquely and peculiarly visible for the reader.

What if today's churches were to seek to be visible in ways that seemed counterintuitive to conventional thinking and maybe just wrong, but, paradoxically, were profoundly right? Mixing economics with ecclesiology? Sexuality with security and covenantal living? What if the website were less important to the church than the way it interacted with its social and political soil? What if survival, along with repentance and prayer among others, was a meaningful category within the life of the church? How would the church choose to organize its budget if survival for the "outsider" community were paramount? What would it mean to value the security of the poor and the marginalized above the traditional orthodoxies of church membership? Or perhaps, in the spirit of Ruth, would it be possible for a marginalized community to welcome the "citizen" church, to help it unlearn the rules of patriarchy, capitalist addictions, and heterosexual prejudices? Would a "citizen" church welcome Ruth or, like Naomi, turn away from her in silence?

Could the church anticipate Christ in the shadows of survival, seeing Christ amid the struggles of marginalized peoples? Might the salvation of the straight community and that of the LGBTQ community be bound up together? What if the church instead of being passive in socio–political space was, in faithfulness to God's incarnational presence in Jesus Christ, enlivened and intensified to become an agent in space, exposing injustices with lament even as it clothed those wounds with the story of God's unusual love? What if the church's peculiar narrative, its identity as a Moabite woman taking upon her lips and into her heart the language of God's unfamiliar faithfulness, were to become its binding vocation? What if the visibility of the church took form as public mime of hope and lament, witnessing to God's steadfast love amid adversity? And what if that vocation swept up the church into a place where every encounter was a teacher and every enemy already, by God's grace, a friend? What if participants in the life of the church acted as midwives to one another, citizens and non–citizens, in the labor of a deeper and more authentic return to a flourishing humanity?

The next chapter picks up these questions and themes as it explores how communities of solidarity and economic alternatives are taking shape in the borderlands of the United States and Mexico.

3

Desert Shrines

Liturgy and Life in the Borderlands

They often build them where they find rest.
–THE REVEREND JOHN FIFE

If you were to visit the shrine built by the No More Deaths (NMD) volunteers at the Arivaca Camp in Arizona's Altar Valley, you would see an upturned tree stump, its root system exposed, almost churning, as if alive, with the things heaped around it. Among these are a half dozen or so white crosses, some bearing the word "*Niños*" or asking "*Cuántos más?*" A tall figurine of Mary stands precariously at the upper left edge of the shrine, surveying her cloudburst kingdom of things with uncanny serenity.

You might also begin to notice the scattered, bleached bones of animals; the shed antlers of a deer; a cow's skull, vertebrae, and ribs. You would see other remains too: abandoned shoes and sandals; a purse with a pink floral design; a shirt reduced to rags; a framed picture of a family, its glass face cracked, the photo discolored; a water bottle wrapped in dull canvas, the color of the desert; and an oxidized credit card inserted into a shoe, creased in the middle, Chase Visa emblazoned on it, a few pesos scattered nearby; and at the far edge of the shrine, almost like an afterthought, a broken necklace of white beads, some of the beads loosed from their thread, melting into the memory of the borderlands.

Other things are left behind as well, more haphazardly than what migrants leave as carefully arranged shrines. On the migrant trails, both north and south of the border, one sees the shed skins of a life being left behind: a pair of women's embroidered jeans, opened packets of strawberry-flavored electrolyte powder carrying the image of a smiling baby, empty water bottles, worn-out shoes, discarded food tins. These trails betray an experience of hurry, of danger, of no time to rest, of living in a manner that cannot sustain life for very long.

While I walked these trails in the light of day, the people who walked them ahead of me were probably moving at night; they were probably people unused to desert heat; they were people who were told by the coyotes (human smugglers) that crossing the desert would be easy; they were people who perhaps imagined there was only one border to pass, the six-meter-high fence that stretches across 344 miles of the U.S. border with Mexico, rather than multiple borders, the most impassable border being one of fear and invisibility; and they were also, significantly, people of prayer and hope.

Arivaca Camp Shrine and migrant trails stirred up a lot of feelings for me, many of them conflicting. Among these was a sense of outrage that people should be reduced to this condition; fear for those who were crossing even at that moment; and a sense of helplessness, knowing that some would die as they attempted to cross, that predators, both official and unofficial, hunted for the poor who made their way along these paths. But it was also the peculiar proximity of creation and financial system, of bones and pesos, that gave me pause. I also felt a sense of awe, of wonder at the spirituality of the desert places and the courage of those who do cross, or try; perhaps it was the sense of being dangerously close to a life, or to a death in life, close enough to touch the clothing once worn by another, close enough to make out the faces held in a pendant, close enough to imagine the girl who wore the necklace, close enough to imagine the girl who wears it no longer.

The contrast between the shrines and the trails might be the paradox between pilgrim and migrant, between home and far country, between the furtiveness of shadows and the plaintive, open spirit of prayer. A pilgrim takes to the path with a sense of hope while the migrant takes to the road out of a sense of desperation, danger, or hunger—both take to the road. The road and the forces that haunt it may tear people apart or, as in the case of the shrines, may bring them together, witnessing to the subversive power of the Spirit, insinuated into and disruptive of the powers and principalities, existing where it ought not, crossing boundaries of spirituality and politics, entangling the flesh and the prayer, offering the gift of hospitality and hope where neither were sought nor expected. In the larger way of gesture, the metaphor of the shrine suggests how the church may come to inhabit the far places of exile as people who strive to reconcile seemingly opposing forces, financial system and creation, home and far country, loneliness and communion.

FRONTERA DE CRISTO

On the border I witnessed unlikely communities being formed through practices of gathering, of confronting prejudices and, in some measure, being reconciled to the image of God in the other. Whether I was with No More Deaths volunteers in the Altar Valley or visiting a bus depot with volunteers from Casa Mariposa in Tucson to offer hospitality to recently released (and often disoriented) female detainees, I saw potent signs of community formation through ministries of compassion and mercy. Like the shrine, they form resting places, sanctuaries alongside migrant trails: they offer shelter, hospitality, and a place to pray. Also, like the shrine, they seem almost weed-like, growing in the cracks of a borderland system. They may be opposed by the system, but, like a weed, they find ways of reproducing amid hostile environments, almost delighting in the way hospitality, hope, and faith erupt unapologetically and unimpeachably in sociopolitical monocultures. With creeping tendrils of mercy, the communities I visited seemed to have an uncanny instinct for finding the systemic rupture, the crack in the borderland machine, a place to grow with unlikely promise.

The shrine metaphor also supplies a way of holding these very diverse and sometimes seemingly contradictory constituencies together. Frontera de Cristo, a bi-national mission of the Presbyterian Church (USA) and the Presbytery of Chihuahua, Mexico, gives concrete expression to the shrine metaphor. As an organization it focuses on a joint effort to nurture church development, health ministry, family ministry, a community center, mission education, just trade, and migrant resources. What links these diverse ministries together is a commitment to "cross borders" or, put another way, to make borders porous enough to support life. According to their website, Frontera de Cristo "facilitate[s] the crossing of physical, cultural, political, linguistic, and economic borders, through the interaction of people of diverse backgrounds, and through biblical reflection in the light of our realities." This practice derives from the conviction that "we are all to 'welcome the resident alien, because we too once were aliens.'"[1]

Immigration, poverty, and border enforcement policies, both north and south of the U.S. border with Mexico, represent a dominant motif for Frontera de Cristo. Yet the border is not a simplistic reality but one shot through with the theological conviction of God's presence in Christ crossing the most complete and indomitable border, the one between God and the human being. Rev. Mark

1. Frontera de Cristo, "Building Relationships and Understanding between People of Our Two Nations," http://www.fronteradecristo.org/en/responding-to-the-immigration-crisis/building-relationships-and-understanding.

Adams, a mission coworker with Frontera de Cristo, liked to say, "Our battle is not with flesh and blood but with principalities and powers." Distinguishing the work of Frontera from that of activists that might organize on the basis of an issue or concern, Mark offers instead a profession of faith that entails an explicit landscape for discipleship: "I would describe myself as a Christian. I am seeking to follow Jesus in all areas of life, including economically and politically."[2] It is a faith that, by nature, becomes public because Christ himself has gone public, "crossing" the border separating "religion" and politics.

Conditions of politicized and militarized exile add to already unhealthy polarities. Mark believes these kinds of dualities contribute to some of the thorniest issues confronting ministry on the border: "The biggest problem on the border is blaming some group of people [migrant, border patrol, or activist] for what's wrong." According to Mark, the root problem is the temptation to *simplify* the borderland culture through the "demonization of entire groups," which in effect absolves stakeholders, north and south of the border, of their particular hand in the immigration crisis: "What I want is for all of us to ask, 'How can we all turn our backs on that [unjust] system?'"[3] Enlisting very different conversation partners in that journey helps to subvert the simplistic polarities created by the global financial system, implicating *all* people (the undocumented, human smugglers, activists, consumers, and narco armies) in the new thing of God.

It would be incorrect, however, to say that the community of Frontera views exilic experiences as "essentially equal," as if a "neutral" position or a middle ground between those who are driven by the financial system and those who drive it were a faithful response. Moderation seems like the gospel of the status quo. It is hard to believe in the gospel of the status quo when you have bandaged a migrant's blistered foot or grieved with those who have undergone prolonged separation from their loved ones. The people who form the community of Frontera de Cristo choose to walk with those who experience the physical and emotional abuse caused by the borderland culture on a daily basis. Much of the ministry of Frontera de Cristo tends to the physical, legal, and emotional needs of migrant peoples. Some of their strongest leaders were, within their lifetimes, migrants themselves. Yet, theologically, the confession that Jesus Christ dwells in that place, fully God and fully human, radicalizes the commitment to trust in Christ's desire to create community where no trace of community seemed possible or desirable, not only among friends and family but also between enemies. If Christ shows God's fullness

2. Mark Adams, interview by author, written notes, Tucson, AZ, 18 February 2013.

3. Adams, interview by author, 18 February 2013.

through his humanity, undermining the power of the cross to terrorize and dehumanize, should we anticipate anything less than God's Spirit doing the same alongside a twenty-first-century border, creating an improbable community amid principalities and powers? Should we anticipate anything less than a community as improbable as Isaiah's vision of lambs and wolves eating together (Isa. 65:25), joined together not as predator and prey but as a new creation altogether? And what if we should hope only for the possible? Perhaps then, as one theologian said, we would achieve the all too possible.

In a way similar to how I was struck by the desert shrine of Arivaca, I was often thrown off balance by the kinds of community I encountered in the borderlands. Perhaps most of all, I became aware that being fully human with God and neighbor in the inhospitable spaces of the borderland system was the "impossible" community, the community we could not on our own imagine. It also proved to be the most profoundly real form of community. Supplying food and water, medical supplies, and legal support to undocumented migrants and deportees was of a piece with that experience, but it didn't stop there. It also extended to the border patrol agents themselves. Communities were about forming the roots of a new society, and to be truly new they had to subvert the easy polarities of good and evil, polarities they themselves could fall prey to. They would have to confess their own complicity in attitudes and behaviors that scatter the human community, creating enemies rather than sisters and brothers through Christ. Similarly, if churches were to contribute to meaningful alternatives to the financial system, they would have to experiment with entrepreneurial activities rather than merely condemning financial inequities. Their practices reflected a determination to remain different, to be visibly alternative in the way they gathered and how each was included in the broader witness of reconciliation. They sought out and tried to cultivate spaces where reconciliation and formation might, by the grace of God, take place or at least have an opportunity to grow.

The people involved in these communities did not experience "perfect" moments of reconciliation, but rather difficult, often painful, and always exceedingly human exercises in being made one with each other. It was more pilgrimage, where the destination is often to be found in the journey. But it was pilgrimage over real land and real conflicts.

Over the course of this chapter, I will try to gather some of the stories of the people I met, their activities, and a glimpse of who they were, at least so far as I was able to grasp their humanity in my short time with them. However briefly, I witnessed a bold, realistic, and often difficult attempt to be the beloved community in conditions of real exile. If nothing else, the communities I met along the U.S.-Mexico borderland demonstrate that being the church in the twenty-first century will involve more than our belief systems, our pronouncements—it will involve our bodies bound together, inscrutable and conflicted though they may be. Despite all appearances, we are still being reconciled through the activity and radical hospitality of the Spirit.

"Joshua"

The morning I arrived, Mark Adams gave me the number of "Joshua," a border patrol agent who lived in Douglas, Arizona, a border town with Agua Prieta, Mexico.[4] This, I thought, was peculiar: why would Mark put me in contact with, of all people, a border patrol agent? Nonsense, I thought. My stated purpose, after all, was to see how community was being formed amid exilic realities and leaving me with the border patrol seemed like the exact wrong way to go. A visit to a detention center or even to the Migrant Resource Center (which I did visit later on) seemed logical enough, but an agent who helped to enforce the militarization of the border? While I thought it peculiar, I said nothing at the time. I never asked about Mark's reasoning. Maybe he didn't have any. I asked him several times, "What is your given day like?" His reply, "I don't have a 'given' day. It's different every day." When I pressed him on it, he would only repeat that he had no pattern. So I finally stopped asking him about patterns and went along for the ride. Maybe this was just another one of those "random" happenings. Perhaps. However, if his days had no pattern (and this turned out to be true), there were clear patterns of intentional community. And this, to my mind, suggested a kind of logic to this as a starting place: it seemed so remote from anything I had anticipated it *had* to be logical. Like the shrine, the prospect of meeting a border patrol agent seemed to be joining things together that we would ordinarily keep separate. What I would discover during my visit is that these categories, while bearing some truth, come at a great cost. They tend to obscure deeper truths about our common need of each other, how our salvation is wrapped up in the other. This is no less the case for a border patrol agent than it is for a migrant or an activist—or a consumer.

For his part, Joshua, a devout Christian, found his way into U.S. border enforcement through a failed marriage and a job loss in his native home of Michigan. As he began to put his life together again, he decided to join the U.S. Border Patrol, an agency that was about to grow exponentially. After

---

4. "Joshua" agreed to this interview on the condition that his name not be used. In order to honor his request, I have also changed identifying details to protect his anonymity. "Joshua," interview by author, audio recording, Douglas, AZ, 17 July 2011.

his training, he was assigned to the Southwest region. Now, almost ten years after his graduation, serving as a border patrol agent in Douglas, he arrests and deports undocumented people. He clings to the conviction that he can bring "nobility to the job" even if the job is often inescapably ignoble. But because of Joshua's faith, he has also been drawn into the circle of Frontera de Cristo, along with its concerns, which he, as a border patrol agent, negotiates from a deeply personal place. Without prompting from me, as we drove around town in his beat-up sedan, Joshua quickly seized on the question of *his* identity, whether resident or alien: "I, as a Christian, I don't know if I would say that I'm in exile or found sanctuary here in Douglas, but ten years now, living in this city, and knowing both sides of the border fairly intimately . . . whether [or not] I've found exile or sanctuary here, *I've found a home here.*" He says that during the time he has lived in Douglas, many of the people he graduated with from the Border Patrol Academy have come and gone, and many others, the undocumented, he arrested and deported; but he has remained.[5]

As Joshua spoke of his experience of the borderlands, he referred to job opportunities more than once: "Others have come here to work as firefighters, border patrol agents, police officers, sheriffs, teachers, and many other lines of work." Living on the border, or near it, entails a culture shock, in that Douglas is not an ordinary place; its dynamics are what some refer to as "border town culture." It is a small town, but it is in close proximity to the borders of the modern nation-state and global financial system. There is a criminal element, too, as has been well-publicized. Some people who migrate, Joshua reminds me, are the "bad guys"—running drugs, prostitution rings, working for cartels. Surprisingly, however, the criminal element seems less pronounced in Joshua's account than the economic conditions that lead people to migrate, including the conditions shaping his own life story. He recalled, for example, working as a laborer for a landscaping company as a teen: "I was the only White boy on the crew." Arriving one morning with an "empty tank of gas and an empty stomach," a coworker, a Latino, gave him something to eat and said he would have lunch for him that afternoon: "That was my first experience of undocumented migration that I knew of." Today, he says, the opening of a textile factory in Agua Prieta "warms the cockles of my heart." Even if most will work for just eighty dollars a week, it's a job, he says, better than nothing.[6]

Beyond the economic features of the border, there are, he says, unlikely graces, as some get arrested and some deported, some escape, or in the context of meetings between officials and migrants, something happens, an epiphany,

5. Ibid.
6. Ibid.

perhaps. Joshua says these experiences give him a connection to the people he meets:

> [These experiences are in my mind] when I meet them [detainees] either in a cell in our station, in the back of a truck, or somebody arrested as a group in a house here in town, or possibly somebody I chased down an alley, tackled, and handcuffed. Now I can talk to that guy and ask him some legitimate questions: Hey, where were you born? Where do you live? How is it right now in the pueblo where you live? . . . and then he and I have an adult conversation about some real problems that he's trying to leave.

When asked if he experiences a contradiction between his faith and his duty, he acknowledges a "fracture" but quickly minimizes its significance: "Although there is a fracture there [between the Christian vocation and border patrol activities], we can look in the Bible and see Paul in the prison and yet he sang with the guards. I've experienced that. . . . At the same time, I don't have a problem exercising force: that's part of my job. So although the dichotomy is there, I don't always see it."[7] Not always, maybe, but sometimes.

Perhaps unwittingly, Joshua surfaces a tension that he does indeed feel as a border patrol agent:

> I try to do what Paul said, somewhere in Galatians or Ephesians . . . where Paul says put on the full armor and above everything put on love. So I got my badge, I got my gun, I got my radio, I got my baton to break somebody's ankle. I've got everything I need today . . . well where's my love? Well, it's in my heart and I need to bring it out here at work. . . . I need to be a Christian at work [regardless] of what may have happened that day.[8]

Joshua seems to be naming the tension between his vocation and his faith: "*I've got everything I need today.*" Everything. *And, ironically, nothing at the same time.* Wearing the uniform authorizes a form of total power over the life another human being, a form of state-sanctioned violence to be executed on the body of the undocumented migrant who, at present, is insufficiently protected by U.S. Border Patrol policy.[9]

---

7. Ibid.
8. Ibid.

By the same token, however, border patrol agents as individuals step into a system that prescribes their actions and their loyalties. They do not exercise absolute agency. Between the "badge and the gun," an agent's activities are no longer his or her own but, in the logic of law enforcement, belong to the state. The agent's person mirrors the totality of the nation-state, and this entails a suppression of the humanity of the agent, his or her ambivalence about the job, and perhaps how the agent practices his or her faith in that place. Mark tells me that, given a change in immigration law, many border patrol agents would rather help migrants fill out immigration paperwork. Joshua is no exception. As it is, he goes on patrols in desert regions in order to enforce U.S. immigration law. Ambivalence suggests itself regarding whether his oath to enforce U.S. border security is entirely complete in itself, as if the symbols of state power were insufficient or, at heart, in fundamental conflict with his own human identity.

If conflict it is, it only begs the question: how then does his Christian identify find outlet in his work? Although he acknowledges a tension between work and faith, Joshua expresses his faith through "civil rights in action," something not inconsistent with U.S. laws—namely, his duty to supply food, water, and dignity to detainees: "That part of my day [is] to reaffirm that he [the detainee] is a human being, he still has rights, still valued by God, and I might not do that verbally but by giving him a gallon of cold water . . . and even though I've arrested him, he's loved by me too, you know. And I've had many, many of my [detainees] tell me, '*Usted es un buen official*' (you're a good officer), and every time they tell me, I almost want to cry."[10] As he speaks, his voice quavers with emotion. Perhaps his emotions surface just here because he hopes to salvage something of his own humanity against the ravages of a system that imperils both migrant and agent.

Although the migrant bears the bruises, Joshua wears the uniform that authorizes sometimes violent acts of coercion. Which is the more harmful is hard to say. Like a victim, he can never remove the skin that authorizes physical coercion, not really and not completely. According to the psalmist, the garment of violence can leach into our very being: "He clothed himself with cursing as his coat, may it soak into his body like water, like oil into his bones" (Ps.

9. The Border Patrol is undergoing increased scrutiny in light of charges that it uses excessive force in its apprehension tactics. See for example, "Border Patrol Under Scrutiny for Deadly Force," *USA Today*, 14 November 2012, http://www.usatoday.com/story/news/nation/2012/11/14/border-patrol-probe/1705737/. See also Mark Adams et al., *A Culture of Cruelty: Abuse and Impunity in Short-Term U.S. Border Patrol Custody* (No More Deaths, 2011).

10. Joshua, interview by author, 17 July 2011.

109:18). Mark believes that being a good officer, or "redeeming what they do" as officers, is one thing; but the prospect of *leaving* what they do, that is, taking off the uniform and all it signifies, poses far deeper challenges.[11]

I didn't go that far in my conversation with Joshua, but it was probably not too far beneath the surface. Violence may erupt suddenly in the borderlands, perhaps the way the arroyos, previously empty, can suddenly transform into raging waters during the monsoon season. Violence may threaten to sweep up one's identity, rendering those who are daily exposed to it especially vulnerable. The desert may seem barren, but it is not and it can change dramatically, in an instant.

While I was south of the border in Mexico, tending to the water stations set up along a migrant trail about twenty miles or so from Agua Prieta, my hosts gave me a pair of binoculars and pointed to a lookout on top of the ridge, about a quarter mile away. They told me that it belonged to one of the narco armies that controlled the area. The Mexican army had destroyed it once, but the narco traffickers had quickly rebuilt it. I wondered if, at that very moment, someone might be watching us as we made our way along one of the sandy paths used by migrants and drug smugglers alike. When we came to the wall, my companions stood up on the ridge and told me to watch the road that ran parallel to the wall, just north of it, in the United States. In a matter of minutes, we could see a white border patrol SUV roaring down the road, coming toward us, as if to warn us that we were being watched. For me, this was just one day, one three-hour experience. Joshua thinks about these realities every time he goes on patrol. Flesh and blood issues of justice and dignity, violence and hostility, present themselves regularly. By contrast, supposedly "objective" or "middle of the road" people—those of us, for example, who take the "good deals" of cheap labor while turning a blind eye to our own complicity in the perpetuation of the global financial system—see borderland violence only as a report or perhaps a statistic or a problem for the border rather than the whole of society.

A convenient illusion, of course. Joshua understands himself as a participant in a daily reality rather than one who merely opines about an abstract issue. His relationship with displaced peoples and displacing economies is far from metaphorical. According to his own testimony, thirst, medical needs, fractured narratives, and the threat of violence appear regularly in his day-to-day work on the border. The body of the exile and his own body may be literally locked together in a life-or-death struggle. If so-called ordinary people were to subject their own activities as consumers to the kind of reality testing present in Joshua's

---

11. Adams, interview by author, 18 February 2013.

struggle with faith and vocation, we might be in a very different kind of society; more importantly, perhaps we might begin to feel the more bracing urge to foster a different kind of church community. Maybe it would even come to resemble something like a home, complete with real tensions and bonds, rather than merely aping the certitudes and routines of a financial system.

But Joshua's narrative is instructive in one more way: Joshua wants to be a "good officer" not only for the detainee but among those who offer scathing criticism of U.S. immigration policy. His longing leads him to keep some unlikely company, especially among the people of Frontera de Cristo. Joshua's determination to be part of this community continues to impress me, and perhaps it is a testimony to the kind of community that Mark has tried to cultivate through the ministries of Frontera de Cristo. At the same time, the church does not always welcome the kind of conflict Joshua's presence creates. His determination to be the "good officer" was, and remains, bewildering and, perhaps to some, offensive enough to reject him completely. When this happens, not only does Joshua lose but so does the community. If communities of faith jettison his place in this conversation, not only do they lose his perspective, which has its place, but they also lose the way the church in North America, as passive beneficiary of the global financial system, uses soldiers and border enforcement personnel as abstract proxies in a conflict that it keeps at arm's length (sometimes in the name of "theology"), thus washing its hands of any real sign of understanding its complicity.

This kind of moral and ethical cleansing takes place regularly in church communities that pursue a clear picture of victim and victimizer. As I listened in on a meeting between activists, church groups, Frontera de Cristo representatives, and Latino and Hispanic residents of Douglas, the offense of his inclusion was evident. The group, which included about a dozen or so people from out of state, had gathered for a meal and information gathering, seeking to understand what is happening at ground zero of the immigration crisis, what progress or challenges still remained in the struggle for justice, and so on. There's often a sense of unanimity in these sorts of meetings, of being on the same "side" in the struggle of good versus bad, and usually the "bad" are not invited. Most of the time, they're not interested, either. Unless, perhaps, there is something else going on, as there was on that particular night in the shape of Joshua's longing to be fully human. As we sat at tables arranged in a rectangle, Joshua shared his perspective as an agent *and* Christian. Some did not welcome his perspective and said so; others listened politely but said nothing in response. Afterward, however, little huddles engaged in the predictable chatter: "What's the Nazi doing here?" Maybe by labeling him as the "worst" some believed they could remove the conflict his presence created: an agent among activists, a person at the opposite end of the immigration debate but one who was also deeply embedded in an attempt at an authentic encounter with faith-based communities.

Listening to Joshua, I often found myself responding with frustration, uneasy with his willingness to think of instruments of violence as just one more piece of the armor of God: "I got my baton to break somebody's ankle." Particularly grieving to me was the ease with which he married violence and Scripture, but my time with him was disquieting in more significant ways: he embodied violence in a way that is ordinarily all too easy for someone like me to ignore or, if not to ignore, to treat as an object outside of my reality. That's my illusion. The nation-state and global financial system—which I support through taxes and unchecked consumerist behavior—contributes to this violence. Meanwhile, the church's quiet acquiescence to injustice ends up aiding and abetting that violence while its theology is usurped by a nation-state hungry for theological validation. As a citizen and member of the church, Joshua believes (not without a particular kind of reason) that he wields his "baton to break somebody's ankle" as an expression of my own life and commitments as a U.S. citizen and follower of Christ. It's all a bit too close for comfort. One is tempted to simply suppress his presence altogether, to "cleanse" our identity of any complicity in that kind of violence. Such were my feelings at the time, and perhaps these were not dissimilar to the reactions I witnessed during the church meeting in Douglas.

Resisting that temptation, the community of Frontera de Cristo negotiated the kind of complexity Joshua presented in more theologically disciplined ways—ways that required not just one meeting or one interview, but instead a long journey. Something of that journey, its ordinariness and complexity, appeared in what seemed like an off-hand remark by A. Tommy Bassett III, one of the members of the Frontera community and the Director of the Just Trade Development Center of Café Justo (more on Café Justo below). Just as Joshua was leaving the U.S. site of Frontera de Cristo, Tommy called out after him, "Don't bring any bullets," and then, pausing, added, "except one." Later, when I asked Tommy about his comment, he explained that he was opposed to the violence of U.S. border policy, represented by the sidearm Joshua would carry that day, but he was also trying to acknowledge his affection for him, his exposure to dangers on the border, where drug cartels and smugglers are armed and often operate with impunity.

Agents can quickly turn into victims. The U.S. Border Patrol reports a 70 percent increase in assaults against agents. For both migrants and agents, the border is becoming an increasingly violent place. U.S. Border Patrol agents have been shot and killed while patrolling the border. But the escalation of violence seems grossly asymmetrical, even according to the U.S. Border Patrol: "Rock throwing," says one U.S. Border Patrol official, "is probably the most common form of assaults [sic]."[12] Stones or not, the risk is real enough; crucially, however, the community of Frontera de Cristo strives to be even more real, more determined than the violence of the system itself.

This is no easy journey, not for Frontera de Cristo and not for Joshua. The culture of the border and border enforcement policy makes being a "good agent" especially difficult. As our conversation was about to end, Joshua admitted that things do not always go well on the border: "Cops get pissed off when people run from 'em, and they hit 'em, and we shouldn't do that if we've already got 'em restrained."[13]

Agents shouldn't assault detainees, but they sometimes do. No More Deaths sets out to demonstrate what Joshua hints at as a broader culture of violence. According to the authors of "A Culture of Cruelty: Abuse and Impunity in Short-Term U.S. Border Patrol Custody," a report that culls through thirty thousand incidents of abuse and mistreatment by border patrol agents, abusive treatment is not an aberration "attributable to a few rogue agents" but instead reflects an institutional and systemic culture of abuse:

> The abuses individuals report have remained alarmingly consistent for years, from interviewer to interviewer and across interview sites: individuals suffering severe dehydration are deprived of water; people with life-threatening medical conditions are denied treatment; children and adults are beaten during apprehensions and in custody; family members are separated, their belongings confiscated and not returned; many are crammed into cells and subjected to extreme temperatures, deprived of sleep, and threatened with death by Border Patrol agents.[14]

---

12. Greg Bledsoe and R. Stickney, "US Border Patrol Reports 70 Percent Spike in Assaults on Agents," NBCNews.com, 14 March 2013, http://usnews.nbcnews.com/_news/2013/03/14/17315534-us-border-patrol-reports-70-percent-spike-in-assaults-on-agents#.

13. Joshua, interview by author, 17 July 2011.

14. Adams et al., *A Culture of Cruelty*, 4. The report concentrates on twelve areas of concern: denial of sufficient water, denial of sufficient food, failure to provide medical treatment or access to medical professionals, inhumane processing center conditions, verbal abuse, physical abuse, psychological abuse, dangerous transportation practices, separation of family members, dangerous repatriation practices, failure to return personal belongings, and due process concerns.

The report's authors go on to assert that the abuse is "part of the institutional culture of the Border Patrol, reinforced by an absence of meaningful accountability mechanisms."[15] Among their findings are the following:

> Border patrol agents denied food to **2,981 people** and gave insufficient food to **11,384 people**. Only 20 percent of people in custody for more than two days received a meal. Agents denied water to **863 people** and gave insufficient access to water to **1,402 additional people**. Children were more likely than adults to be denied water or given insufficient water. Many of those denied water by Border Patrol were already suffering from moderate to severe dehydration at the time they were apprehended. Physical abuse was reported by **10 percent** of interviewees, including teens and children. The longer people were in custody, the more likely to experience physical abuse. Of the 433 incidents in which emergency medical treatment or medications were needed, Border Patrol provided access to care in only 59 cases—**86 percent** were deported without necessary medical treatment.[16]

The list of abuses goes on. The report shows an agency that lacks real external accountability but also an agency that, as part of the Department of Homeland Security, chooses the migrants' bodies, their flesh, as its primary theater for enforcement activity.

According to one Homeland Security document, "The intensification of border enforcement activities creates impediments to illegal entry that *increase the costs incurred by migrants*," including the "physical hardship" of a desert crossing.[17] By forcing migrants farther out of the city centers, Homeland Security uses the desert to expose the body of the migrant to ever-greater levels of vulnerability and exploitation. The idea of the desert as "deterrent" of "increased cost" is euphemistic for its cost in flesh and blood. Recent data confirm this relationship, especially in light of the doubling of the U.S. Customs and Border Protection forces, which contributes to migrants' decisions to cross in ever-more-remote and risky areas: the ratio of deaths to apprehensions has

15. Ibid.

16. Ibid., 5; bold in original.

17. Bryan Roberts et al., "An Analysis of Migrant Smuggling Costs along the Southwest Border," Working Paper, Department of Homeland Security, Office of Immigration Statistics, November 2010, http://www.dhs.gov/xlibrary/assets/statistics/publications/ois-smuggling-wp.pdf; emphasis mine.

increased from 0.046 percent in 2007 to 0.112 percent in 2011, according to a statistic provided by U.S. Customs and Border Protection.[18]

Although there has been a 62 percent decrease in the number of illegal border crossings between 2007 and 2011, a closer look at the numbers points to a less than rosy condition on the border. The increasingly militarized status of the border, with growing numbers of "boots on the ground" and "drones in the air," makes crossing even more deadly, according to Isabel Garcia, cochair and founder of the Tucson-based *Coalición de Derechos Humanos* (Coalition for Human Rights). She says, "We never thought that we'd be in the business of helping to identify remains like in a war zone, and here we are."[19] The bodies of the poor, not the financial system that often makes undocumented migration the only real alternative to poverty, serve as the targets of the exceptionally well-financed U.S. Department of Homeland Security border enforcement activities. Intensify border control in the cities, drive would-be undocumented migrants farther out into the wilderness, terrify those who attempt to cross, increase the risks and expenses of using human smugglers—this is deterrence.[20] Or, in plain English, make the poor pay with their only possession: their skins.

Maybe we wonder how Joshua's story relates to the story of the migrant. It is not immediately self-evident since on the surface the two seem opposed. On the one hand, they could not be more different: one walks into the desert with backup and weapons and the support of the U.S. Department of Homeland Security. By contrast, migrants act like exquisitely vulnerable prey, hiding under cover of scrub brush or walking through the night in order to avoid detection, undergoing famine and thirst, suffering terrible injuries, and depending on poorly financed organizations like No More Death to offer help. While all are exposed to risk, the risk endured by a migrant is exponentially larger than that borne by an agent. There is much that separates these two identities. Yet financial need provides a commonality: border patrol agents are by and large not vigilantes who enjoy "stalking" migrants but people who found work in a system they themselves did not create. While this does not

18. U.S. Customs and Border Protection, cited by Carolina Moreno, "Border Crossing Deaths More Common as Illegal Immigration Declines," *Huffington Post*, 17 August 2012, http://www.huffingtonpost.com/2012/08/17/border-crossing-deaths-illegal-immigration_n_1783912.html.

19. Moreno, "Border Crossing Deaths More Common."

20. Reports of border patrol agents and/or vigilante groups slashing the water containers left by No More Death members and other migrant activists are not uncommon. Activists have been arrested for "littering" (leaving full containers of water along migrant trails), and other groups have been "dusted" by border patrol helicopters, an especially deadly tactic used against migrants because it instills fear and confusion, leading migrants to scatter and become disoriented in remote desert areas.

absolve them (or the larger public they serve) from moral and ethical reflection on their vocations and actions, it does supply an understandable frame of reference. One can understand a particular action without blessing it. Much of what happens on the border—and well within the borders of the United States—points to the global financial system. Financial need appears to be a common thread between the two, between border patrol and migrant peoples. Migrants do not come to the United States because they "love America" but because they want to feed their children. Not entirely unlike the people who are paid to track them down in the desert.

But the connections go deeper than the financial narratives alone would suggest: like the migrant's shrines, mostly invisible to the larger public, the faith of people like Joshua is concealed in the poverty of the uniform, beneath the imperatives of the financial system and only intermittently present as coherent witness. Like the undocumented person who crosses, the border patrol agent may well struggle between the coherence of pilgrimage and the way the "far country" of empire imperils faith, identity, and community. While the destitution of the one is self-evidently that of the victim—a victim "disappeared" into a desert and xenophobic culture—the destitution of the other is hidden behind the guise of the nation-state and the financial system that animates it. The bodies of each are, in a sense, "disappeared," and to that extent both remain tragic. Maybe part of the purpose of a community formed amid exiles, communities that include people like Joshua, is to keep the question alive, the possibility of change going.

Perhaps most instructive is the sense that Joshua presents the community of faith with an enormously complex problem: authentic Christian community cannot get along either by scapegoating entire groups or by abandoning radical convictions of justice and prophetic witness. They belong together, but the company they keep is never easy, never without some form of creative tension. While I was visiting the Altar Valley with John Fife, cofounder of No More Deaths, I asked him if a border patrol agent had ever shown an interest in joining him on one of the migrant trails where No More Death's teams walk and attempt to offer help to migrants they meet on the trail. "Yes," he said, "there was one. I said sure, you can come along. He was welcome. But only thing is, I said, you *cannot* wear that uniform." Whether the agent ever followed up on that offer, I don't know. Most agents probably wouldn't. But Joshua seems like one who is trying, in an imperfect way, to walk the migrant trail. Perhaps more significantly, there is a community that is trying to walk with him. At least in one agent, there is more than a uniform at work.

A LITURGICAL WORLD

The conviction that there is more than a uniform at work on the border could easily be set to one side as a matter of individual conscience and forgotten. That is, it could be seen as a matter primarily for the individual to enact. Something I *choose to do as a matter of personal conviction* rather than seek to *embody as a matter of liturgical habit*. Something held in the individual conscience rather than shared as the collective body. Those who grieve the state of the border might point to promising exceptions, perhaps like Joshua. But if we left it there, we would rob the church of its most profound expression: being the body of Christ in the world. As Paul would have it, the whole body operates together, and it is nothing short of heretical to imagine that Christian witness can be reduced to the private conscience of individual believers doing the best they can under the circumstances. One part of the body cannot act on its own but always acts in concert with and to the edification of the whole. Moreover, the complexities of exilic conditions call on a much more theologically expressive imagination than could be reproduced by one individual showing mercy. Theological imagination expressed through corporate performance entails the whole body gathering in order to dramatize an alternative world.

Sadly, it often seems the church operates in just the opposite way, returning people to the world as *individuals* as soon as it enters into the public square, virtually guaranteeing a sense of paralysis in the face of complex challenges. While it acted as a body in worship, its movements synchronized by a shared liturgy that underscored its deepest hopes in God, it undergoes a reverse transformation, or rather it scatters, its body dividing into discrete, and hopefully conscientious, individuals. Where does it scatter? Supposedly, into a nonliturgical and politically neutral public square. There we operate as individuals, making decisions based on rational calculation, for instance, rather than through liturgical practice. Apart from the church, we imagine that we live as "free agents" in a world bereft of liturgy.

Not so, writes James K. A. Smith: "We are what we love, and our love is shaped, primed, and aimed by liturgical practices that take hold of our gut and aim our heart to certain ends. So we are not primarily *homo rationale* or *homo faber* or *homo economicus*; we are not even generically *homo religiosis*. We are more concretely *homo liturgicus*. . . . "[21] Smith uses language like "embodiment" and "ultimate concerns" and "pedagogies of desire" (i.e., practices, rituals, and liturgies that act as tacit forms of education, shaping the body according to an

---

21. James K. A. Smith, *Desiring the Kingdom: Worship, Worldview, and Cultural Formation* (Grand Rapids, MI: Baker Academic, 2009), 40.

ultimate yearning or hope) to get at what he means by liturgy. Smith shakes up our thinking of liturgy as principally a religious act in order to gain a more generous and expansive understanding of those patterns of embodiment that shape the human identity. Formative liturgies may be secular, economic, or military, as well as religious.

While he offers a more nuanced description of liturgy than I will repeat here, the crucial character of liturgy is not that it belongs to a particular church or religious tradition, but that it serves as a ritual of ultimate concern: "Liturgies are the most loaded forms of ritual practice because they are after nothing less than our hearts."[22] They "inculcate particular visions of the good life, and do so in a way that means to trump other ritual formations."[23] In other words, liturgies express an almost Darwinian spirit as they "compete" to provide the ultimate account of our deepest desires as human beings: "Our thickest practices—which are not necessarily linked to institutional religion—have a liturgical function . . . that aim to do nothing less than shape our identity by shaping our desire for what we envision as the kingdom—the ideal of human flourishing."[24]

Smith points to the "liturgy" of the mall as an example of the way consumerism has exploited the *homo liturgicus*. A mall, he says, seems like a temple of sorts, its nearest historical antecedent being the medieval cathedral. In most communities, it stands as the central gathering place of the town or city. People come not only to purchase items, but to eat and to fellowship with one another, to see and be seen. Others take their daily exercise in the mall, padding back and forth through the cavernous, always well-lit structure. At the center of the mall, there might be an open steeple of ceiling windows. This supplies the "center" for the religious pluralism of consumerism. The walkways and food courts, he might say, are the outer courts of the temple, where the masses gather. However, if we desire a deeper identification with the thing we love, we enter one of the side temples, where we meet with the high priests and priestesses of that particular god, usually smiling, attractive, eager to help. If we make an offering, we receive not only the purchase but also a bag, much more important as a public marker than the purchase, which remains private. The embossed bag announces the particular kind of consumer we represent: an Abercrombie consumer, for example. [25]

Such routines, rites, and liturgies, whether economic or political, are freighted with competing messages about what is ultimate and who we are

22. Ibid., 87.
23. Ibid., 86.
24. Ibid., 87.
25. For a more extended description of the "mall as liturgical space" see ibid., 19–24.

in relation to that ultimate. If this is the case, says Smith, then Christian communities need to critically assess the liturgies that shape society in the public square. Alongside that process of critical assessment, church communities need to become "intentionally liturgical, formative, and pedagogical in order to *counter* such mis-formations and misdirections." Practices of Christian worship will remain at heart aimed at the restoration of a "creational desire of God," but they will also practice liturgies of counterformation, challenging and competing with the "mis-formation of secular liturgies into which we are 'thrown' from an early age."[26]

As communities of faith find the exilic landscape encroaching on them more and more each decade, the call for intentional counterformation in the public square will become increasingly critical. One could liken it to the expanding deserts or the rising waters associated with climate change. These liturgies seep into the liturgical space of the Lord's Day worship; without challenging those liturgies in specific ways, they, as competitive and well-financed productions, could very well overwhelm our best intentions. There's little doubt in my mind that communities in the borderlands of the Southwest understand this fact more so than other congregations that view the border as something vague and indistinct. Misformation through the militarization of the border and the dehumanization of migrants alerts communities like Frontera de Cristo to the dysfunction at work in the public square.

The Healing Our Borders Vigil, described below, suggests how the communities around Douglas, Arizona, and Agua Prieta, Mexico, have sought to develop a counterliturgy to border intimidation and a shocking "wake up" against the routinization of a deportation regime. It acts as counterpedagogy as it shows the poverty of the financial system, exposing the hidden costs of U.S. border policy, and even awakens onlookers to an identity that is not conformed to the systems of consumer, commuter, and nation-state.

HEALING OUR BORDERS: A PUBLIC LITURGY

The liturgy begins almost innocuously. A passerby would barely notice it, its beginning almost indistinguishable from everything else going on around it. Yet, to the careful observer, something would appear out of place, especially when members of the group start to transfer a truckload of white crosses into a waiting grocery cart. It seems awkward at first, comingling these sacred signs with a grocery cart, perhaps from Wal-Mart. The space around us does not authorize this kind of beginning. We're not commuters or consumers. Even

26. Ibid., 88.

so, begin it does, each Tuesday evening, at around five o'clock, as those who will keep the vigil begin to gather at the edge of a McDonald's parking lot alongside the Pan American Highway in Douglas. It may seem small, transient in nature, especially when compared to the imposing structures of the border and interstate highway, but the concern at its heart casts a very long shadow. The vigil represents a memorial for those who have died while crossing the desert in Cochise County, a witness against the injustices of U.S. and Mexico border policies, and a public lament at the costs exacted by the global financial system. The groups vary in size, from three or four to a dozen or more, and they are usually composed of different faith and ethnic groups. As the vigil progresses from the north to the south, the participants carry crosses with the names of the deceased written on them. Moving in leapfrog fashion, each participant hoists her or his cross into the air when reaching the head of the southward end of the line and calls out the name of the deceased, then the rest of the vigil participants cry out in unison "*Presente!*" The person at the head of the line faces oncoming traffic as he or she announces the name of the dead. Once the other vigil members have responded, the person bearing the cross places it on the ground, between the curb and road, and the next person in line repeats the liturgy.

Finally, as the participants near the border (about thirty or so feet north of it), they form a circle. The leader of the vigil gathers together three crosses, one with a woman's name, one with a man's name, and one "*No Identificado*" (unidentified). Participants share these three crosses, holding each cross in hand and heart, as vigil members prayerfully contemplate the persons of the deceased, where they died, their age at the time of death, their gender, and to whom they may have belonged. Traffic and sirens sound off in the background. Prayers are offered in silence. The group sings a simple song, calling on themes of the Spirit.

As the finale of the service, each of the crosses is placed in the middle of the circle. Then, taking hold of the cross marked "*No Identificado*," the leader of the liturgy turns to the north, the south, the east, and the west, crying out each time, "*No Identificado!*" And on behalf of that one called, on behalf of those who cannot answer, the congregation thundered in prophetic reply: "*Presente!*" In this way, Mark explains, the vigil claims the presence of Christ crossing borders of principalities and powers, triumphing over these borders of death with the promise of the empty tomb, the stone of separation rolled away.[27]

---

27. Adams, interview by author, 18 February 2013.

The liturgy ends almost as it began, almost casually. Participants talk, visiting as they collect the crosses from the side of the road. Later the group gathers at a local church in Douglas to enjoy a meal. But the way it appears and then suddenly vanishes into ordinary life, the life of fellowship and friendly conversation, does not lessen its influence on the life of the community afterward. I found this experience intriguing: how was it possible to move from this drama to the very ordinary actions of gathering and eating? Of course, I didn't have far to look: the life of the church frequently follows that pattern as it witnesses to the life, death, and resurrection of Christ and then gathers in the fellowship hall for cookies and coffee. If anything, the liturgy's habitual character supplies the accent, the aroma to every meal, illuminating every glance or shared word with something much deeper, unspoken perhaps except through the liturgy itself, which continues to speak in the memory of the participants.

While the liturgy itself is simple, the ironies of the liturgy and its immediate surroundings are dramatic and lasting. To the east of the vigil, traffic moves along the Pan American Highway, going to or coming out of Mexico. The older part of Douglas sits just beyond the highway. A strip mall stands on the west side of the highway, housing a variety of big-box stores, among these a Wal-Mart as well as several different fast-food chains. The border crossing is about a quarter mile south. When the vigil starts, around five o'clock, commuter traffic has already started to pile up. Sirens go off incessantly, saturating the area with what seems like a constant state of alarm. Even as this is in the background, the ordinariness of the place is striking, as people come and go, mostly as consumers or commuters and mostly without any trace of alarm. While the desert is an ecologically complex place, the border crossing in and around Douglas seems to have achieved a "monoculture" of sorts, with people mostly adjusted to the routine experience of either the "commuter" or the "consumer" or the "alarm" of the border—this state of affairs is almost surreal when, at any single moment, you can be assured that coyotes are smuggling people across the border and, alternatively, people are being deported south.

Together, it makes for an unsettling impression, as if there were a profound disconnect between the trauma and inhumanity of the border and the routine way in which people pursue their interests. But the vigil has a way of speaking into this place in a manner conditioned by neither the nation-state nor the financial system that seems to be otherwise taken for granted. Nor does the vigil allow the routines of border culture to mask the violence that takes place there. The vigil plays a small but crucial part in bringing into public what otherwise remains invisible, hidden in the routine quality of deportations or in the all-too-familiar reports of yet another body found in the desert.

You could say that the vigil "complexifies" the area as it mimes a liturgy of proclamation, lament, protest, intercession, and prayer. It does so through a form of salvage, drawing on something related to consumerism—namely, a shopping cart—to carry the crosses, hundreds of them, to the border itself. In fact, the shopping cart looks for all the world as if it had been abandoned, forgotten, left beneath a small vine-invested tree growing in a rocky island in the middle of an asphalt sea. But on Tuesdays, even this forlorn shopping cart is sanctified as holy salvage, like a modern version of Simon of Cyrene, carrying its unusual burden, crosses memorializing the dead. The crosses, painted white, almost look like bones, jutting out at odd angles, pushed along in a cart where we, as consumers, ordinarily place our purchases, our "things" which are not yet our things, but imminently our things; now, this cart carries a grisly purchase, bristling with the names of the dead. In a sense, the cart and its sacred memories become a shrine, salvaged from its ordinary function and reinterpreted in the context of protest, lament, and prayer.

With the juxtaposition of these images—crosses and grocery cart, evening commute and solemn lament—one gets an awkward feeling, an out-of-place feeling. Perhaps this is why Tommy Bassett began the first vigil I attended by telling us, "Nothing we're doing here is illegal." What he meant by that expression, I suppose, was that our activities would not be breaking any laws. Perhaps this was also a way of saying that this would be a nonviolent protest. But one could hear it in another way as well: the place we were standing was not accustomed to the acts, words, or peculiar juxtapositions of symbols within the vigil. The vigil did not "belong" here since it was neither a consumer nor a commuter, and yet, in a most significant way, it was profoundly appropriate just there, in that place, as it witnessed to the whole human community, especially that part that the financial system itself would have us forget or ignore. Given its peculiar visibility, it required some sort of explanation, if not an apology, for its existence. No, we were told, nothing we did that day would be illegal. But it would be profoundly visible—rather like the Word made flesh or as lambs among wolves.

If border enforcement activities restrict space and shape people, the liturgy operated in a different way, often exposing the system and liberating people who conformed to its powers to an alternative way of being. For example, a common interpretation of Jesus' word to the disciples that he is "sending them as lambs among wolves" stresses their vulnerability to persecution. However valid that interpretation may be, it should not exclude the visually shocking idea that the church deliberately acts as a lamb among wolves. Luke's Jesus stresses the dramatic alternative expressed by those sent in his name, how they bring to expression an unambiguously vulnerable love.

Of course, to be among wolves is also to be in the environment dominated by the culture of wolves. Although the vigil participants were the primary "congregation" for this gathering, the boundaries between the gathered community and the "outside" community were porous. As members of the vigil hoisted the cross, their gaze was met not only by other vigil members but also by commuters. Some drivers would nod, others might turn away, but each person, whether vigil participant, commuter, or even customs agent, could "hear" the address of this unique proclamation. Children were almost always wide-eyed as they watched the vigil group parade down the road. One young boy leaned out a car window to cry out, in unison with the vigil group, "*Presente!*" as they responded to one of the names of the dead. Another family walked along the sidewalk, rolling a small trolley behind them loaded with things bought at Wal-Mart. The husband nodded to one of the vigil participants, saying, "Thank you." And they continued on their way home, to Mexico.

Whatever else may have been thought about the vigil, it was "ill fit" to this space, in a sense far too large for the border as it has been constructed by the financial system and nation-state. Indeed, it split the space open as it mimed the drama of sacred memory, lament, and radical promise and return. On the one hand, it helped to expose the injustices of the border, memorializing the dead whose remains society would too quickly forget, but, on the other hand, it also contributed to the humanizing of the living, whether vigil participant or not. In a sense, like the crucifixion itself, onlookers and disciples were addressed by the cross, which ceased to be merely a Roman cross or the cynical betrayal of religious powers. Maybe the vigil, like the cross itself *and perhaps as a logical consequence of the cross*, became a sign not only of the injustices of the borderland, but also a sign of the resurrection, God's promised victory over powers and principalities.

CAFÉ JUSTO

What grows out of the church's testimony? Do these "counter-formations" and attempts at forming shrines of reconciliation ever produce something more tangible than moving witnesses? Is the life of the church limited to courageous liturgies and stirring struggles for justice in the deserts of injustice? When does the proclamation of the good news take root in an actual reality that contributes to meaningful economic alternatives and not just heroic and all-too-momentary stands for justice? When do the church's prayers manifest in real flesh and blood alternatives, capable of sustaining body and mind after the benediction has been given? When do the two, the church's testimony and its role in economic life, come together in close proximity so that they are, in a sense, engaged in a dynamic and holistic event of community, entailing both the call of witness and the response of social action? When does the church claim not only the language of protest but also the migrants' cry for survival and dignity?

Answers to at least some of these questions appear in the story of Café Justo, or Just Coffee, a small coffee-roasting cooperative owned and operated by the people of Mexico and closely affiliated with the Presbytery of Chihuahua (Mexico) and the Presbyterian Church (USA). As in the story of Ruth, the relationship between cultural insiders (U.S. citizens) and migrants was a reciprocal one: the genius and courage of this small enterprise and its potential to begin reshaping the economic map through faithful alternatives derives from both sets of voices and experiences. It would not be an exaggeration to say that the faith of the migrant as pilgrim and the willingness of those who have access to wealth through citizenship and skin color were midwives to one another, contributing to the total sense of the human being. At the same time, as in the story of Ruth and Naomi, the economic assumptions of the U.S. participants continue to be shaped and reshaped by the economic worldview of those from the southern hemisphere. A measure of security will surely be achieved, but it will not be without significant changes in worldview and questions of ultimacy.

The company's website introduces the cooperative and tells its story, accenting the product but also the social vision: "Café Justo is a coffee grower cooperative based in Salvador Urbina, Chiapas, Mexico. We market a pure, organic coffee which is grown, harvested and marketed in the spirit of justice. Our goal is to provide incentives for people to remain on their family lands." The company strives to create an alternative to migration by creating a bond between the coffee growing community (farmers and roasters) and the communities that purchase their product. Instead of an anonymous farming community (their anonymity making their lives and dreams easy to ignore), Café Justo stresses actual economic relationships and not merely financial ones. While operating within a global financial system, the cooperative rejects global aspirations, instead adopting a commitment to "provide the training and resources necessary for farmers to create and maintain a sustainable, small-scale, international coffee company."[28]

---

28. Café Justo, "About Us," http://www.justcoffee.org/
index.php?option=com_content&view=article&id=10&Itemid=7.

However, a mission statement could never fully tell the story of Café Justo because it actually arises out of testimony and pilgrimage, lament, mutual collaboration, and hope. In September 1999, Eduardo Perez Verdugo stood up before a church gathering, telling his story of migration from Chiapas, two thousand miles to the south, to work in one of the factories in Agua Prieta. He also told the gathering that he had been approached by someone who said that he could have a job in Phoenix paying many times what he earned in the factory and that further, with that income, he could quickly return to his home in Chiapas. Although he initially resisted, he finally decided to cross the border without documents:

> I have decided I will cross the border in two weeks, on October 4th [1999] after worship. I have found a coyote and he will help us get across to the other side without problems. We will have to walk for three days. . . . I ask you to pray for the Mexican government that we will find a better way. I ask you to pray for the United States that we will find a better way.[29]

The date arrived and the group began walking north, but they would not be on the migrant trail for very long:

> Three days later Eduardo was back at the church building in Agua Prieta, battered and bruised both emotionally and physically. He had not achieved the "American Dream." The limp in his walk testified to the twisted ankle and the banged knee he suffered falling down an embankment during his night hike. The scrapes on his face gave witness to the tight passage through the unforgiving mesquite forests of the Sulphur Springs valley.

He also "received a kick to his face and a boot on his neck" after he protested to an abusive border patrol agent that "the same blood ran thorough both of their veins and that both had the same need to provide for their families." At the end of this ordeal, Eduardo cried, in Spanish, "To leave our land is to suffer."[30]

Eduardo's cry was not lost on those who live day in and day out along the border, but it was difficult to see beyond the outrages against humanity inflicted by U.S. immigration policy. As Mark Adams and Chuy Gallegos, a

---

29. Mark S. Adams and A. Tommy Bassett III, *Just Coffee: Caffeine with a Conscience* (Douglas, AZ: Just Trade Center, 2009), 30.

30. Ibid., 32.

border ministry colleague, spoke in Colorado about migrant issues, someone in the conference challenged them, saying, "It's easy to talk about how bad things are. You need to do something about it!"[31] The challenge lingered with Mark and the Frontera de Cristo community. I suppose they knew this all along and were groping to name it; these two incidents, along with innumerable other experiences on the border, catalyzed their determination to do something no seminary ever trained ministers to do: become economic entrepreneurs. However, under Mark's leadership, Frontera was determined to be more than an entrepreneur, aping capitalist models. When it finally came to fruition, Café Justo would even go beyond the model offered by Fair Trade, the progressive end of capitalism.[32]

As it evolved, the vision for Café Justo aimed to do something different and more just; they wanted to establish an economic model that encouraged stability rather than instability, and ownership rather than financial captivity; and crucially, they wanted a model that was genuinely collaborative in spirit and practice. Following Eduardo's vision, they dubbed their business model "Fair Trade PLUS" because it would bring to fruition his "hope that farmers would be able to participate in the whole process—from cultivation to roasting to packaging." This model provided fair prices for the beans but also the added benefit of greater profit and employment in their home communities.[33]

A brief description of those who began this company serves to demonstrate the ethical, ecumenical, and collaborative spirit at its roots. In December of 2000, Frontera had no one with any business expertise, but they did have an idea as well as a small community of people to whom they were bound in the Spirit of Christ. Significantly, that community, though animated by decision to follow Jesus Christ across borders, did not stop at the boundaries of religious dogma but instead joined hands with people of different religious traditions, or even multiple religious traditions, or perhaps even no religious tradition, around the common concern of human dignity. Thus it was not insignificant that a pivotal meeting between Mark, an ordained Presbyterian minister originally from South Carolina, and Tommy Bassett III, originally from Minnesota, would take place at an atheist/Hannukkah party in the artist

---

31. Ibid., 36.

32. The latter, while attractive, suffered from two crucial problems: first, Equal Exchange, a pioneer in the Fair Trade coffee industry, was not entering into any new relationships with new communities; and second, although they bought the raw beans at "fair" prices, they effectively cut the farmers out of the most profitable end of the business, the final product, roasted coffee beans. Ibid., 37.

33. Ibid., 38.

colony of Bisbee, Arizona. According to Tommy, the party was being held to "protest Christmas."[34]

Though it was an unlikely meeting, an even more improbable friendship began to form between Mark and Tommy. Tommy had come to the Southwest to manage one of the largest border manufacturing plants in Mexico (plants owned by companies in the United States and given special tax breaks by both countries), in some ways representing the very antithesis of the kind of company he would eventually help to form in Café Justo. Moreover, when asked about his religious identity, Tommy answers, "My religious orientation [is] a Contemplative Roman Catholic Buddhist . . . with the emphasis on universal. . . ." For his part, Mark calls South Carolina home and understands himself as a disciple of Jesus Christ serving the Presbyterian Church (USA) in the Southwest. Perhaps more significantly, according to Mark, Tommy was initially not interested in issues on the border. That would begin to change after Mark invited Tommy to the Healing Our Borders vigil. The experience clearly impacted his views, and he started looking at the question more closely, and more religiously.[35]

Tommy says his involvement with the lives of migrant peoples has led him to a deeper engagement with the prayers of the church, prayers that had, at one time, begun to feel empty or somehow rang false:

> You can only pray so much when people are dying in the desert every week. And here it was a real killing zone. . . . A person [a 23-year-old woman] actually died in my yard. It was soon after we had started Just Coffee and the woman was from El Salvador. A day or two after she died, I got a phone call from her sister who was waiting for her in Houston. She knew she had crossed through Agua Prieta, and got my phone number from the Just Coffee website. It was a very traumatizing event. She was about a 100 yards from a water faucet.

Tommy wanted to do more than "gather" within a faith community to receive the mass or participate in a religious service disconnected from the world; instead, he longed to participate in a more worldly expression of his faith. Tommy wanted to use his business skills in a different way than they were being used by the financial system of the borderlands. As for faith, he cites Jesus'

34. A. Tommy Bassett III, interview by author, audio recording, Douglas, AZ, 19 July 2011; Adams and Bassett, *Just Cofee*, 38

35. Adams and Bassett, *Just Coffee*, 39.

words, "I was hungry and you gave me food, I was thirsty and you gave me something to drink, I was a stranger and you welcomed me" (Matt. 25:35). Setting water tanks out for migrants and using his gifts in a way that created spaces of hospitality "seemed like a natural thing to do."[36]

One more narrative led to the formation of this unique venture: In January 2002, an exile from Chiapas, Daniel Cifuentes, began to offer his expertise to the Fair Trade Plus vision team. Like others, Daniel came to the north for jobs at the border factories, or perhaps to cross into the United States. He had fled economic privation in Chiapas, where coffee bean growers were being destroyed by low prices. With three generations of experience as a coffee farmer, Daniel, who was also a Presbyterian, broadened the partnership to include exiles in the North of Mexico and their families and neighborhoods Salvador Urbina. Now with Mark, Tommy, and Daniel, as well as others in Agua Prieta, and members of the Lily of the Valley Presbyterian Church, they had strong cell to launch their vision. Eventually, they acquired a $20,000 microfinance loan from a missionary branch of the Presbyterian Church, to create a meaningful alternative to economic migration.[37]

Such was the beginning of Café Justo and today it has brought together many more stories, including the story of Pedro Maldonado Lopez, who works in Café Justo's roasting plant in Agua Prieta: "I am a Mexican," he says proudly, "a Chiapan."[38] Pedro, a man of slight build, his face betraying the high cheekbones of his Mayan ancestry, was devastated economically in the 1990s and migrated north in 1994 (the same year that the North American Free Trade Agreement was approved). He was not alone in this migration from the south to live in towns like Agua Prieta: "The majority of these folks left their lands, not because they wanted to live on the border or in the United States, but because the price they received for their coffee and farm products had fallen dramatically." During this period, prices for coffee had dropped from about $130 for each 125-pound bag to about $33 per bag—a 70-percent reduction.[39] Agua Prieta, like other border towns, saw its population quickly swell with Mexico's poor, the population growth rapidly outstripping the city's infrastructure.

36. Bassett, interview by author, Douglas, AZ, 19 July 2011.

37. Ibid., 37–38.

38. Pedro Maldonado Lopez, interview by author, trans. Mark Adams, audio recording, Agua Prieta, Mexico, 20 July 2011.

39. Adams and Bassett, *Just Coffee*, 31.

Coming this far north was no small undertaking, and it literally required Pedro to sell everything his family owned as well as things that he had cherished as a younger man. His migration included a lengthy separation from family:

> There in Chiapas, I had materials to build a house. I sold all that material . . . [to leave] money for the family and to be able to bring money for the trip. I had a very beautiful guitar as well and I had to sell it in order to get my passage paid. . . . I was here for about two years without my family and then they came in 1996. And then, as a family, we established ourselves here and I was already paying on this land here.[40]

Pedro left Chiapas not in his youth, but well into his mid-forties, at an age when getting new work proves more difficult, especially in a region where he would be a stranger, thus indicating just how severe the economic conditions were. He counted himself blessed to find a job in a *maquiladora* (a foreign-owned assembly plant) where he worked making seatbelts: "In Chiapas the economic problems were great and we could see in Agua Prieta a favorable change. We had money to buy food to eat, and clothes to wear, and to sustain the family, and also to pay rent."[41]

Initially, like many others who migrated north, Pedro imagined he would return to his home region:

> I had thought I would be here [in Agua Prieta] for six months and then return, but the blessing of work was great. . . . I felt like I would be able to sustain the family better. And [so] we started putting roots down here in Agua Prieta and erased the idea of going back to Chiapas, but even now, if there was an opportunity, we would go back. It is our native land; the majority of our family is there. [While we are not rich here in Agua Prieta] we have our house, we have our work, a salary and thanks be to God we've been able to survive.[42]

Although he had applied for a visa to the United States, his application was denied. Today, he says, he has no desire to enter the United States.

---

40. Lopez, interview by author, 20 July 2011.
41. Ibid.
42. Ibid.

Although he is not migrating again, he knows the migrant's path and, at the level of theology, he understands his identity in Agua Prieta as well as his work in Café Justo as an expression of God's life in the world as a stranger:

> People saw [Jesus Christ] as a stranger and he lived as a stranger. . . . [I]n the beginning, being in my own country [in northern Mexico], I felt like a stranger. [Until then] I'd never contemplated the history of our Lord Jesus Christ. The owner of all the universe, he came and lived here as a stranger and was a stranger. Even his own creation rejected him. . . . I think, as the Apostle Paul says, we are foreigners but God is giving us the opportunity to rejoice in the time here on earth. [As a] reality, this is very difficult to explain but it is very worth it to confront the situation. Who is this? [they asked of Jesus]. Where did he come from? The Pharisees asked this and Jesus seemed to be an unknown, not of his own people. . . . They've said that to me as well. There are many people who believe that Chiapas is not Mexico. It's another country. Some people don't recognize us as Mexican; we are strangers.

Speaking of the wall separating the United States and Mexico, Pedro says he "admires the situations of the Americans. [They have documents] and [because of this] a very good road." Why, he wonders, should Mexicans enter in a "hidden way" (i.e., illegally)? He says the wall is a show of power, a strategy to humiliate a weaker people. "The wall," he says, "is really not a solution for the U.S. because people still jump [cross illegally] and [poverty] is one of the reasons."[43]

When Pedro finally decided to put down roots in Agua Prieta, he and his spouse determined to build, as he put it, a "big house." Mark became curious about the "big house" Pedro had in mind, thinking this was out of character for him, a modest person by all accounts. For Pedro, it turned out a "big house" was code for hospitality and the spirit of pilgrimage:

> When I first arrived . . . there were people who searched me out as someone who could be trusted and I wouldn't deny them help when they were going north. In the same way, when we built this house, we've had an opportunity to house many people going north. Hundreds of people, probably two hundred, three hundred people have come through this house, [receiving] shelter and food

43. Ibid.

and economic help too. And we have had this opportunity to serve them in this way because God has given us the opportunity to have this house. People who search us out, we provide them shelter [and] welcome because I felt like a stranger when I got here and I think people who come here from outside felt like strangers, so we open our hands and arms and open our door and share our roof and table as well.[44]

Pedro, according to Mark, built for himself and his family a small house, but with a big vision.

Not long after Pedro migrated to Agua Prieta, he would become a member of the Lily of the Valley Presbyterian Church, a congregation consisting of many who came to Agua Prieta as economic exiles from their home state of Chiapas. It is within a stone's throw of the Café Justo roasting facility, where he works today. Although themes of exile recur in Pedro's testimony and that of others, there is another sense in which the church evokes the story of exodus as well. It is an exodus not only out of captivity to economically forced migrations, but also out of a particular financial system, an exodus represented by the more inclusive and just model of economic activity employed by Café Justo. According to Mark, when the group first developed the idea of linking farmers in Chiapas to the production facility in Agua Prieta, providing both farmers and workers with a partial share of the business's profit, they thought about keeping the idea to themselves, given that it was so revolutionary. But among the people in Chiapas, it was different, according to Mark: they wanted to share this model with their neighbors and other families of farmers so that it would foster something quite distinct and counter to the model of capitalism that otherwise seems to reign supreme.

Pedro's conviction that there is an exodus at work, that the ongoing exile of famine is not the only thing, is also reflected in his commitment to show hospitality to those moving farther north. The image of exodus supplies a significant metaphor for the experience of the faithful pilgrims of Agua Prieta. When I visited the Lily of the Valley Church, it was under construction, and someone, perhaps trying to beautify the otherwise plain concrete, had painted a mural on one of the side walls near the Lord's Table. The mural showed Moses descending Mount Sinai with the Ten Commandments. Suggestively, the artist used the outline of the mountain Cerro Gellardo, which dominates the skyline of Agua Prieta, in place of Mount Sinai, thus showing Moses coming down a mountain both familiar to actual life and yet also overlaid with the memory of

---

44. Ibid.

God's faithfulness. The mural seemed to announce that Lily of the Valley was not only born of suffering but also, as people recently liberated, continuing the pilgrimage for the home and society promised to them by God.

On Tuesday morning at the roasting plant, I joined the weekly Bible reflection that "interrupts" the regular work schedule at Café Justo. Although it is a business, this enterprise roots itself in the notion of God's presence and activity in the borderlands, not only in the church proper, but in the whole network of relationships that makes up the ecology of faithful community in pilgrimage. On that day, as we gathered in a room adjacent to the roaster, the text before the group was Matthew's parable of the mustard seed. We were each asked to reflect on what we heard God saying to us in the parable. Pedro's comments were memorable. He likened the church to a large tree, rich with foliage for shelter, food, and rest. "Many birds," he said, "land in this tree. They come and stay for a while and sometimes they go, fly away." This is the nature of trees: they extend hospitality to all, thriving in a complex ecology, which they reflect. The point of the parable, he continued, is not only that shelter would be offered, which is natural to the tree, but that we might grow closer to one another through the story of Jesus Christ. Rooted in the community forged on the cross, the church born of the mustard seed gospel exhibits a diversity of shelters, a capacity to welcome stranger and friend alike, and even enemies.

MI CASA ES SU CASA

It would seem that, at least in fits and starts, and in some quarters, the church is awakening to itself, returning to its life. What is it returning to? Perhaps, unlike the churches of Christendom where institutional affiliations or doctrinal commitments were the primary signature of the worshipping community, the church evoked by the stories of this chapter reflects a renewed sensitivity to geography, place, personhood, survival, and economy. A worshipper knows the church's particular expression of worship and witness not primarily through its denominational affiliation so much as through symbols of common life, what it salvages for faithful doxology. The story of God in these communities interacts in deliberate and vital ways with the surrounding communities, sometimes exposing idols, sometimes expressing a corporate and public lament, sometimes engaging in strategic efforts that contribute to the formation of meaningful economic alternatives. This church crosses borders boldly, intentionally, and prophetically.

Just as the Word became flesh, a scandal to some and foolishness to others, these communities are grappling with that reality, taking the visibility of the church in its fleshly expression as basic to the covenant of God. Such visibility means that the church is not the only community to "behold" the Word made flesh, though it may be the community that testifies to Christ's peculiar glory. Some will hear thunder while others will hear the voice of God. The church's voice and its visibility come together as a vocation of right speaking and right seeing. With that vocation, the walls of the church of Christendom suddenly become too narrow. The church, as Pedro understood it, is vastly more complex than we imagine even as it remains profound in its simplicity of devotion. Like Ruth, the church clings with its whole body to the desolation of Naomi, and yet, at the same time, like Naomi, it neither wholly denies its capacity to broker meaningful change nor remains unchanged in its own right. A community forged amid deep exilic realities will, if it takes those conditions as a matter of vocation, reflect a heterogeneous quality. Reconciliation takes practice, patience, and openness not only to the other but to the way the other may show Christ more clearly than we imagined possible.

Return clearly means something different to different people. For some, like Pedro, Joshua, and Lucia, it means continuing to live in the place they now call home. Whether in the United States or Mexico, in Chiapas or Agua Prieta, a theology of return is at once partial and incomplete, and yet, in the spirit of the promise, always confirmed as a present reality. Perhaps the church needs to expand its vocabulary to include not only return, in its radical sense, but also survival and stability, thriving in the city where we live for the time being. Each story of this chapter supplies a small but significant glimpse into this narrative of return.

Giacomo Danesi, writing of migration and its close connection to survival, suggests that those who undergo migration are "gradually forming a new social fabric, a new body, which the Gospel message is called to animate."[45] This new fabric contains a "tragic aspect," but, at a prophetic register, it signifies transformation, appealing for community in places where profound intimacy and radical estrangement are brought together in the fierce testimony of God's steadfast love, a love that clings to us despite our circumstances. Likewise, it means growing in the land of Babylon, actually prospering there. It is ironic that the prosperous mainline church often eschews what it dubs a "prosperity gospel" while the poor often seem to gravitate to a gospel that promises not only "spiritual" and "therapeutic" comfort but also material security. You don't have to baptize the prosperity gospel to grasp the significance the Scriptures assign to

---

45. Giacomo Danesi, *Church and Migration*, WCC Fifth Assembly Dossier 13 (Geneva: WCC Migration Secretariat, 1981), 10–41, at 35, quoted in Gemma Tulud Cruz, "Between Identity and Security: Theological Implications of Migration in the Context of Globalization," *Theological Studies* 69, no. 2 (June 2008): 369.

prosperity, the book of Ruth supplying but one example. Another more well-known text appears in Jeremiah:

> Build houses and live in them; plant gardens and eat what they produce. Take wives and have sons and daughters; take wives for your sons, and give your daughters in marriage, that they may bear sons and daughters; multiply there, and do not decrease. But seek the welfare of the city where I sent you into exile, and pray to the Lord on its behalf, for in its welfare you will find your welfare (Jer. 29:5-7).

Perhaps the legitimate caution between the biblical language of well-being and the "prosperity gospel" comes in a warning: do not confuse Zion with Babylon. For Jeremiah, Babylon remains the butcher it is even if the community of faith remains faithful to whose it is.

A practical theology of return clearly means much more than confronting geographic or political borders, but the theology of return is incomprehensible without geography through which to anticipate the promise of God's return. Just as Paul found talking about the resurrection without a body impossible, we could say that talking about return without geography is impossible as well. It matters that we live and work in a particular place, and especially that we worship and witness in a particular place. The church is the first expression of local politics, the best kind of politics since it takes its beginning at the cross, where nothing but the politics of the principalities and powers seemed to be at work. The promise of the resurrection catalyzes our understanding of that moment and that place.

Finally, these stories evoke the spirit of a church committed to community formation and not primarily to cement buildings. Buildings do, in fact, appear as an expression of the worshipping community, but the building is an open one, a continuing one, a "migratory" building, its basic identity found in and through the narratives of movement and encounter. A "migratory building" reflects the contrariness of the metaphoric logic represented by the shrine, as it signifies the stability of shalom and, at the same time, the restive spirit of social revolution. Community formation of this kind asks the people of God to gather, to foster security and stability but also to look out, to see where the Lord has gone, to follow God more radically and faithfully into the world—whether that leads onto the migrant trail, as strangers in a strange land, or into a parking lot alongside the Pan American Highway—in all cases open to the diversity of shelters blossoming in the body of Christ, the church. The building of the church is never a sealed tomb but an open calling, where borders remain porous rather than closed.

Maybe this sense was somewhere behind the words of Pedro, when, holding my hands in his hands, he said, "*Mi casa es su casa.*" *My house is your house.* I stammered, embarrassed, as I repeated his pledge in his modest home holding a big vision, a vision too big for the world or seemingly for my reciprocation of his pledge. My words sounded hollow to my own ear and I wonder if he heard the words that way, too unbearably thin to carry the burden of our day and our lands. Pedro will probably never sit at our table, never enjoy the view of Dubuque's Mississippi valley. My words seemed like exiles, shorn from the hospitality he showed me and would show again and again to many others.

In spite of these realities, this was a statement of faith wrapped around a reality. While Pedro may never cross the border between the United States and Mexico, in that expression he welcomed me into his home, welcomed me as a friend who would otherwise remain a stranger in a strange land.

Two migrants joined hands to become pilgrims. We are not there yet. Lucia is not there yet. Neither is Joshua. Even so, we walk together beneath a great canopy of grace: "Mi casa es su casa."

4

A Broken Benediction

The Gospel of Matthew and Homelessness in Dubuque, Iowa

> *Beauty is often hidden, particularly in the places abandoned by Empire. It's covered by crumbling bricks and swollen bruises, stained jeans and tall weeds, leaking roofs and rotting wood. Here, beauty has been marred by concrete and violence, graffiti and neglect. When people visit our neighborhood, the lack of beauty is one reason they feel less welcome or safe. When I tell people where I call home, they often respond, "You live there?"*
>
> —Chris Brennan Homiak, Cherith Brook Catholic Worker[1]

If you walk down the southern end of Main Street in downtown Dubuque and look above the overhang of the thrift store there, you might see a little neon cross glowing through a window, as we did. Still new to Dubuque in 2003, my spouse and I were out walking, exploring our new home, when we noticed the neon cross gazing down on the street from a third-floor window. We saw people inside, their profiles outlined by light.

"Maybe a storefront church. Or maybe a charismatic church," we speculated. "Probably not Presbyterian," I added dryly. "Not with that neon

1. Chris Brennan Homaiak, "Seeds of Beauty," in Cherith Brook Catholic Worker (Lent 2012): 4.

cross." And we continued walking. Later, we learned that this "charismatic church" was actually a group of men gathering for worship in a side chapel of a homeless shelter.

Several years after this, but now as a volunteer, I became more acquainted with the shelter, particularly with its chapel. It's an interesting room. Worship leaders know just where to go, to the wall opposite the entrance, where someone has painted a mural showing a series of cathedral arches, royal blue, white, and gold. The symmetries of the arches suggest coherence, balance, as if they captured the natural order of the universe. A yellow trim outlines the arches, as if it were a portal of heavenly light splashing into the otherwise drab space of the shelter. Central to the room is a battered looking crucifix, a forlorn figure, bereft of the usual accoutrements of churchly glory.

Maybe, to some, it was cheesy, this crucifix and the mural, but when I arrived to lead worship for the first time, these symbols told me where I was supposed to sit, where I might "belong" in a shelter for those who do not belong. And this, I suppose, was where my comfort with those symbols ended. This particular "visualization" of church came from somewhere or, really, *someone*, perhaps reflecting the faith of one of the residents of the shelter who, when he was asked to "imagine" the church, saw something resembling a cathedral. Perhaps the mural suggests what many of us want: a world that makes sense, a place where beauty is exalted, where the doors are open rather than closed, and a place set apart for something different, deeper than merely survival. A place open with the generosity of hospitality. And yet, against this hope, the residents were *required* to attend the shelter's worship service, a service broadly ecumenical in content but essentially Christian in character.[2]

This was not lost on the residents. I came once to see how the service was conducted before I started volunteering. During announcements, prior to the beginning of the service, "John" (not his real name), a one-time resident of the shelter and now a paid employee of the shelter who had done some prison time for the sale and possession of drugs, was confronted by a younger African American man who, like me, was also attending for the first time. Unlike me, though, he was *required* to be there: "Why I am required to be here?" he demanded. "You can't force me to do this. This isn't my religion. This violates my constitutional rights, my religious freedom." John, who was known as the "captain" at the shelter, reminded him that as long as he was living in the shelter,

2. Given the nature of its work, a shelter may impose a variety of requirements, among these an expectation of sobriety among the residents, a commitment to a "drug free campus," hours when the shelter is closed during the day and when residents need to be back, length of stay, perhaps some kind of rent, work expectations, and so on.

he was required to attend the service.[3] And that was it. No one said anything. A whimper of protest gave way to quiet resignation.

That episode led me to reflect on that mural, the message it conveyed in its context—namely, the contrast between the church it imagined and the lives of the residents. The residents were required by the shelter to participate in worship, something pastors would never require of any church member, much less any nonchurch member. Yet homelessness was sufficient reason to strip this basic dignity from the residents and to do so almost exclusively on the basis of their poverty. Perhaps the shelter reasoned that they, unlike the middle classes, "needed encouragement" or the "comfort" or "wisdom" that a chapel service might provide. Charitably, some did derive comfort from those services, finding them redemptive. But the contradictory messages of the mural, which signified hospitality and generosity, and the less than generous requirement of chapel attendance made for a particularly unhappy form of Christendom.

What I saw at the shelter may have been raw, but it was not, by extension, isolated to that community or even original to it. The discrimination faced by the poor went beyond the shelter and was, in fact, of a piece with other forms of discrimination. An especially memorable interaction occurred during a sermon I was preaching from Jeremiah's letters to the exiles (29:1-7). I was trying to convey how difficult Jeremiah's sermon was to hear: "Pray for those who abuse you? Persecute you?" The sermon was safe so long as it was in Bible-land, but the next move was risky in ways I hadn't anticipated. I shared how my mother, for a brief time, had been homeless as a young teenager. Perhaps thinking about this experience and the homelessness she now sees on a regular basis, she commented, "Being poor in America is illegal. You have nowhere to go." When I related this to my "coerced" congregation, the reaction was swift: a resident who appeared to have only been half-listening, bolted upright. "What?" he demanded, in disbelief. Opposite him, an African American shot back, "Shit yeah, you can't go anywhere!" It was a lightning-fast exchange, a "dialogue" sermon where the truth rang out in an unalloyed manner. And the residents laughed a hard, knowing laughter.

That exchange brought into focus a problem broader and more complex in scope than a particular shelter, though, to be sure, it includes the shelter. The requirement to attend the worship service did not so much reflect a shelter as it did a larger church and society, more comfortable with coercion and

---

3. Several residents told me that this particular mission was actually more liberal in its application of the worship requirement. Shelters often have some form of work requirement, and others, including the one I served, included a worship requirement as well. That requirement was received by some with greater willingness than others, but whether welcomed or opposed, it was required.

discrimination than maybe either is prepared to acknowledge. It brought into focus what was there all along but, given the chance, we could politely ignore. By contrast, the Gospels are full of episodes you simply cannot ignore, not only because we care about their outcomes but because, at a deeply personal level, we know our hopes and dreams are at stake as well. When the crowds bring to Jesus a paralytic, the paralytic provides the focal crisis but not the only crisis. Reader and crowd alike stand in need of God's healing and reconciliation. Likewise, this community, in its brokenness, is only more visibly broken than the churches that support it.

But even here, amid the inconsistencies and the contradictions of such a community (or rather *communities*), one gets poignant glimpses of hope. The crucifix in the chapel, posed in the style of *Christus Victor*, shows Christ reigning from the cross as if it were his throne, his arms extending up and outward in the gesture of perfect benediction. But this particular crucifix does not offer a "perfect" benediction: a closer look at Jesus' right hand, the right hand of *Christus Victor*, reveals that his index finger has been snapped off, perhaps after being unceremoniously dropped to the floor.

RECEIVING MATTHEW'S BROKEN BENEDICTION

What would it mean to stand beneath that benediction, to receive this "broken" benediction as a church? To cross the borders of Christendom, borders that keep churches secure in gated communities of privilege and authority, into more just and inclusive communities of Christ? What would it mean to receive and pronounce, as a church, a broken benediction? To announce the church's complicity with principalities and powers and, at the same time, be joined together with the church Christ creates out of the broken and the bruised bodies of the exile? To recognize our own exile with the exile? What would it mean to anticipate Christ among the poor, the disabled, to anticipate Christ's appearing in the words and companionship of people for whom the street, the overpass, and the park bench may be more hospitable than the pew or fellowship hall or the occasional "religious" volunteer who acts more like a "stray" than a companion?

This chapter explores these questions using a perhaps unpromising conversation partner—namely, the Gospel of Matthew. Why would Matthew be unpromising? To begin with, Matthew seems, among the Gospels, to be very churchy. According to Raymond Brown, it represents the quintessential Gospel of the church: "It is the only gospel that uses the word 'church.' Of all the gospels it was best suited to the manifold needs of the later church, the most cited by the church fathers, the most used in the liturgy, and the most serviceable for catechetical purposes."[4] Based on that assessment, Matthew would seem most likely to authenticate the institutional climate of assimilation and colonization, both characteristic of Christendom models of the church. Second, Matthew's so-called Great Commission stands behind much of Christendom expansion and the modern evangelical movement. Third, many scholars view the writer of Matthew as focused on personal behavior, religious community, and purity codes rather than on politics as such, rather like many "conventional" expressions of church, which focus more on institutional maintenance and personal piety than they do on questions of justice. Like the co-opted mural described above, Christendom models of church neatly segregate interior preoccupations from actual conditions confronting the poor, the downcast, the mentally ill. It often treats these concerns as isolated to one population or demographic, a virus that it tries to contain through charity, segregating *need* from *doxology* and cross from community.

Compared to the other Synoptics (Luke and Mark), Matthew might look like a stained-glass version of the gospel that produces a church turned inward to its own religious and personal life. There are enough of these around. A downtown church advertises its life to the public with a banner announcing, "If you think our windows are beautiful, you should meet our people!" Maybe we could say that this church is formed by a Matthean tradition of community, at least as we have received it, with an understanding of the church as closed (barring the stained-glass windows) and mostly preoccupied with institutional religion rather than raw social inequities. Assimilation rather than mission seems the most dominant motif. The mentality of stained-glass windows would seem to barely rattle in the frames of post-Christendom realities. But what if, in Matthew, we were to find a Gospel capable of subverting the very patterns it seems to underwrite? What if the reading of Matthew that the conventional church has inherited is a reading made at the expense of Matthew's word to the victims of imperial domination? In short, is it possible to salvage Matthew for the church as exile, among exiles, and as antidote to exile? To recover Matthew's Gospel as a witness to nonviolent community, a parabolic expression of the new creation, global in its scope but profoundly disruptive of violent methods? And if such a recovery were possible, what would be the distinguishing features of a community formed out of the fabric of Matthew's Gospel? A church primarily concerned with religious questions, moral and institutional, or something different altogether, or perhaps in some way

---

4. Raymond Brown, *The Churches the Apostles Left Behind* (Ramsey, NJ: Paulist Press, 1984), 124.

representing both as necessary and concomitant to authentic expressions of Christian community?

TEASING APART MATTHEW FROM CHRISTENDOM

Answering these kinds of questions requires, as a first step, a critical assessment of how we have received Matthew's Gospel. We might start with the thorny issue of Matthew's seemingly triumphalist masthead, the so-called Great Commission of 28:18-20: "All authority in heaven and on earth has been given to me. Go therefore and make disciples of all nations, baptizing them in the name of the Father and of the Son and of the Holy Spirit, and teaching them to obey everything I have commanded you. And remember, I am with you always, to the end of the age." We cannot hear Matthew's commission without hearing the echoes of missionary colonialism, how it took up this text as a Christendom mandate, complete with assumptions about Western superiority and American exceptionalism.

Today, if you come from an evangelical strand of the Protestant church, you might have heard this text used as a scriptural warrant for a global, evangelistic crusade: subdue the nations to Christ. Maybe this language is shocking to some, but to many others it will be familiar. This call almost always assumes the benign assistance of the nation-state, especially for those who subscribe to a form of American exceptionalism. When read through this interpretive lens, Jesus' pronouncement that we are to be "a city built on a hill" (5:14b) suggests nothing so much as an American city and an American empire. Although the formal apparatus of Christendom may not shape the global stratagems of the nation-state and financial system, the church, particularly the American church, never broke decisively with the culture of the modern nation-state. This actually spans the conservative and liberal divide. The number of churches with the U.S. flag flying in the sanctuary, for example, reinforces this tacit alliance, one that the nation-state happily receives. But on the left there is a similar form of this flag-flying when national denominations take a so-called stand on an issue, which it then sends to the Associated Press, and then, since no one else is listening, congratulates itself on being prophetic. Well-meaning denominational executives end up aping what the denominations once were, power brokers among the principalities and the powers. Denominational pronouncements, weighty on the surface, go no deeper than the sheets of paper they're written on.

And what's more telling: Herod is unmoved.

TWO FAMILY TREES

In Matthew's world the birth of a child makes Herod shudder with fear: "When King Herod heard this he was frightened" (Matt. 2:3b). What are we missing in the church today, that church pronouncements barely cause a ripple in the social and political consciousness of the principalities and powers? Have we, in a sense, missed the political and economic dimensions of this text? A clue to recovering the political and economic quality of Matthew's Gospel appears in its two "family trees," the genealogy and the cross. A closer look at these two "family trees" may help recover something of Matthew's "broken benediction" for the church today.

Beginning at the end, in Matt. 28:18-20, Douglas John Hall takes aim at the so-called Great Commission. Hall claims we misunderstand this text when we use it to underwrite vast programs of ecclesial expansion, especially those of Christendom. He points, first of all, to the parables—namely, those of the mustard seed, of salt, of yeast, of the light of a beloved community shining amid the dread darkness of empire. All these metaphors of God's heavenly reign share one thing in common: although small and insignificant by the world's standards, they play an essential role in the production of remarkable fruits that benefit both the just and the unjust, since they are given by God rather than by empires. In a similar way, the communities presupposed by the Matthean parables are not large, self-replicating communities; rather, they are communities formed in and living out the logic of the cross. Hall offers this succinct statement of how he understands mission through a theology of the cross: A theology of mission formed by way of the cross "is a theology of *faith* (not sight); of *hope* (not finality); and of *love* (not power)."[5] When the church casts its lot with the king makers (or job creators) of the world, it resembles the very sort of empire that Matthew opposes in its narration of Jesus' birth, preaching, and death.

This line of sight informs how we read the "genesis" of Jesus, the genealogy. According to Warren Carter, Matthew's genealogy shows the beginnings of an alternative to the *pax Romana*, the peace of Rome—namely, the beginning of the "empire of heaven." Carter makes four observations about the genealogy. First, Carter draws our attention to the unnamed giant—the Roman Empire—in a genealogy chronicling the rise and fall of tyrants and powers. The genealogy's astonishing silence regarding the Roman Empire, he says, does not suggest its irrelevance to Matthew, but quite the opposite: the audience of Matthew well knew Rome's imperial claim that it was the agent of

---

5. Douglas John Hall, *Cross in Our Context* (Minneapolis: Fortress Press, 2003), 193.

the gods, that it and it alone was the agent of divine activity throughout the world. And yet, on this point, the genealogy thunders with an unmistakable silence: the writer of Matthew says nothing about the gorilla in the room, Rome. The powers are nothing, almost not worth mentioning, compared to the sovereignty of God that continues through and despite all obstacles.[6]

Second, the genealogy attests to God's determination to persevere through trial and adversity. At first glance, the genealogy's *theological* character might be obscured by the frequent mention of Israel's kings. Thus, a reader might conclude, "The kings advance the purposes of God!" However, Carter points out that of the thirteen kings named after David, just four are elevated as "good" kings in 1 and 2 Kings and 1 and 2 Chronicles. Most of the kings are evaluated as "bad" by the biblical historians. Additionally, the repeated references to exile in 1:11-12 reflect language used to describe God's punishment for Israel's sin within the Old Testament. Thus, it is not Israel's faithfulness (or its kings) that has brought God's purposes to fruition in history, but rather God's own steadfast purpose. And, crucially, if God has overcome the failures of the kings, the unfaithfulness of Israel, and the adversity of empires and exilic conditions, Rome can no more resist God's purposes than can any other earthly reign.[7]

Third, the three references to Abraham (1:1, 2, 17) underscore the way God blesses all the peoples of the earth. Matthew attests to God as the one who blesses the whole earth, even in spite of so-called good kings. By asserting the radical sovereignty of God's heavenly reign, Matthew undermines nationalistic claims on God's favor. Abraham's blessing extends to the whole human family.[8]

Fourth, the references to the Davidic line recall God's promise to David and how those promises actually surpass David's own flawed kingship. Carter asserts that the reference to David's failure as a king (6b) reminds the reader of David's failure to fulfill the kingly ideal of justice and opposition to oppression and exploitation held up in Ps. 72:4: "May [the king] defend the cause of the poor of the people, give deliverance to the needy, and crush the oppressor." Carter believes the audience hearing Matthew's genealogy would make the connection between Rome's violence and exploitation and the failure of kings in general.[9]

Matthew, then, promotes another sort of king, a messiah who will "save his people from their sins" (1:21b). "What sins?" asks Carter. Ordinarily, we

6. Warren Carter, *Matthew and Empire: Initial Explorations* (Harrisburg, PA: Trinity Press International, 2001), 77.

7. Ibid., 78.

8. Ibid.

9. Ibid.

take "sins" to signify the separation between God and the fallen human being, and Jesus' salvific purpose as tied to some theory of substitutionary atonement. Being saved in this view is to be saved, usually as an individual, from categories of religious and moral sins. Carter's reading of Matthew suggests that this is too narrow to be plausible, especially given Matthew's world, one up to its neck in an imperial bloodbath, a reality that surfaces almost immediately opposite the birth of Jesus in the slaughter of the innocents (2:16-18). Everything from sexual exploitation to murder to xenophobia to corrupt kings populates this peculiar tree: "All of this expresses a rejection of God's will. The sinfulness is simultaneously political, economic, social, religious, and moral."[10] The fruit borne by this tree mixes God's purposes alongside the express rejection of God's purposes by kings, empires, Israel's unfaithfulness, and, by implication, Rome's assertion of itself as the agent of the gods.

At least one other feature of this genealogy should be mentioned—namely, the stories of women listed in the genealogy, especially since each of these women faced sexual violence, whether threatened by rape (Ruth), a captive of the sex trade (Rahab), or sexually exploited by men of power (Tamar and Bathsheba). What, if anything, might these stories have to do with Matthew? According to religious studies scholar Davina C. Lopez, Roman language about conquest was gendered and perpetuated through metaphors of sexual violence. The agents of Rome's empire were known by some as "the rapists of the world," with whole nations feminized in the imagination of Rome, who projected "control" through "sexual violence, real or metaphorical."[11] Rome imagined other nations as effeminate and subject to violation, figured as passive amid the aggressive powers of Roman hypermasculinity. [12]

If this was the metaphorical construction of women and of the Jewish people in particular, as Lopez suggests, then Matthew's genealogy may suggest a profound activation of that so-called passive sexuality. Tamar, for one, employs her sexuality subversively, refusing to be passive as successive men, including Er, Onan, and Judah, failed in or blatantly chose to ignore their covenantal obligations to provide her security through the birth of children. Refusing passivity, she sets out to gain her security: "[She] put off her widow's garments [her victimhood] and put on a veil, wrapped herself up" in the clothing of a temple prostitute (Gen. 38:14a). When approached by Judah for sex, she demands not a generic payment but the particular payment of Judah's

10. Ibid., 79.

11. Davina C. Lopez, *Apostle to the Conquered: Reimagining Paul's Mission* (Minneapolis: Fortress Press, 2008), 109, 172.

12. Ibid., 172.

identity: his signet ring, cord, and staff, the authentic "signs" of his covenantal obligation to Tamar (18).

With the bold assertiveness that was evident in Ruth's determination to achieve security, so also with Tamar: she subverts the norms of sexuality, showing that she, and neither Judah nor the system, really represents the covenant promise of God. Through her ironic *disguise* as a prostitute she *exposes* Judah's faithlessness: Judah wants to pay off his debt to the temple sex trade, a trade he recognizes as normative system while showing a shocking indifference to his covenantal obligations to Tamar. This extends to the village, too, because when Tamar begins to show, "three months later" the people accuse her of "play[ing] the whore" and being "pregnant as a result of whoredom" (Gen. 38:24b). As a mob, they prepare to burn her alive until she presents the "signs" of Judah's obligation, which, in the end, he admits show Tamar was "more in the right" than he (38:26a). In a manner similar to the way Boaz responded to Ruth, Judah will finally give to Tamar what he himself did not volunteer.

Bathsheba represents an especially tragic memory in that her name not only recalls her sexual exploitation by David and the subsequent machinations of royal power to effect a cover-up but also recalls the rapes of other women in the Old Testament, including the rape of Tamar by David's son Amnon. After she is raped by Amnon, the royal household "put out" Tamar. She flees, covering her head with ashes. Another irony-laden image appears: she tears her robe, places a hand on her head, her body simultaneously covered and uncovering the act of rape in a state of shame and pain. And the un/covering of violence would not be removed: "So Tamar remained, a desolate woman, in her brother Absalom's house" (2 Sam. 13:20b).

Unearthing these particular stories suggests a pattern that Matthew's audience would recognize in their own setting, but it also suggests that the writer introduces these narratives to accent the story of Jesus' birth, especially his mother's pregnancy. Mary, pregnant without a "public" explanation (so far as Joseph and the rest of the village was concerned), does not, in light of the genealogy, suggest some moral trespass on Mary's part. Nor should we retreat too quickly into doctrines of Immaculate Conception unless those doctrines are given a healthy dose of Matthew's sociopolitical realism. If the genealogy may be said to echo in the birth narrative of Jesus, then this birth is best understood neither as Joseph's response to village rumors of a moral failure nor within a decontextualized doctrine of the virgin birth, but rather in a context of sexual exploitation, shame, and violence. It almost seems as if in Matthew's account it were routine, that this sort of thing happens, and "being a righteous man" Joseph was going to spare Mary from "public disgrace" by covering her pregnancy (and, by implication, the sexual violence of empire) in secrecy—just as had been done to victims of imperial rape in the past. Matthew, however, uses Jesus' birth narrative to expose the secret violence of empire, doing so by "uncovering" the name of Jesus, Emmanuel, God with us, activating Mary's sexuality as the mother of God, subverting every power to kill and to disguise. Mary will not remain a victim, she will not be passive, but she will be the mother of God.

This reflects the "seed" that produces the fruit of the crucified God—Matthew portrays neither a God removed from politics nor a community of "pretty people" hidden behind stained-glass windows. Instead, Matthew's vision for community entails a church intensely involved with the world around it and yet, at the same time, because of its theological origins, never reducible to that world. It operates at the level of a community "borne" by God and carried into the world by God's promise, which it seeks to reflect in actual life practices. Crucially, it is a Word conceived in a woman by the power of the Holy Spirit, a woman whose pregnancy will forever join her not only to God but to every other woman victimized by societal rape. Indeed, most reports of a pregnancy are accompanied with rejoicing, but this one was almost covered up, hidden by the community. Yet, this text testifies that the passivity of victims assumed by the rapists of the world has come to an end in Mary's radical receptivity to God. According to the angel of the Lord, "Look, the virgin shall conceive and bear a son and they shall name him Emmanuel, which means, 'God is with us'" (1:23b). "Mary is not the initiator," writes the theologian and Jesuit priest Avery Dulles. "Her Yes is a response, an Amen to the saving initiative of God." Yet Dulles also underlines Mary's agency through receptivity: "Mary's receptivity was active, not passive. God deals with her as a free agent, not as a mere object to be manipulated. As St. Augustine put it, she conceived the word in her mind before giving the Word a body in her womb."[13]

With the violent character of Rome in the background of Matthew's genealogy, Mary's response reflects a peculiar form of agency, conceiving a community that receives suffering not to valorize it but to make alive and to make whole. Mary's receptivity and agency supplies the analogy for the shape of the church as it receives in community (not as isolated individuals) the cost of discipleship.

---

13. Avery Cardinal Dulles, "Mary's Yes and Our Response to God," *Living Pulpit*, October-December 2001, 30.

SHAPE OF COMMUNITY

Significantly, the community of faith lives in tension between its "secret discipline" and its public expression. Matthew evidences this sort of secret discipline in Jesus' Sermon on the Mount:

> Beware of practicing your piety before others in order to be seen by them; for then you have no reward from your Father in heaven. So whenever you give alms, do not sound a trumpet before you, as the hypocrites do in the synagogues and in the streets, so that they may be praised by others. Truly I tell you, they have received their reward. But when you give alms, do not let your left hand know what your right hand is doing, so that your alms may be done in secret; and your Father who sees in secret will reward you. (Matt. 6:1-4)

The intimation of a secret discipline appears, too, in the parable of the hidden treasure and the "one pearl of great value" (13:44-45). The "hidden treasure" or the "pearl of great value" represents the gift of God given to the world in Jesus Christ, who empties the riches of heavenly empire onto the field of the cross. A community persuaded of the gospel of Jesus Christ engages in practices of self-emptying that would appear, on the surface, to be utterly insane among worldly empires and systems but, to those being saved, reflect nothing less than the saving activity of Jesus Christ in the world, a radical triumph subverting empire.

On the flip side, this community, according to Matthew, is irresistible and richly abundant, its good self-evident to the public: "Every good tree bears good fruit, but the bad tree bears bad fruit. A good tree cannot bear bad fruit, nor can a bad tree bear good fruit" (7:17-18). The gifts produced by the community do not discriminate because they are too expansive for discrimination, bearing a likeness to God's own providence: "The kingdom of heaven is like a mustard seed that someone took and sowed in his field; it is the smallest of all the seeds, but when it has grown it is the greatest of shrubs and becomes a tree, so that the birds of the air come and make nests in its branches" (13:31b-32). Again, the parable of yeast speaks to the way the community "leavens" the whole community (13:33), enriching not only the "community of believers" but the whole body.

When read in that vein, as a tangible alternative to the peace of Rome, one sees the dramatic tension between Matthew's "empire of heaven" and that of the Roman Empire. The community arising out of Matthew's challenge to the Roman Empire brings to light a parabolic expression of the beloved community of Christ. Instead of extending control, the "empire of heaven" intensifies taste and texture. New Testament scholar Douglas Hare, for instance, suggests that we paraphrase "You are the salt of the earth" (5:13a) as "'You are red hot pepper for the whole earth!'" This metaphor, according to Hare, does not relate to status but rather to function. Matthew represents the church as a small but intense community that activates unusual alertness, a sharpness of perception, and an acute sense of place.[14] If you stumble across this church, you're likely to sweat, your pulse will jump—there will be something edgy in its activity. Empire, by contrast, tends to propagandize space, monopolizing it into a "common flavor" whose only trait is its uniformity. It mass produces (or coerces) empire, turning the particular identity of community into ciphers imposed by imperial systems. Matthew's vision of the community arises from a small but potent expression of life that intensifies the experience of life in ways that are affirming and liberating.

Matthew resists the temptation to create communities preoccupied with deciding who is in and who is out, the very preoccupation of empire (and denominations), where citizenship (membership) is nothing more than a revenue stream or a "blood" infusion, bodies for use in wars both religious and secular. Given the frequency with which Matthew addresses the "mixed" character of the heavenly kingdom, it is possible that some in Matthew's community would like to live in an "ideal" world of religious purity. Against that tendency, the community Matthew evokes in the parable of weeds (13:24-30) does not provide perfect clarity on who belongs and who doesn't. Ambiguity, questions, and betrayal are mixed together in almost equal measure with the gifts of bread and wine. But crucially, God in Christ gives bread and wine enough and more to live fruitfully, creatively, and inclusively in a world that God so loved—or so we might read the feeding of the five thousand (14:13-21), the four thousand (15:32-39), and the Lord's Supper (26:26-30). The eucharistic practice, bread broken and cup shared, tip the balance of Matthean community in favor of inclusion. So also the ending of Matthew, the climax where presumably we might see the wheat and tares finally separated yet witness instead a vision of inclusivity that transcends but does not exclude confession: "When they saw [Jesus], they worshiped him; *but some doubted*" (28:17).

By now, it may be evident that Matthew operates with some kind of border, but it is not a Christendom border. One senses that Jesus speaks and

---

14. Douglas R. A. Hare, *Interpretation: Matthew* (Louisville, KY: John Knox Press, 1993), 44.

acts in such a way that the message of the gospel is "overheard"—the wall of the church is, in a sense quite literally, just skin deep and just as porous: "When Jesus saw the crowds, he went up the mountain; and after he sat down, his disciples came to him. Then he began to speak, and taught them" (5:1-2). Crowds and disciples, Christ and the projection of imperial power in the crucifixion remain almost breathlessly, skin-on-skin close. The body of the Matthean church breathes, interacts with the world around it, betraying something at once different and yet profoundly responsive to the surrounding political landscape: "While [Jesus] was still speaking to the crowds, his mother and his brothers were standing outside, wanting to speak to him. Someone told him, 'Look, your mother and your brothers are standing outside, wanting to speak to you.' But to the one who had told him this, Jesus replied, 'Who is my mother, and who are my brothers?' And pointing to his disciples, he said, 'Here are my mother and my brothers! For whoever does the will of my Father in heaven is my brother and sister and mother'" (Matt. 12:46-50). Faithfulness trumps the privilege conferred by blood relations. While the empire exalts the deity of the ruler, the heavenly reign of God assigns kingship to Christ and Christ constitutes a new kind of family.

While conventional interpretations of Matthew might accent the way the sick and weak were "impure" according to synagogue standards, they were also, as Carter points out, unwanted by empire. And yet such persons become the building blocks of Jesus' new community. Carter believes they are not "accidentally" ill: "Jesus heals people who have been made sick by the imperial system. *Imperial power is bad for your health.*" City life for the nonelite, according to Carter, was rife with disease, malnutrition, overcrowding, and so on. This was not an accident of an individual's health or Jesus' particular fondness for sick people, but a dramatic expression of an alternative to the Roman imperial system.[15]

Almost invariably, Matthew's Jesus claims a special kinship to those persecuted or marginalized by empire, especially women and children (19:13-15), the diseased and chronically ill (8:1-4; 9:18-26), the physically challenged (9:2-8, 27-34; 12:9-14), those judged to be deviant or mentally deranged (8:28-34; 17:14-18), and the unelect, both in terms of gender and ethnicity, for example, the Canaanite woman (15:21-28). Carter also draws our attention to classes of people who would be used by the Roman Empire, albeit contemptuously, so that Matthew speaks of "tax collectors and sinners" in the same breath. Sin, in this case, carries an ethical accent rather than a merely

---

15. Carter, *Matthew and Empire*, 71.

moralistic one. This figures into the call of Matthew, simultaneously a traitor and a Jew, beholden to Rome but now responding to Christ's call, subverting both the scandal of his vocation and his captivity to the Roman Empire (9:9-13).

The fact that Matthew includes the apparent "interruption" of the work of the disciples as fishermen (4:18-22) is often interpreted as the way clergy or missionaries come to full-time ministry, in effect leaving economic labors to pursue a "holy" vocation. However, if we view this text from the vantage point of people working passively under the manacles of a financial system, the calling of the disciples might strike us a bit differently. Those who would follow Jesus do so from deep within the financial system; they are perhaps even numb to its exploitative nature or at least resigned to it. However, when they follow Jesus, the financial system, an emperor in its own right, is turned on its head because they will never again submit to a system that claims the power to pacify, to turn people into nothing more than "consumers" or "job creators." Likewise, the cross is not merely atonement theory but also the power to pacify a population in order to secure the stability of Rome's financial system of revenue and taxation. And yet, in Matthew's Gospel, the cross exposes both the disease of empire and, ultimately, its impotence.

It is not too far a stretch to imagine that Jesus' disciples, like David's ragtag refugees, were debtors, fantastic failures as consumers, and nowhere near resembling the coveted "job creators" of empire. But, as in the account of David fleeing from the insane kingship of Saul, this new people turns out to be a crazy quilt of community formed from "everyone who was in distress, and everyone who was in debt, and everyone who was discontented" (1 Sam. 22:2a). This very crowd of castoffs, malcontents, drifters, and the fit for nothing but crucifixion, including the "two bandits . . . crucified with [Jesus], one on his right and one on his left" (27:38), were the parabolic substance of the new community, the mustard seed, the yeast that would leaven the imagination and hearts of all those who heard and responded in faith. This empire will be peculiar in its inception, inverting power with weakness and violence with peacemaking.

Of course, once the community begins, how will it be distinguished from the empire it is an alternative to? Is there a sense in which by *responding* to empire the church is destined to repeat its shape, in a manner of speaking, becoming the very thing initially opposed? This could be true of Matthew's Gospel, according to Carter: "As much as the Gospel resists and exposes the injustice of Rome's rule . . . it cannot, finally, escape the imperial mindset. The alternative to Rome's rule is framed in imperial terms."[16] In a sense, we are brought back to the so-called Great Commission. It seems to license the imperial ethic, the parables and the metaphors of Matthew notwithstanding. Robert R. Beck, a priest and religious studies scholar, provides an interesting interpretive possibility. Beck believes that Matt. 28:18-20 may actually reprise the temptation narrative in Matt. 4:1-11. The devil probes not the *extent* of Jesus' power, which seems to be taken for granted, so much as Jesus' *restraint*, his willingness to not exercise power, to refrain from coercing, even for good reasons (turning rocks into bread or saving his own skin or having the chance to set up a "better" civilization). Jesus invokes a different kind of power, the power to love one's enemies, a nonviolent power that breaks with what has been known since the days of the kings. This power extends the global witness of the church not through coercion but through love as it is signified in the sacrament of Baptism.[17]

Cracking the Stained-Glass Windows

Imagine a church as a community dedicated to the interruption of the status quo. Imagine a community more focused on living intensely and intentionally as an alternative community, visibly different and engaged in practices of radical presence. What would that community look like? Would we be able to detect a glimpse of how the Matthean community may have looked? Or perhaps how the church looks today when it takes its starting point from a reading of Matthew that is alert to the political and economic dimensions of community as well as to its moral and religious dimensions? This brief reflection on Matthew's Gospel and the community it envisions forms the background for the next chapter, which explores how a small group of people formed around a commitment to be salt, yeast, and light have created a new kind home in the old world of homelessness.

---

16. Ibid., 171.

17. Robert R. Beck, *Banished Messiah: Violence and Nonviolence in Matthew's Story of Jesus* (Eugene, OR: Wipf and Stock, 2010), 192.

5

A Labyrinth of the Streets

Gospel Obedience in Cherith Brook, Kansas City, Missouri

> Today's paper with its columns of description of the new era, the atomic era, which this colossal slaughter of the innocents has ushered in, is filled with stories covering every conceivable phase of the new discovery. Pictures of the towns and the industrial plants where the parts are made are spread across the pages. In the forefront of the town of Oak Ridge, Tennessee, is a chapel, a large, comfortable-looking chapel benignly settled beside the plant. And the scientists making the first tests in the desert prayed, one newspaper account said. Yes, God is still in the picture. We have to remember it. We are held in God's hands, all of us, and President Truman too, and these scientists who have created death, but [God] will use it for good. . . . [God] is our creator. Creator.
>
> —Dorothy Day, September 1945[1]

My first contact with the Cherith Brook Catholic Worker House in Kansas City, Missouri, was by phone. I called to see if I could visit the community. Rev.

1. Dorothy Day, *Selected Writings*, Robert Ellsburg, ed. (Maryknoll: Orbis, 1983), 268.

Eric Garbison was the name I had been given, and when I called the house I asked if I could speak to him.

"No," came the reply, "he's in jail."

"Oh," I said, trying to sound natural, "any idea when he might be out?"

"Hmm," he said, "Not really sure."

"Does he have a cell phone?" I asked, only realizing too late the lameness of my question.

"No, I'm afraid not," he answered. "*He's in jail.*"

Such was my introduction to Cherith Brook, a community determined to live as a coherent expression of the reign of God in Kansas City.

I later learned that Eric, along with other members of the Cherith Brook community, had been arrested during a protest for trespassing onto the construction site of a plant that made parts for nuclear weapons. Grasping the background to their arrest supplies not only a context for this specific situation but also a sense of how the community critiques the theology of the principalities and powers and offers an alternative account of the way of God in the world. As for critique, this 1.5-million-square-foot nuclear weapons parts plant, estimated to cost $673 million, helps America make bombs faster. Antinuclear activist Ann Suellentrop put it this way as she described the core producing sites at Los Alamos and Oak Ridge: "They make the bullet and we make the gun."[2]

A privately owned and city-financed construction of a weapons site represents an unprecedented incursion of militarism into community life. Sadly, however, it was also familiar, as Kansas City had served as the site of another older facility for decades. Cherith Brook took the "new normal" of militarization as a call to action. While its advocates billed it as an infusion of jobs during the Great Recession, Cherith Brook, along with many other Catholic Worker communities and other antinuclear activists nationwide, asserted that it benefited the poor very little and probably harmed that population by draining city finances away from the crisis of poverty in the actually "blighted" urban areas of Kansas City. The very people who could stand to benefit from this sort of stimulus were, in effect, turned away while those who enjoyed material resources and political influence (middle and upper middle classes) were given a generous infusion of federal- and city-financed

2. Adam Weinstein, "A Privately Owned Nuclear Weapons Plan," *Mother Jones*, 29 August 2011, http://www.motherjones.com/politics/2011/08/nuclear-weapons-plant-kansas-city. For additional information see Lawrence Wittner, "Kansas City Here It Comes: A New Nuclear Weapons Plant!" *Huffington Post*, 14 September 2011, http://www.huffingtonpost.com/lawrence-wittner/kansas-city-here-it-comes_b_949165.html.

welfare designed to subsidize a financial system dedicated to the perpetuation of violence.

These developments eventually led to what the Catholic Workers call an act of "gospel obedience"—these acts, they would say, are not the same as acts of "civil disobedience" because this expression assumes the sovereignty of the nation-state rather than the sovereignty of God. As in Matthew's Gospel, their first and most important expression of citizenship is theirs through the reign of God announced in Jesus Christ. And, indeed, the shape of their "gospel obedience" witnessed to God's sovereignty through worship and liturgical activity in a place—the construction site for a nuclear weapons part plant—where it was all but denied by the civil sovereign. Nick Pickrell, one of the members of the community arrested for trespassing, described the event as part theater, part worship: "Part of our peacemaking work involves looking to things that are harmful . . . things that go against peace, the peaceable kingdom." The court charged them with an act of trespass, but the community viewed it as an expression of faith and prayer, more liturgy than law breaking. Nick stresses that they began with a "beautiful" gathering, suggesting the character of Christian worship and community in concrete spaces of exile:

> We gathered as [different Catholic Worker communities from all over the country]. . . . It was around Easter time. . . . [O]ur theme for that weekend was "The Hope of Easter in a Disarmed World." We were there to celebrate the resurrection. The whole weekend culminated with a piece of satire highlighting the fact that for many people the bomb is their idol. The bomb is our god that we worship. That's the thing that makes us feel safe and secure rather than God. And so we satirized that with a little street theater. And then we experienced a resurrection moment where we laid down; we rose again, confessed our own complicity, . . . and vowed to not be silent again. . . . [As we drew to the end of the liturgy, we] called for repentance and prayed that this would be a life-giving place, a place of resurrection rather than a place of death. With that said we [made a procession] onto the land and . . . were arrested for trespassing while singing songs, singing hymns.[3]

They represented with their prone bodies the fruit of an ideological and financial system built around the perpetuation of violence. As part of this, they also gave expression to repentance for our collective acquiescence to such

---

3. Nick Pickrell, interview by author, audio recording, Kansas City, MO, 25 January 2012.

systems. And then, as a response to the promise of God's triumph over the powers, they figured the resurrection, rising as a community of hope amid protest and repentance, as a community taken up by God's future rather than one held captive to principalities and powers. During their court trial, members asserted their innocence of any crime, and they refused to pay bond as a protest against the way bonds fund a spiraling poverty among the poor. As a consequence for their acts of gospel obedience, they were sentenced to time in jail. Some were even ordered to do community service—another irony, given that the very life of the community is, at minimum, a service to the community.[4]

While they laughed at the irony of being "sentenced" to community service, they trusted in the paradox of their vocation. The community might not object to the idea that their life is a baptism in trust, a baptism that immerses it in the waters of its namesake, the Wadi Cherith, east of the Jordan: "The word of the Lord came to [Elijah], saying, 'Go from here and turn eastward, and hide yourself by the Wadi Cherith, which is east of the Jordan. You shall drink from the wadi, and I have commanded the ravens to feed you there" (1 Kgs. 17:2-4). The act of gospel obedience the community sought to represent at the weapons parts site entailed trust in God: the ravens that seemingly cared not a whit for Elijah, nor perhaps even about the drought, would at the Lord's command supply him with sustenance. The community at Cherith Brook seems to have adopted this faith, that the world belongs to God and that God activates the entire creation in preserving and growing the peaceable kingdom in the midst of a larger famine of compassion and imagination. As this community attempted to express gospel obedience, it found itself, naturally, even predictably, in prison. Indeed, the community of Cherith Brook lives in the scandal of the cross, in the geographic space of things that many "normal" and "conventional" churches would call a zone for charity but would resist as a place to call home. Amid the catacombs of the normalization of famine, the community attempted to live out the reality and richness of the resurrection.

Cherith Brook walks in that paradox: it is a community that engages in almost spontaneous worship, but it has neither steeple nor pews nor formal set-apart clergy; it is charitable but it is not a charity; it is revolutionary but it is not violent; it was animated by a rich vision of the church but as a community sought to name its own boundaries by which it could sustain its particular

---

4. See "Transformation not Annihilation" for Nick Pickrell's video account of this act of gospel obedience at http://www.youtube.com/watch?v=T-s329ZW97k. See also "Report on Nuclear Weapons Plant in KC," Cherith Brook Catholic Worker, 12 May 2011, http://cherithbrookcw.blogspot.com/2011/05/report-on-witness-against-nuclear.html.

vocation in Kansas City. If you just glanced at the community, you might see a maze of seemingly contradictory activities and identities. However, a longer reflection on their life suggests another metaphor, that of the labyrinth, which to the uninitiated seems at first to be a maze. According to Lauren Artress, a maze reflects a "multicursal" pattern while a labyrinth employs a "unicursal" pattern: the former tests our decision-making skills by inserting "false" paths and includes hedges to make it more difficult for the walker. By contrast, the unicursal pattern of the labyrinth "invites our intuitive, pattern-seeking, symbolic mind to come forth."[5]

Ancients used the labyrinth as a model of walking prayer. In this model, there are no "dead ends" and all paths lead to the center and out again, linking beginning and ending into one patterned expression of the journey. It is not designed to trick the person who walks its path but rather to cultivate a spirit of trust through walking, through movement and place. Viewed through the lens of the labyrinth, the community at Cherith Brook brings into focus important characteristics of a church formed amid conditions of poverty.

In the subsequent pages, I will introduce the paradoxical relationship between the community at Cherith Brook and the poverty it has chosen to inhabit and describe how as a community it contributes to something like God's shalom in the city. This community prompts the church to understand streets of precarity not as a maze of "lostness" but as representative of the mystery of God's presence, a mystery into which the church is called to live as companions on the way of the Christ. By implication, as a community, it may alert us to ways in which we have become addicted to the financial system and the violence it perpetuates. It also challenges us to begin a journey that we may not feel is possible, that we may reject out of hand, but that may in the end hold the promise of new life.

FIRST STEPS

"Solvitur ambulando. . . . It is solved by walking. . . ."[6]

Each time I have contemplated a large journey, I am almost overwhelmed by a feeling of dread or the sense that this is *not* the way to go. In 1999, I called my parents from Paris, France, where I was studying for a summer, and announced that I would be walking the Camino de Santiago, a pilgrimage road that winds

---

5. Lauren Artress, *Walking a Sacred Path: Rediscovering the Labyrinth as a Spiritual Practice*, rev. ed. (New York: Riverhead Books, 2006), 51–52.

6. St. Augustine quoted in Artress, *Walking a Sacred Path*, 69.

almost five hundred miles from its beginning point in St. Jean-Pied-de-Port in France to Santiago de Compostela in Spain. When I told my father I would be walking this distance, he laughed: "You'll be crippled," he said. That was the evening before I left Paris to begin the pilgrimage. I recount this because, as I drove to Kansas City, I felt similar feelings of dread. I don't know that I understand these feelings completely. But they seem to come upon me any time I begin something new, something that does not quite conform to what I have grown to take for granted.

Coming to visit Cherith Brook stirred up similar feelings. It was a journey, in a sense, away from the church I had known all my life and perhaps, even more dramatically, a challenge to how I understood community itself. It threatened to "cripple" my assumptions and that, I think, must frighten anyone, at least anyone paying attention. I know that I am not alone in these kinds of responses: a similar ambivalence surfaced during a visit by a presbytery committee, a regional governing body of the Presbyterian Church. The presbytery listed Cherith Brook in their budget as a line item, but the committee members soon bogged down with the question of how to classify it as a community: a charity? church? or political advocacy group? It seemed to slip through or overflow the carefully arranged universe of the church and its charitable activities, and, in so doing, the community challenged each one in its own way. And yet the Cherith Brook community itself seemed to shrug these questions off, apparently more interested in the journey than in abstract definitions. Like the Camino where I was joined to the lives and paths of other pilgrims on the first morning of the walk, Cherith Brook quickly gathered me along for the journey, our footpaths being joined together in a different way.

My "little" pilgrimage with Cherith Brook began as I walked up to the house, trying in vain to be at peace with the free-range chickens and their droppings. I felt immediately the sense of life being lived. Eric and Jodi, founders of the community, met me at the door and invited me into the kitchen where members were cutting up vegetables for that night's meal. Most introductions are formal, stiff, but this one was more like stepping into a small boat, floating in a small river or stream. Everyone seemed active, participating in the delicate, joyful balance and banter of meals and fellowship, of activity and reflection.

A similar feeling went through me the next day, on Monday morning, when the community was serving breakfast and I was signed up to serve the guests. It was as though I were stepping into a body in movement. Indeed, what I witnessed at Cherith Brook was more organism than organization, an expression Dorothy Day used to describe the Catholic Worker Movement.

The shape of their weekly life suggests what this organism looks like in terms of practices, of repeated activities and gatherings. On Mondays, Tuesdays, Thursdays, and Fridays, Cherith Brook offers showers from 8:30 a.m. until 11:00 a.m. On most days breakfast is served. Then, on Thursday night, there is a community meal, where the doors of the house open to their friends from 5 p.m. until 7 p.m., and, at least when I was there, singing and fellowship continue later into the evening. Garden workdays, roundtable discussions, early morning devotions—this weekly rhythm demonstrates the simplicity of the works of mercy and the life of prayer but also shows a complexity that defies easy description.

For example, although I had "volunteered" to help serve their friends during the Monday morning breakfast, I was encouraged to visit. It was not long before I met Greg, an African American, probably in his forties. I introduced myself, extending my right hand. As he took my hand, I almost didn't notice that his right arm hung limply by his side. I asked if I could join him for breakfast and he motioned for me to take the chair opposite him. I asked him about his arm. He was robbed, he told me matter-of-factly, at gunpoint, shot three times in the arm and shoulder and once through the stomach. His attacker was a young man who, he said, was "jumpy" with the pistol. His assailant had gone to prison but had been released. Not long after Greg heard about his release, he saw his assailant leaving a grocery store in the neighborhood. Before the attack he was a mechanic making a good wage, but after the attack, Greg says, "What good was I as a mechanic? I couldn't work with just one hand." Later, as I was serving the friends, a man in his fifties asked me to read the newspaper, the astrology table, pointing to the entry under Virgo. He explained that his eyes were bad and later, for some reason, complained to me that he had an ulcer. Carl, an older friend of the community, caught my attention and began to tell me that he needed to get out of the apartment he was living in, that the people he lived with were stealing from him and doing drugs. Unprompted by me, he laid out how much support he got each month: $90 in food stamps, $496 in Social Security, and $225 in supplemental aid. Any food he has, "they eat it up," he said in disgust.

Later that morning, after most of the friends had eaten, someone began to playfully tease an openly gay man, Terry, to sing a hymn for everyone. Later in another encounter Terry would tell me that he was not welcome in the church but here, at least, he was willing to share his voice in worship. When he finished singing, a hush fell over the room. Afterward, Steve, wearing a black hairnet, started rapping a song based on the prodigal son: "If I never lost my place, I'd never know his grace. . . ." While he rapped the story of the father receiving the son, he folded his arms as if to receive the robe and put his hand into the air as if receiving the "ring of honor." At the end of breakfast, before everyone departed, Jimmy W. Clarke, a Native American, offered a Cheyenne benediction.[7] After breakfast, Julie arrived at the door. An older woman, she wore layers of coats that not only kept her warm but seemed to be an unsuccessful attempt to disguise her frailty. She walked into the dining area, visibly shaking, unsteady on her feet. Somebody went back into the kitchen and fixed her a plate of food. As she sat at the table, she told us that her clothes had been stolen. She ate quietly, listening in as the volunteers shared a Scripture reading and prayers following the meal.

As Julie sat with us, a volunteer from a supportive congregation in the area wondered if they should bring more food given the number of people arriving to be fed. Eric's response surprised me, and probably the volunteer: no, he said, the amount of food they brought that morning was "perfect," and he went on to remind the volunteers that Cherith Brook was not a "soup kitchen" that tried to feed as many as possible as often as possible. If Cherith Brook tried to do that, he explained, they would lose their unique vocation in this area of Kansas City— namely, to be an agent of humanization and genuine, personally expressed hospitality. Simply handing out food, he seemed to say, was not the answer. Supplying food with authentic fellowship and shared humanity was their vocation.

This commitment to a peculiarly Christ-like function within the community bore distinctive fruit: the people who came to breakfast and to the showers were part of a community of prayer and common concern. At one of the breakfasts, we had heard that José Lugo, one of the Latino men, had been jumped and savagely beaten by four men. He was admitted to the hospital where, using plates and screws, they put his jaw back into place. Eric had gone to visit him and told us that it was not clear why he was beat up. The street itself was silent on who was responsible for the beatings since "snitches" might be targeted for reprisal. For its part, given his poverty, the hospital quickly released José, returning him to the streets where, according to Eric, he was probably self-medicating.[8] Eric tells me that José was formed by the streets, but as he continues to age he is entering a phase of poverty in which he will

---

7. Jimmy Wayne Clarke was murdered on 13 June 2013. His body was found in a makeshift shelter behind a BP gas station on Independence Avenue, not far from Cherith Brook. See Christine Vendel, "Homeless Man Is Found Dead behind Gas Station," *Kansas City Star*, 13 June 2013, http://www.kansascity.com/2013/06/13/4290639/body-found-behind-gas-station.html.

8. "Self-medicating" refers to how the poor will take some of the drugs given to help with physical or emotional ailments, but will sell most of it on the street.

be increasingly vulnerable to beatings by younger men. When José arrived at breakfast, he said nothing (his jaw was wired shut and he was badly bruised), but the Latinos asked for prayer for José. The prayer was offered and translated into Spanish by the Latino community. The beating and the dehumanization was very real but so also was the prayer and involvement in the life of the neighborhood. While a larger shelter or soup kitchen might supply what they could, Cherith Brook offered an alternative to the silence, anonymity, and exposure of the street. José belonged to this community more than he did to the streets, or to the hospital, or to his own destitution. Boundaries did not mean exclusion so much as they reflected a commitment to the clarity and deepening of Cherith Brook's collective vocation in that place.

Indeed, walking the streets and narratives of Cherith Brook as a labyrinth suggested that the street acts both as figurative expression and concrete habitation. It supplies both a sense of being lost but also, as a matter of faith, the foretaste of being found. As expression and reality, it often signifies something akin to a maze: Addiction says Jeffrey New, a friend of the community, "sends you on a road that you get a long way down before you know how you got there."[9] Another guest of the community, Paul Newman, reflected on his experience of homelessness saying, "it has no time frame"—no point in time when it is clearly going to be over.[10] Interestingly, this sentiment is reflected not only among the friends of Cherith Brook but also among its founders: "Jodi and I moved five times in the first ten years of our life together. . . . At the time we thought little of our transience. It mostly felt logical (education), necessary (a job) good (a call to ministry), and at times a little adventurous. Yet looking back [from the perspective of intentional community] it feels very different. It's as if we have lived in the middle of everywhere but aren't from anywhere. No roots."[11] Perhaps this sense of being without roots contributes to a deep connection with the place in and around Cherith Brook. People on the streets know Cherith Brook as "the Shower House," a place where you can get breakfast, a change of clothes, and a hot shower. Volunteers call it "a community within a community," and to their regular friends, Cherith Brook seems like church, the church of real presence, where they come not only to find nourishment, but to fellowship, to sing, and to pray. To those who covenant together as Catholic Workers, like Allison Rozga, trained as a nurse but now a member of the community, it is what church was always meant to be

9. Jeffrey New, interview by author, audiovisual recording, Kansas City, MO, 23 January 2012.

10. Paul Newman, interview by author, audiovisual recording, Kansas City, MO, 24 January 2012.

11. Eric Garbison, "Being Placed: More on Stability," *Cherith Brook Catholic Worker*, Ordinary Time 2012, 1.

but often failed to be: "I was surprised because the things they were doing here and the things they believed in . . . all really coincided with what I wanted for my life but didn't really know how to make them happen. . . . [Here] I felt . . . this *is* what church is."[12] For Nick Pickrell, who grew up in what he described as a "spiritual" and "emotional" evangelical tradition, Cherith Brook made his faith tangible:

> Maybe my faith has become more earthy and concrete as opposed to being . . . over-spiritualized. And so there's now a concrete aspect, a day-to-day living out of my faith in Jesus in very mundane things, like doing laundry, cooking food (a lot!), doing dishes afterwards, having simple conversations, growing things, and learning how to do all these things . . . more [sustainably]. . . . I now consider Cherith Brook to be church. For me, it's by far [the place] where I have the deepest relationships. . . [T]he work is really hard and I experience the whole range of emotions but I know I'm alive, and that tells me I'm on the right track.[13]

The street was not only a symbol but also a reality, reminding the faith community of its historicity, its social location, its deeply rooted vocation in the ordinary acts of making a home amid homelessness.

THE CHERITH BROOK CATHOLIC WORKER

When talking about the spirituality of Cherith Brook, Eric recalls the tradition of Dorothy Day: "Dorothy Day believed deeply in a spirituality of precarity. We're not here to establish an institution that will continue to repeat itself. Houses are born, and they die, and they're reborn and they die. . . . [I]f it happens that way, that's OK because . . . you're living more organically, living into call rather than into institutional commitments."[14] While a complete description of Day's vision is more adequately treated by others, a brief introduction to her understanding of poverty is important to grasping the tradition at work in Cherith Brook.[15]

---

12. Allison Rozga, interview by author, audiovisual recording, Kansas City, MO, 24 January 2012.

13. Nick Pickrell, interview by author, audiovisual recording, Kansas City, MO, 25 January 2012.

14. Eric Garbison, interview by author, audiovisual recording, Kansas City, MO, 25 January 2012.

15. For further reading, see Jim Forest, *All Is Grace: A Biography of Dorothy Day* (Maryknoll, NY: Orbis Books, 2011); Dan McKanan, *The Catholic Worker after Dorothy: Practicing the Works of Mercy in a New Generation* (Collegeville, MN: Liturgical Press, 2008); and Robert Coles, *Dorothy Day: A Radical Devotion* (Boston: De Capo Press, 1989). For primary sources, see Dorothy Day, *Loaves and Fishes*

Beginning in 1933, during the Great Depression, the Catholic Worker is most often recognized for its houses of hospitality, frequently located in urban areas blighted by poverty. They have also been formed in rural areas as farming communities. Cofounded by Day and Peter Maurin, a French immigrant, the Catholic Worker tradition formed around a philosophy of communitarian self-determination, voluntary poverty, personalism, nonviolent action, houses of hospitality, and agricultural communities.[16] Other influences include the study of Catholic saints and the Gospel of Matthew, especially the Sermon on the Mount.[17] "Our rule is the works of mercy," said Dorothy Day. "It is the way of sacrifice, worship, a sense of reverence." "We try," explained Day, "to shelter the homeless and give them clothes, but there is a strong faith at work. We pray. If an outsider who comes to visit us doesn't pay attention to our prayings and what that means, then he'll miss the whole point."[18] It is also, according to Day, a way of revolution:

> "The greatest challenge of the day is: how to bring about a revolution of the heart, a revolution which has to start with each one of us? When we begin to take the lowest place, to wash the feet of others, to love our brothers with that burning love, that passion, which led to the cross, then we can truly say, 'Now I have begun.'"[19]

Day believed that poverty was both the enemy and the key to faithful revolution. Day admits that poverty is "an elusive thing" and a paradoxical phenomenon: "If we are not its victims," she warns, "its reality fades from us." "I condemn poverty and I advocate it; poverty is simple and complex at once; it is a social phenomenon and it is a personal matter."[20] Precarity, then, refers to a

---

(Maryknoll, NY: Orbis Books, 1963) and *The Long Loneliness* (New York: Harper and Row, 1952); for an edited selection of Day's writings see Robert Ellsberg, ed., *Dorothy Day: Selected Writings* (Maryknoll, NY: Orbis Books, 1983).

16. *Personalism* is a term used by Day and Maurin to convey the emphasis on the human person as created in the image of God: "According to Emmanuel Mournier, the French thinker who coined the term, personalism began with the affirmation that the human person, created in the image of God, is 'an absolute in comparison with any other material or social reality . . . and can never be considered merely as a part of a whole, whether of family, class, state, nation, or even humanity.'" McKanan, *Catholic Worker after Dorothy*, 9.

17. For a brief description of influences, see McKanan, *Catholic Worker after Dorothy*, 13–16.

18. Jim Forest, "The Catholic Worker Movement," in *Encyclopedia of American Catholic History*, ed. Michael Glazier and Thomas J. Shelley (Collegeville: Liturgical Press, 1997), 310.

19. Day, *Loaves and Fishes*, 215.

20. Ibid., 71.

contradiction or paradox residing deep within the logic of the community itself, between promoting stability through voluntary precarity and, at the same time, condemning systems that demoralize human beings by refusing, in as much as it is possible, to participate in those models of society.

Day urges the ideal of the early church fathers: "The ideal is for every family to have a Christ room, as the early fathers of the Church called it." If people of faith returned to this practice, she claims "there would be no need for huge institutions, houses of dead storage where human beings waste away in loneliness and despair."[21] Day's model resembles more the way a family, in the shadow of famine, breaks bread than the way an institution builds an endowment: "We must often be settling down happily to the cornmeal cakes, the last bit of food in the house, before the miracle of the increase comes about. Any large family knows these things—that somehow everything works out. It works out naturally and it works out religiously."[22]

Day's advocacy of poverty is located in Christ's poverty, in Christ's self-emptying. However, she does not valorize poverty for the sake of poverty; instead, she believes it reveals God's determination to overcome poverty with love. Destitution, she insists, is blasphemy and an offense to God. But the poverty incarnated in Christ, who made his home in our midst as a homeless and persecuted refugee, supplies a radical response to destitution, effectively adopting its condition but doing so with the coherence of God's reign, seeking to live as a new creation amid the ruins of the old. A community, then, formed in the shape of Christ adopts precarity as an expression of "gospel obedience"—acting in the spirit of faith rather than reacting in a spirit of scarcity. The latter produces predictable results while the former leads us in a way we did not know or even particularly desire.

At the time of my visit, the community was just five years old, having been founded in 2007. Eric talked a lot about the question of stability in the still-young community and what it would mean to continue past the five-year mark, whether there would be a future for Cherith Brook. But while those questions lingered, the reality of the weekly rhythm seemed the strongest. Like the broader Catholic Worker tradition, Cherith Brook attempts to live its life in solidarity with the poor, married to the poverty of Christ. In this way, they differ from those who experience precarity of destitution. A yearly covenant and a common purse, close and caring relationships, shared meals and work, learning—all these help bring the community together. However, given the voluntary poverty of the Catholic Worker, the question of the future is never

21. Ibid., 198.
22. Ibid., 92.

far removed from the present, just as it is for people who live from day to day in poverty.

The youthfulness of the community makes an interesting contrast to the depth and richness of the faith represented by its members as well as its collective interest in the history of the church, the monastic movement, and the lives of the saints, modern and ancient. Eric and Jodi, along with their two children, founded the house. Eric describes himself as always having been on the margins, having come from a fundamentalist background before fundamentalism gained political ascendancy in the United States. He grew disenchanted with his fundamentalist roots and became a Presbyterian, attracted, at least initially, to its polity and Reformed theological perspective. The latter remains among his theological influences but by no means the only influence: today, as a community, they are exploring the Benedictine monastic traditions. Eric graduated from Duke Divinity School in North Carolina and was exposed to Stanley Hauerwas, but at the time it was mostly Hauerwas' ideas on ecclesiology that interested him. He didn't begin, he says, as a peace and justice person; rather, those concerns evolved, especially as he moved further from academic theologies to theologies espoused through intentional communities.

Eric's first ministerial call was as an associate pastor to Knox Presbyterian Church in a Kansas City suburb. The Willow Creek model of seeker services, relevance, and so on was key to the vision of the senior pastor. In that context, since it was just after the attacks of 9/11, Eric thought, "What's more relevant right now than a class on Christian responses to war?" So he introduced an adult education class using a "generic" textbook presenting different perspectives on the Christian response to war. Previous classes he had developed had enrolled around twenty-five people, but surprisingly this class, following 9/11, attracted just six or seven people. This prompted Eric to question what "relevance" actually meant: was there a profound disconnect between the so-called relevance campaign and the actual reality of escalating violence in the United States and wider world? Just as discouraging, however, was his sense that people left the class with the same views they had when they came: if they were pro-war, they left pro-war, and if they were against war they left with the same point of view. There was no real dialogue, no real change.

Eric and Jodi had also both been exploring alternative communities, like the Open Door Community in Atlanta, Georgia, a place where they would live for two years. They also count the Church of the Savior in Washington, D.C., among their influences.[23] Instead of going to academic conferences,

---

23. For further insight into the Church of the Savior movement, see http://www.inwardoutward.org/.

Eric sought out immersion experiences in communities that were attempting a more radical expression of gospel obedience. Intentional communities did not reserve theological education for the classroom but fostered theological reflection through solidarity with the poor and the marginalized. Jodi says that, as a result, the things that preoccupy many congregations, the style of music for example, are simply not what she cares about.[24] Faithful practice, especially nonviolence, peacemaking, and the works of mercy, she might say, prompts the theological root of their worship and life at Cherith Brook. While Eric often speaks of theological influences, he underscores the practitioners of nonviolence, such as Clarence Jordan of Koinonia Farms and André and Magda Trocmé, as being by far the most influential in his theological development.[25]

Eventually, others joined Cherith Brook, contributing to its evolution. It is a small house, running from two to three members at its beginning all the way to six or seven members. Each of the people I met with—especially Eric and Jodi, Allison Rozga, Josh Armfield, Elisabeth Rutschman, Nick Pickrell, and their guest at the time, Paul Newman, as well as Jeffrey New, a friend of the community—shared something in common even while being quite different. Josh Armfield, for instance, came to Cherith Brook by way of a background in the Nazarene Church and then, decisively, through a relationship that began while he was deployed in Iraq. Feeling more isolated than ever, a fellow soldier who claimed conscientious objector status became a crucial teacher as Josh migrated from a more or less conventional Christian view of violence and U.S. military power into the Catholic Worker's position on nonviolence. Probably the best description of that common center comes from Cherith Brook itself:

> Our daily lives are structured around practicing the works of mercy as found in Jesus' teachings. We are committed to regularly feeding the hungry, clothing the naked, giving drink to the thirsty, welcoming the stranger, visiting the prisoner and the sick in the name of Jesus. As followers of Jesus we understand our lives to be centered in God's Shalom. Cherith Brook strives to be a "school" for peacemaking in all its dimensions: political, communal, and personal, working constantly to undo poverty, racism and militarism. All of

24. Jodi Garbison, interview by author, audiovisual recording, Kansas City, MO, 27 January 2012.

25. For an introduction to Koinonia Farms see http://www.koinoniapartners.org/. For an article-length introduction to the legacy of André and Magda Trocmé, see Alicia Batten, "Reading the Bible in Occupied France: André Trocmé and Le Chambon," *Harvard Theological Review* 103, no. 3 (July 2010): 309–28. See also Philip Paul Hallie, *Lest Innocent Blood Be Shed: The Story of the Village of Le Chambon and How Goodness Happened There* (New York: Harper & Row, 1979).

these can be summed up as the struggle to connect with the God of life. We pray that Cherith Brook can be a space where all of us—the broken—can come to learn and relearn the ways of Jesus; a place to struggle together for God's call of love, mercy, peace and justice.[26]

Guests are invited to enter into the common life as deeply or as little as they are inclined. The members of the community share a covenant together that they renew each year, and some share in what is called a "common purse," a fund from which each member receives a modest monthly stipend. They contribute to that fund through income earned in part-time employment. As a community, however, Cherith Brook depends on donations to support its activities. In order to maintain its autonomy from the state, Cherith Brook does not claim tax-exempt status, although not all Catholic Worker Houses take this stance. Members adopt poverty not only to "strip" themselves as the poor are stripped, but also to avoid supporting U.S. military activities around the world.

An (Un)Remarkable House

In the mornings, I would sit in a side room and listen to the sound of the trucks and cars going by: the whine of tires a barely interrupted series of Doppler shifts, of overlapping pitches of departure and approach. They sounded mindless, indifferent to the place and the people they passed. They sounded efficient, too, moving so quickly and purposefully that my murky, often uncertain thoughts seemed something like litter by comparison. I was lonely with my thoughts but I was, paradoxically, in good company. Indeed, Cherith Brook, an unremarkable house, would probably not give anyone pause, unless perhaps they caught a glimpse of the gardens that surround the house or one of the banners they sometimes hang outside, announcing an upcoming event in the community. Otherwise, it's mostly unremarkable: a simple red brick house with an adjoining property, chickens roaming the grounds, surrounded by a smattering of storefront churches and bars.

But the ordinariness of the house is part of its beauty, its charm. During one of their evening talks, when members are invited to share both a "high point" and "low point" of the previous few days, Josh reflects on his feelings about being the only protester out at the construction site of the nuclear weapons facility mentioned above. He rode his bike partway and then caught a bus for the rest of the distance. Holding his sign at the site, he made up songs

---

26. Cherith Brook Catholic Worker, "Who We Are," http://cherithbrookcw.blogspot.com/.

that he sang out loud for whoever was there to listen. The group laughs at the image of him being out there singing, marching alone, as traffic passed by.

"They're building so fast," he sighs. "It doesn't seem like our protests accomplished much."

Smiling, Nick Pickrell reminds Josh of how they had protested one of the training sites of Blackwater USA, the military security contractor: "They left that site," he says hopefully. "Maybe we had something to do with *that*!"

More laughter and perhaps an even deeper folly.

Compared to the multimillion-dollar war effort, Josh's protest must have seemed like I felt that morning ten times over: a futile exercise. At least the muddle of my thoughts was hidden in the security of my notebook. There was no such cover for Josh or the cause of peace, which stood out, embarrassingly and uselessly exposed. Everything else glistened, shone clearly in its paramount importance. If there was a gate at the site, I suppose it would have been staffed by a guard, by a well-financed security detail. Comers and goers could pass by Josh and his singing without more than a second thought.

Perhaps this impression was not too far removed from the reality of the streets themselves, the city and the financial system, particularly the way we pass through communities, anonymously and without reflection. Everything about our society moves too quickly to reflect, too rapidly to ever second-guess the system in which we participate, too fast to reflect critically and practically on what we take for granted as the only possible way. One begins to wonder whether this is intentional or simply an accident of nature. Perhaps we are incapable of thinking about the present except as we pass it. The present and the people in it appear only in the periphery of our social vision, a blur at best, a momentary glimpse of need or a question never quite heard. A nascent question aborted by hurry, we move on, too busy to pause for very long. Questions of justice, violence, poverty, and the role of faith drift out of sight.

Slowing the system down forms a significant part of the life practices of Cherith Brook. The other part is the creation of an alternative space, where human flourishing has a chance to take root and grow. Perhaps that is why, not long after my arrival, Eric, Josh, and Elisabeth invited me to join them on a walk through the neighborhood. It was a strange sort of walk, not only because of the places and experiences they shared during that time, or my own direct experiences of the street that I could not begin to relate in their entirety, but also because it seemed that through the *streets* they were introducing me to the *house*. It was as though small openings of understanding on the street, seemingly far from hospitality, returned the community to the heart and practices of hospitality. Cherith Brook, in short, became a mirror of the encounters they had "away" from the center, in the far-flung places of addiction and violence. The streets were simultaneously center and margin.

As we began our strange walk, Josh tells me that it is known as a peacemaking walk:

> There's a few specific spots in our neighborhood where we always go, places where . . . violence happens, prostitution and drug dealing, and that sort of thing. . . . [W]e stop at these places and interact with folks. [We meet] lots of people who come to the Shower House . . . and lots of other folks who we just see on the streets every once and a while, and then [there are also] lots of others we don't know who are . . . coming to buy [or sell] something. . . . [W]e . . . try to interact as best as we can. And if there's a violent situation, we . . . intervene, if we think we can intervene in peaceful ways.

"Mostly," Eric adds, "we hope that [violence] doesn't happen, we hope that our presence here changes business as usual." According to Eric, the history of the walk evolved, like other practices in Cherith Brook, through trial and error: "When we first started [the peacemaking walk], that's how we knew people wanted showers, by hanging out on the streets." At one stage in the evolution of the walk, in order to "let people know where we were" and about the showers that were available, they would give away sack lunches at one particular hangout. While that seemed OK at first, it also introduced a "certain set of dynamics" that they found unhelpful to establishing a deeper level of interaction with the people in their neighborhood. While conversation may have happened in some instances, many just took the sack lunch and disappeared; whatever they were doing—drugs, prostitution, and the like—went on uninterrupted. Perhaps, too, it resembled the practice of charity that is a common feature of street ministries.[27]

With this concern, they stopped bringing the lunches but continued to interact with people they met. "It came as kind of a shock to some folks," according to Eric. They were surprised, he continued, that members actually wanted to know about their lives, why they were engaged in prostitution, for example: "Often they . . . would say [about working as a prostitute], 'I'm doing this because of economics . . . and this is the way I feed my babies.'" For others, without the sack lunches in hand, it became a question: "What are you doing here, in *our* space?" Others were simply curious: "Why are you here?" The

---

27. Josh Armfield, Eric Garbison, and Elisabeth Rutschman, interview by author, audio recording, Kansas City, MO, 24 January 2012.

question itself prompts what Eric calls a form of "reverse hospitality" where the community of Cherith Brook is welcomed into the community of the streets, where genuine sharing can perhaps begin to take place. Indeed, this had already happened when, only a few minutes before, we met Carl, mentioned above, and his friend Roy. After bantering back and forth with them for about five minutes, Carl gathered us in heartfelt prayer on a street corner a few blocks from Cherith Brook. Eric explains that the purpose of these encounters was to try to "create a new way of being in that space," a sort of place where more human flourishing might emerge, both their own and that of others.[28]

Before going too much farther on the street walk, they shared with me some guidelines or rules they live by on these walks: they never go off alone; they don't go into anyone's home without the group; and if there is ever a point where anyone is uncomfortable with a situation, instead of saying, "I'm uncomfortable with this situation and I need to get out of here," one says, "I'm thirsty. I'd like to go get a drink of water." Finally, they don't tolerate either violence or aggressive behavior toward women. I am told that we, the men in the group, will be seen by the street as prostituting Elisabeth. In the space of an hour, we were approached on two separate occasions, once as a car slowed down while the driver motioned to Eric, and, in another instance when a young man ran across a four-lane road to demand to know "who" Elisabeth "belonged to," as if she were property. It was routine.

And it was violent. Along a busy thoroughfare we met a woman, a regular friend at Cherith Brook, at the bus stop. She stood with her partner, her eye and face badly bruised. As we chatted, I asked, "Where are you going?" She motioned toward her partner, saying that he had a court appointment for charges of domestic abuse: "She came to our house the morning that happened," Eric says later. "She woke up with him choking her. And now she's back with him again. Going with him to the bus station so he can go to court." A couple of years ago, another woman, probably being prostituted, was raped, tortured, and finally murdered, her body thrown out the window:

> *We see this every day, this is not unusual.* For a while, there was a
> serial rapist who was targeting prostitutes, throwing them in the car,
> stabbing them with a screwdriver and then he would rape them.
> And one of the girls we know, she escaped, except that she got a
> screwdriver through her shoulder blade. Dora [not her real name]
> had been raped by this man. . . . Probably she prostitutes, I don't

28. Ibid.

know, but at this point, she doesn't [prostitute] or at least I hope not. And she was raped. It was clear to her she was raped.

Elisabeth says that one of the victims told her, "'I can't go to the police because they know who I am.'" Early during their time at Cherith Brook, Eric recalls a woman they met on the street and never saw again: "We came up to her, she talked to us, I asked her, 'Are you safe?' She said, 'No, I'm not safe.' Her earlobe had been bitten off by a john and the other john had pinned her in the car and took a ball-peen hammer and shattered her kneecap."[29]

Eric says that many women feel they can't go to the police because they are "known" as prostitutes, as if prostitutes can't be raped: "Some police are more aware of this dynamic of the streets," how some see the rape of a woman being prostituted as a contradiction in terms, "than others." However savvy the police may be to what is happening, they have to surmount enormous obstacles just to seek help. "They often don't go," says Eric. "The fear factor is huge. Would an undocumented person call the police? No. It's the same dynamic." Even that morning these kinds of events were being related, as Elisabeth shared: "Today a woman came in [and] she had a terrible story. . . . I asked her how she was doing. 'Better,' she said. But she had been trapped in a barn and raped by six men for two days and she had just been able to escape."[30]

Eric believes that at least some of the women they meet on the street show the symptoms of post-traumatic stress disorder. He admits that he and the other members of the community have only a faint comprehension of the violence faced by women who live on the streets each and every day. And yet, however brief their interactions with this violence, the community often finds it needs to recover from the experience. Eric speaks of the "in your face" nature of the violence they meet during their interactions with the larger community: "In the Shower House we're somewhat protected, but to see what they have to deal with every day is overwhelming for all of us."[31]

These experiences led to the formation of Women's Day, a time and a place at Cherith Brook exclusively for women, a place in which women are given some space away from the violence of men and the streets themselves. More bluntly, as Nick Pickrell puts it, "It's a time to give the women a break from the men." Volunteers come to do hair, to provide massages, or simply to talk if women are willing to talk, and, wherever possible, to offer help. Sometimes women who have been on the streets and came to Women's Day for a little

29. Ibid.
30. Ibid.
31. Ibid.

shelter from the exploitation and violence of the street return not to be sheltered so much as to offer shelter to other women. Like the Shower House itself, there is a sacramental logic to Women's Day, where there is a laying on of hands as the gift of God's compassion, an expression of holy touch. It does not remove the violence of the streets, but opens up a little way for an alternative expression of community to take root and grow.

Becoming New

"I'm fifty-four years old and I don't know what a healthy relationship looks like." This is something Jeffrey New tells me several times as we sit outside on the front deck of the house. When he says this, I feel a sense of frustration within him, the impression of an intractable estrangement, one that he finds difficult to name: "It was easier to let go of the booze and drugs than to face what came after." He never said what he meant by "what came after," but I suppose he meant facing the reality of what one has lost. He refers to it as facing the truth, perhaps of what one has yet to try to rebuild, the feeling that maybe it will be impossible to rebuild. After "white knuckling" himself off alcohol, he began something like a return: "So that's what I had been doin', I kind of pulled myself away from a lot of stuff—the way you have to exist on the street—and started getting help with my depression, then, [laughing] I came out here to take showers every day. From where I was living it took me about an hour and fifteen minutes to walk here every morning, but I learned there was a shower and so, to get myself, you know, cleaned up four times a week . . . something to eat, and a change of clothes . . . that's how I started comin' out here." It was not long before the community offered Jeffrey a place to stay and a community to which he might belong: "They offered me a place to get out from under the bridge, in one of their rooms, I don't know what they call it, they got here." He was speaking of the Christ Room, and it was the beginning of a return that even then Jeffrey seemed to still be negotiating. A lot of people, he tells me, come to Cherith Brook. They get a hot meal or a shower, and maybe find a little companionship, but that's as far as it goes. But for others it goes further, as it did for Jeffrey: "They're trying to do the very same thing I am. . . . [It's] their attempt to do what is right in their lives."[32]

Cherith Brook seemed to supply the kind of stability that allowed Jeffrey to begin a journey of return, to make a decision about the kind of person he would be, just as the community tried to make a decision to be faithful to its particular vision of godliness. In a sense, he saw Cherith Brook as a community dedicated

---

32. New, interview by author, 23 January 2013.

to trying to be faithful in a manner not unlike his own attempt, complete with setbacks and successes. He wasn't their "target" so much as their companion on a common way. I get the sense that part of the reason Cherith Brook can convey to the surrounding community its vocation is because its vocation is shared, like the streets themselves. The members of the community that I spoke with had never experienced homelessness directly, but many, as a result of their decision to live in a condition of voluntary poverty, could empathize at a more specific level and therefore at a more humanizing level.

As we finish talking, Jeffrey admits that, "in a way, I'm beginning to feel obligated to them from the point of view of a friendship—that's all new to me."[33] It would probably not be too inappropriate to continue with this pun on his name and say that this experience of friendship and community continues to make new each member of the community, in his or her own way. Eric writes of how, one year earlier, the community had planted pecan trees. He speaks of how, over each year, he feels more invested in their survival and excited to see their fruit, offering it as a parable for the shape of the new community: "This parable of the pecan tree begins with the assumption that I am tending the tree, that I chose to plant it and continue to care for it. In short, I am the cultivator of it. But those thousands of daily acts have their effect on me, too. As the tree roots mine the earth, so my roots are winding their way through the darkness and we are being born anew from the same soil."[34] Garbison evokes the complexity of community, of nurturing place through practical faith and, in the process, being more deeply formed by the whole than we imagined possible.

From Maze to Labyrinth

As I thought about the labyrinth as a way of imagining the shape of the church in exilic realities, I decided to try something. I went home, loaded our children into the minivan, and drove out to the Sinsinawa Catholic Retreat Center in Wisconsin, about twenty minutes' drive from where we live. Specifically, I wanted to see how our children would react to the large labyrinth in the center. As soon as we arrived, shoes and coats came off, barely in time for our two-year-old, Gabriel, who sprinted off across the labyrinth, delighting in a big wide-open space without barriers. Our daughters, a little older at six and eight years of age, were more tentative, noting what looked like a maze but wasn't quite a maze. I tried to explain that a labyrinth was a particular and ancient way of praying while you walk and that no matter where you are, whether you seem

33. Ibid.
34. Garbison, "Being Placed," 10.

to be going away from the center or toward it, you are always connected to that middle part and you will always return to the place where you began, still connected to the center, often symbolized as a rose. With my slim introduction, they began walking, at first a little uncertain and feeling the need to backtrack, to "start over" as it were. At the end, I asked what kinds of feelings they had about the walk. Imogen, our six-year-old daughter, replied, "I didn't know where to go!" Our oldest daughter, Gwendoline, expressed a similar sense of confusion or uncertainty. And both shared a sense of discovering the walk as they walked.

There are many different types of labyrinths as well as different spatial arrangements; for instance, they may be inlaid in a floor for walking or on a wall to be traced by the moving hand. Perhaps the most distinguishing mark of the labyrinth is the labyrs, the double-ax symbol visible in the turns of the path: "They are traditionally seen as a symbol of women's power and creativity," writes Artress. From above, looking down on the labyrinth, labyrs patterns form the shape of a cross. The labyrs conveys a feminine spirituality often lacking in patriarchal theologies: "Matriarchal spirituality celebrates the hidden and the unseen. It is often symbolized by the cycles of the moon that guide the growing seasons as well as the inner map of knowing in women."[35] Hildegard of Bingen spoke of divinity using the symbols of the circle and wheel, the divine holding all in completeness. Hugh of St. Victor believed that visible things guide us into invisible understanding.[36] What looks inscrutable at first glance yields, through active practice, wisdom and trust in the path of life.

People who experience the labyrinth for the first time may believe that, somehow, they may have taken the "wrong" turn, but, as they continue to walk, they discover that the path proves trustworthy, always leading to the middle and out again. The labyrinth, according to Artress, represents an antidote to paralyzing confusion, guiding participants into an active trust in the way: "Labyrinths are powerful blueprints that order chaos, offer a path of prayer, heal deep wounds, serve as a place of solace, and transform human consciousness individually and in community. The labyrinth offers a spiritual exercise that becomes the path of life. It allows the wandering soul to find a way to center, to find a way home."[37] As a spiritual practice, it conjoins the creative symbol of the labyrs to the spiritual act of discernment and community. While people may walk the labyrinth alone, it encourages a communal practice, especially as each participant gains awareness of others who share a similar but distinct journey.

35. Artress, *Walking a Sacred Path*, 55, 60, 67.
36. Ibid., 55.
37. Ibid., 194.

The footpath gathers up its purpose not in grandiose statements but in the almost-plodding way of learning through walking. Dorothy Day reflects on the difficulty of renouncing worldly attachments using the metaphor of walking: "The older I get the more I see that [the life of voluntary poverty] is made up of many steps, and they are very small ones, not giant strides."[38] Day often called on the metaphor of pilgrimage as she described the concrete vocation of the Catholic Worker, a metaphor the community at Cherith Brook would recognize as well.

I had one question that I asked in most, if not all, of my interviews: "Is there a single moment or event that you would say brings into focus your experience of Cherith Brook?" I was looking for evidence of its life through a legendary account of its work as a community. Although they wanted to help me as a guest, the answer came back almost invariably from each person I interviewed: "No, not really." Couldn't you name, I wondered to myself, at least one time or place where the "lost were found" or recall when the dead rose from their graves? One incident in which the gospel was blindingly clear? But as I continued to observe, it began to dawn on me that this community was less about singular moments of transformation and more about surpassingly ordinary and myriad expressions of transformation.

Peacemaking, for instance, which might seem like a word too large to shoulder, surfaced not as an extraordinary activity but an ordinary sacrament, a way of being human. Jodi Garbison admits that she had previously viewed peacemaking as a practice that guided one's response to *enemies*—she did not see it as an expression of how she might interact with friends, family, and neighbors. But she says her experience with communal life at Cherith Brook opened a window on peacemaking that sounded a lot like homemaking, but homemaking externalized into a love of neighbor and enemy alike: "[Peacemaking] is the way I treat Nick and Josh, and welcome Eric, and Steve, and the children. . . . [I]t's the way I practice it on the very mundane kind of daily tasks that will then . . . determine how I handle it when it's bigger . . . more volatile."[39] Peacemaking may appear visibly, as it did in the nuclear weapons plant protest, but it grows in the soil of the ordinary, at table and in fellowship with sisters, brothers, and friends.

No single relationship, no moment where all the pieces coalesced, no one thing captured the community because, in fact, it was more like an organism, with each part connected through ordinary actions of hospitality and gospel obedience. If there was any single narrative to connect their stories, it might

38. Day, *Loaves and Fishes*, 83.

39. Jodi Garbison, interview by author, audiovisual recording, 27 January 2012.

have been found in their frequent references to Matthew's Gospel, especially the Sermon on the Mount, as their manifesto of nonviolence. Moreover, it would seem that theirs is a journey rather than a destination. Members of the community readily and frequently remind me, and even more themselves, that this is a failed enterprise. Faithfulness, not some criterion of success, is their calling, and that requires more than you can see, more than you can understand.

The members of this community are discovering that to live "at home" in the knowledge of Jesus Christ is to live richly, authentically, robustly, and joyfully in the place of the cross, in the place of desolation and loss. They attempt to do so by living sacramentally, which is to say they live physically, the way we receive the sacrament, as persons whose salvation is tied up in the physical well-being and spiritual wholeness of the other. Thus, they anticipate the way human dignity, friendship, sisterhood, and brotherhood quietly release the human spirit from the captivity of the powers and principalities, liberating the flesh from the marketplace, the possibility of a just economy from the tyranny of the financial system, and the holy imagination from its captivity to the modern war machine.

When the women returned to prepare Jesus' body for burial, the path they set out on was familiar even if it was tragic. Like the women who first reported the empty tomb, the church sets out on a path that seems to lead to death but is interrupted by unexpected resurrection. Writers of the gospel point to this path and this journey as foundational to the formation of Christian community. "I die every day," writes the apostle Paul, dies to the order of the world he imagined even as he is awakened to the world God in Christ has already called into being. Perhaps the church should treat its present more like a labyrinth than a maze, electing to step into the precarity of its present not seeking primarily to know but to trust, not to achieve an outcome but to hope in God's future, not to coerce but to love in the spirit and way of the One who first loved us.

6

Changing Clothes
Clothing, Community, and Native Peoples

> *For in this tent we groan, longing to be
> clothed with our heavenly dwelling—if
> indeed, when we have taken it off we will
> not be found naked. For while we are still
> in this tent, we groan under our burden,
> because we wish not to be unclothed but to
> be further clothed, so that what is mortal
> may be swallowed up by life.*
> —THE APOSTLE PAUL (2 COR. 5:2-4)

It was late June 2007 and we had driven from my parents' home in California to a little Nez Perce Presbyterian camp retreat in Idaho, situated between Craigmont and Winchester, atop Mason Butte at about four thousand feet in elevation. Known as Talmaks, which means, "mountain on the prairie," it was established in 1910 and has served as a site for Christian renewal for Nez Perce Presbyterians, but also Native peoples from all over the United States, including Arizona and the Dakotas, and from as far away as the Marshall Islands in the Pacific Ocean. As we drove into the camp, I remember seeing the tipis scattered across the campground. They were taller than I had imagined them, some as high as twenty feet. Each boasted an off-white canvas hide wrapped around a set of wooden poles that converged in a small frond of fingers protruding through the very top of the tipi. Some of the more magnificent ones bore beautiful patterns and colorful prints. At least one was painted in the colors of the U.S. flag. Some had fires burning inside with a slender finger of smoke exiting through the top. There were also cabins, simple structures with bunks and perhaps a porch to sit on in the afternoons, and some campers stayed in modern tents and trailers.

In the middle of the camp stood the church, an open-air structure, its ceiling made of corrugated tin, with folding chairs and a pulpit area. It could hold 200, maybe 250 people comfortably. This is where worship took place each day. Out of sight, among the tipis and often hidden among bushes and hanging blankets, there were sweat houses. These were covered with faded, castoff blankets of different colors and types, which were heaped one on top of another to keep the heat in during the sweats. Nez Perce and guests might enjoy a "secular" sweat, mostly for its health benefits or its social dimensions. Others would participate in spiritual sweats, full of prayer and the anticipation of God's presence, our Great-Grandfather, in the womb of the creation.

With my family in tow, I had come not to sweat but to lead a Bible study for the two weeks of the camp and to contribute to the daily preaching schedule. I had also come for something more, not only to serve but also, perhaps, to understand. As it turns out, I would eventually need to "sweat" for my understanding, but it was more gift than labor. Before taking up that part of the narrative, I need to confess my ambivalence: I've always felt like both an outsider and insider at these meetings, though probably more of an outsider among people who grew up on the reservation than among those who grew up near the village. The source of my ambivalence goes to our family tree. My mother's grandmother, full-blooded Athabascan, married a White man, Whiskey Jack. While his real name was Jack Burchard, I don't know him by any other name. He was a bootlegger, an old-fashioned-sounding word, but no less expressive of the kinds of violence committed against Native peoples in North America. When we visited Nenana, an Athabascan village not far from where my grandmother on my mother's side would have been born, they knew about him. He was notorious. An Athabascan man named Alex took us to the small, out-of-the-way graveyard where my great-grandmother, Evelyn Swenson Burchard, was buried.

According to the family story, Burchard "bought" my great-grandmother with a box of whiskey, which he gave to her parents in trade. I suppose this was how he got his name. He was physically abusive. He struck and killed one of his daughters with a set of dog team traces. It was ruled an accident and there were never any charges brought against him. Some of the White men that Burchard's daughters would marry were abusive as well, as if one cycle of violence begat another cycle with dreary predictability. Of their children, twelve in all, a number of the daughters, including my grandmother, married

White men. Not all of those White men were abusive, but some were. I heard terrible stories of abuse, including of my great-aunt's eyes being burned out with cigarettes by her White husband.

You don't quickly forget such stories.

Or often repeat them.

My mother's father, a White man, I don't know anything about. The only thing my mother told me about him was that he drank a "fifth of whiskey" every day. Once when I asked what she remembered about him, she told me he liked potato chips. That was it. I don't know a lot about my grandmother, either. I do know where she's buried, in a Cordova graveyard. We have one surviving picture of her youth, showing her as a young girl, an adolescent on the cusp of womanhood. Somewhere, I remember seeing a picture of my mother's parents, sitting in a living room, the photo yellow with age. My grandfather disappeared, leaving my grandmother, my mother, and her sister and two brothers to fend for themselves. To my knowledge, no one ever heard from him again. I assume he's dead. Not long after he disappeared, my grandmother died of alcohol-related causes. My mother was thirteen years old.

I often try to understand why the break between my identity today and my Alaska Native ancestors seems so final, irretrievable. Perhaps there's a place you can't go after you've lost as much as my mother and grandmothers lost. Maybe they go back in their dreams, as I sometimes do, but a kind of silence, a pall, falls over the past of those who know exile personally. For my part, exile is more indirect, as I hear of it through them, or rather I hear of it through the silences it produces in them. For me, it's there, but in a different form. Even though my blood quantum level qualifies me for participation in federal programs, and though I am a member of two Alaska Native corporations and some of my closest friends are "identifiably" Native, I still feel far removed from more basic expressions of Native culture, as if something beyond these inclusions suppresses this part of my voice.[1] Of course, part of this distance is not mysterious at all, stemming from the fact that when I was growing up, the cultural renewal activities that are more common among Native communities today were then still largely unknown or in their infancy. Another part of it results from the fact that, after remarrying, our family moved to California, where my stepfather, of Midwestern stock, had family. No less significant is

---

1. As I've talked to others, both those who are "identifiably" Native and those who are not, those who grew up in Native community and those who did not, or those who spent part of their lives in Native communities and other parts in majority culture settings, there is often this sense of historical and cultural estrangement. It appears in different forms and may look quite different from person to person, but it is frequently there.

the role of genetics and skin: I don't "look" Native, not at least to the popular imagination. It goes, too, in a more positive direction, or in the direction of adoption. After spending the last thirty-five years in California, my mother says, "This is my home now. I don't think about the other anymore. This is where I live."

Geography and skin matter, almost like borders become real, especially when you can't cross them legally.

So goes the story. I am not disputing my mother's understanding of home. One cannot live as an exile for very long, if at all. One can mourn and waste away in mourning. Or we cling to something, someone, someplace. We start a new family, something radical arising from a deep rupture or a tear in the fabric of being human. For my mother's part, thankfully, she married a gentle, caring person in my stepfather. Their life has not been easy, but at least it has not been abusive. They genuinely care for one another, as deeply and perhaps more lovingly than what I have seen in many other marriages.

Once, as I pestered my mother to think about her past, to tell me her story, she gently told me that her days of swimming upstream, like the salmon do as they migrate to their spawning places, were over: "I'm one of those salmon who are drifting back," she told me, laughing a little. "I'm finished swimming."

She has her peace. It has been given to her. She wasn't telling me to quit but perhaps, in her own way, letting me know that our journeys were different, albeit connected in the ancient ways of waters. So for me, I am still trying to fight my way upstream, like the salmon we used to watch as kids, trying to return to something that seems lost but real, absent but beckoning. I know it through its absence, a phenomenon that produces in me a thirst for waters that I find to this day elusive

Recently married, I returned to Alaska to visit with my great-aunts, the two remaining daughters of Whiskey Jack; I wanted to know about their lives, what it was like for them growing up. They wondered why I wanted to know about the past: "Leave it," they said. "It's too sad. Too painful. Why do you want to know about all that?" They were genuinely puzzled by my interest in what happened. Perhaps not having words, or words they could speak out loud, they took me, just as my mother had taken my siblings and me to our grandmother's grave when we were small children, to the gravesite where Whiskey Jack, my great-grandfather and their father, was buried. It was a place they hadn't visited in decades. In fact, they didn't know where it was at first, but then, after a bit of searching, they found it at a Catholic graveyard near Fairbanks. One of my great-aunts stood way off, not coming any closer, as if filled with fear or, just as likely, loathing. And I was there, asking questions, wanting to know who or what was hidden in these graves. That's what a lot of the history of exiles is buried in, or clothed in: grave clothes.

But my story is not so terrible or so silent. It is, however, marked with a different kind of loss. Characterizing that loss as being produced by exile may strike some as too much, a culture of victimhood run amok. And perhaps if one only looks at my life, then maybe so. A PhD does not usually show up on the resume of an exile. Because of my skin color and because I was immersed in White culture early, when we moved to California it seemed "easy" to fit in, so long as I didn't mention my story in detail. We were taught, in fact, to tell others we were White, to deliberately suppress our Native background. Whenever I filled out identification papers, like an application for a driver's license, I always reported that my hair was brown; it is actually closer to black. This fact only dawned on me, by now into my early forties, in the last year or so, as I was cutting my hair in the bathroom. To people outside of this experience, it may seem inconceivable that these kinds of intimate and undeniable expressions of identity might be ignored or suppressed. But that's not at all uncommon, at least for one part of the Native experience in North America. While some actively promoted their ancestral identity, many others actively suppressed it and still do. Either way, both its promotion and its suppression extended from the same phenomenon: the physical and ideological force of assimilation. You had to choose what others took for granted.

My mother seldom talked about her ancestry. She obviously learned to do that, to keep that part of her life to herself, even to the point that it was a bit mysterious to me. I can only imagine that this was common among others as well. Once you suppress language, if you invalidate the history of a people, what more is it to simply pretend that it never existed to begin with? And, what is more, maybe my mother, as a mixed-blood person, knew better than I did what might happen if I did share that part of my life.

I would soon discover that firsthand. While at seminary I made the mistake of believing that I could tell parts of my narrative to a group of White students. They looked at me blankly in response. Perhaps they wanted to understand, but for people who grew up in the mostly predictable world of the suburbs, in the middle and upper middle classes, this must have seemed a peculiar thing, particularly given that, at least on first glance, I looked every bit as privileged as they were. And, in a sense, maybe I was and am. For some, your blood quantum is nothing compared to your skin color. One professor asked me pointedly about my mother's Native ancestry: "Then why are her eyes blue?" During a seminar, another claimed I was playing my "Native card" as if it were some kind of superficial fabrication. Yet another expressed shock when she realized that I did not know the traditions of my Native ancestors.

If she had known better, she would have understood that loss or absence is a form of inheritance. Whole generations have grown up without the stability of home and economic security, having lost the umbilical cord that attaches them to the deep wells of ancestral memory. People who have not undergone a loss of this magnitude simply cannot understand the gaping absence left behind, an absence that becomes a thing in itself. I wonder sometimes if this inability to understand exilic loss is especially true of White views of Native peoples. In the White imagination, Natives often seem like the "pristine" national parks that Americans sometimes visit as they get back to "nature" and "purity"—the supposedly pure lands of Native peoples now mostly emptied except for campgrounds and nature trails. Native peoples used to live on these lands, the brochures announce, when they, like the land itself, were pure and remote—and, to that extent, they remain unreal. It's as if the memories of Native peoples were no longer alive, no longer calling. Such an attitude is visible in the way someone will point out a particular weed that Native people used to eat or smoke, then, full of good intention, say, look, here's a great museum with a reconstructed dwelling from North America's indigenous history. By contrast, the living are too untidy, impure. Their boarded-up houses, poverty-ravaged reservation, decrepit trailers, addictions, abuse, and obesity are too much a reminder that theirs is a fantasy. And, anyway, the dead are best kept in the museum. After all, by now, Lord, they stinketh. Leave them in their celebrated tombs, tightly bound in the grave clothes of the irretrievable past.

I am alluding, of course, to the story of the raising of Lazarus in the Gospel of John. As a story it anticipates the resurrection, but it also parables the resurrection as it might take shape in today's communities. The destitution worked by death is named by Martha, as she protests against Jesus' command to roll away the stone: "'Lord, already there is a stench because he has been dead four days'" (11:39b). Jesus persists and they do as he had asked. As the stone is being rolled away, Jesus introduces a prayer to be overheard by those around him so that they understood that what they were about to witness would contribute to their faith in Jesus and his Father.

Yet, oddly, when Lazarus comes out, he does not walk out waving his arms, dancing with joy, or talking, as we might have expected: "The dead man came out, his hands and feet bound with strips of cloth, and his face wrapped in a cloth" (44). Curiously, John calls the now living Lazarus a "dead man" even after he "comes out" of the grave. Perhaps, in the rich symbolism of John's gospel, Lazarus was clothed but in the clothing of death rather than life. He was paralyzed by the clothing, a form of anticlothing that may not close him off to Christ's grace but would impede the community that Christ sought to bring into being. Perhaps one could read this anticlothing as the way in which his humanity and his relationship to others in the circle of life was being utterly closed off, so that he could neither reach out nor be reached. He could not see but neither could he be seen. Shame operates that way, suppressing or sealing the living in the tombs of the dead. And, ironically, the living are also paralyzed by the power of death. Apparently, everyone just stood there, stupid, mouths agape. The pericope ends with a command: "Jesus said to them, 'Unbind him, and let him go'" (44b). This strikes my ear as a liberating word, a word that tells us the things we have buried, especially those deepest memories of our common humanity, are already recipients of the promise of God. Already, we are being born again. We are not being asked to resurrect the dead—that's what God does. We are being asked to shed the clothes of destitution and to unbind and be unbound from captivity to destitution and shame so that we can rejoice together in the freedom of the resurrection, clothed in the naked love of Christ.

As we drove into Talmaks, we saw a community engaged in practices that suggest the shedding of the grave clothes of destitution and being dressed in the clothes of the beloved community. It happened gradually. The first day, when we arrived, we were ill equipped for the cold night that would follow. Perhaps more deeply felt for me than the cold was the sense of difference that I shared earlier. Nancy Half Moon, at the time probably in her eighties, was one of the first to welcome us. She served as the president of the camp and beloved mother to the Talmaks tradition. Not long after that, Connie and Steve Evans came to us and asked us if we would like to stay in a tipi. We were placed not far from Nancy Half Moon, as if to communicate the hospitality that was key to this community. As people who were effectively strangers there, we were graced not with a secondhand robe but with the honored garment of the community. We were adopted, gathered into the hospitality that typifies the Nez Perce in particular and Native cultures as a whole.

This would continue when Adrian Moody, Nez Perce, invited me to join him and a few others for a sweat. It was understood that we would be shedding our clothes but not our deeper humanity, our connection to each other and to our common Creator. In a sense, we were actually being radically clothed and, in that radical expression of human community, being liberated from our captivity to the destitution and paralysis of class and prejudice. Our humanity would be shared as, from a theological perspective, it is not good that we should be alone. It was to be a spiritual sweat, a practice that had, according to Adrian, evolved among Nez Perce Christians from more ancient expressions of spirituality among Native people. Adrian explained the sweat to us as we waited in a semicircle, a group of White, mixed-blood, and Native peoples. It was the first time I've ever been naked in a classroom.

Yet this was no nude beach where people go au natural as a form of recreation. This gathering brought together a pronounced ethical dimension, that of community. We were clothed with nothing but our skins, which would ordinarily render us "naked" (i.e., destitute) but here clothed us in a deeper hue of skin, a community of different skins gathered in order to participate in a rite that parabled a return to the deepest sense of human identity. We were being clothed again, but with a textile that transformed that boundary, marrying our nakedness to our humanity, our solitariness to our belonging within a beloved community.[2]

At the heart of this tradition, according to Adrian, was the act of "reentering the womb," symbolized by the small entryway into the sweathouse. We would enter in the same direction were born, entering backward, retracing our birth. As we prepared to return to the world, we would enter it as we were born, headfirst. As we waited for the rocks to heat in the fire, Adrian talked about the sweat itself. He said we would become as we were before we were born: surrounded by the dark, wet heat of our Creator, particularly as she cleansed and then pushed us with her unbearable heat back into the world, returning us to the world lathered with creation's blood. After we came out into the air and light, we poured a potful of cold water over our bodies, rinsing off. Later, throughout the day and into the evening, I could not stop shivering. I suppose I was suffering from dehydration. But it also reminded me of how, when our daughters were born, they trembled in the seemingly sudden, startling expression of being born.[3]

In the subsequent pages, I try to tease out different qualities—the ethical, theological, scriptural, and cultural dimensions—of being clothed as the church in settings of exile. Guided by the image of the sweathouse, the skins of the tipis, and the open-air chapel, this chapter reflects on how we are "clothed" and "unclothed" or, put another way, how we are *transparently* the church, Christ's own natural body, a reconciled and reconciling people in and for the world. In this regard, Dietrich Bonhoeffer's understanding of the incarnation supplies a Christological framework for my thinking, especially in the way

2. My reflections on the relationship between nakedness and clothing are indebted to the work of Michele Saracino, *Clothing* (Minneapolis: Fortress Press, 2012). See especially chapter 3, "Redeeming Fashion," 83–107.

3. A version of this story appeared in Robert Hoch, "The Season of Epiphany," in *New Proclamation (Year A 2011): Advent through Holy Week*, ed. David Lott (Minneapolis: Fortress Press, 2011), 80.

he distinguishes the incarnation both as Christ's becoming human and Christ being the crucified. I will also briefly introduce the way Scripture, particularly through the psalms, evokes the metaphor of clothing as garment for the body of creation to describe ethical relationships in community. With this background, the chapter introduces the pastoral imagination of Rev. Irvin Porter, pastor of the Church of the Indian Fellowship, a Presbyterian Church that negotiates its identity through Christ's reconciling work, through its and North America's historical relationship with First Nations peoples, and in relationship to non–First Nations peoples.

Back to Nature

While visiting with an organic dairy farmer in Wisconsin, we were talking about gardening and, from my perspective, how difficult it is to keep weeds at bay without herbicides. He gave me a laconic shrug and responded, saying, "The land will cover itself. The earth doesn't like to be bare any more than we do." What I saw as "weeds" or competition with my tomato plants was to the earth clothing by which it preserved the rich topsoil from erosion and wind. Stripping the earth of this garment only inspired the natural way of the earth's expression, to be covered with grasses and fields of trees and brush, which, in turn, support and depend on a complex ecology both above and below the earth's surface. Environmentalists tell us that while ecological systems are hardy, they are also exceedingly delicate. If repeatedly stripped bare of its natural expression, the environment's natural complexity may, finally, be reduced not only to a monoculture but to a noxious monoculture. On a much larger geopolitical and economic scale, that monoculture might be represented by the subjugation of the creation to the singular goals of a financial system—or it may extend to a form of cultural replacement that combines with religious agendas, as it did for First Nations peoples in North America.

As we shared stories from our lives, Dr. Henry Fawcett, a Tsimshian (Alaska Native) and teaching elder in the Presbyterian Church, was reminded of what his father told him before he died: his father would be buried in the cemetery of Metlakatla, but he did not want a gravestone. When asked why, his father explained that when White people came, they took his ancestral name away and gave him a White name in its place. All his life he lived with a name that is more scar than gift, more a reminder of what was torn away than what was given in love. In death, he would take only the name that the earth had given him. He chose to receive the name spoken by the murmurings of the creation, the sound of streams and waters, a name as rich and syllabled as the creation itself. In death, he would cast himself upon the sign of the Creator, the one who creates out of nothingness.

Church leaders among First Nations peoples find that they are confronted by a multitude of questions, including these: How does one form a natural community in a place and among a people for whom the church was not so much a natural expression of their spirituality and history as an instrument of cultural replacement? How can we offer authentic witness in a church that, to use the language of one leader of missions to Native peoples, aimed to "kill the Indian and save the man" in the name of the gospel? What sort of natural Christian community awakens from the apparent namelessness of First Nations peoples? What sort of person walks out of the grave of assimilation, of the namelessness of nothing? What kind of captive and for what kind of liberty? What sort of community rises out of North America's historical amnesia where Native peoples are concerned? Can it be a community whose testimony is Christ and whose body is a natural expression of the world God so loved, diverse and rich, and yet, as a church, clothed with the singular garment of God's salvation?

These questions move from the objection or the no of Christian witness to the yes of Christian community. While these two are inseparable, communities forged in exile are often, for the outsider, primarily known by the way their dramatic no exposes the powers and principalities. However, communities that engage in this sort of activity, witnessing to God's no, are also clothed and are clothing their communities in deeply human hues of being. This twofold dynamic between the no and the yes of Christian worship and witness may be lost on mainline congregations that perhaps only see communities like these as protest movements, organized around issues or historical injustices. To the extent that this is the case, they fail to grasp the manifold importance of these communities.

They do, indeed, protest but they also form community that surpasses in joy and affection the issues themselves. For example, Cherith Brook Catholic Workers never refer to the people in their community as "poor" or "homeless" or "addicts" or "prostitutes"—always, they spoke of their *friends*. They understood poverty as deeply as those who, for example, "specialize" in poverty studies, yet they also undermined even that "expertise" with a new kind of language, the language of friendship and kindred spirit. This in turn led to tangible and expressive forms of community rather than merely sentimental or symbolic or utilitarian relationships. In sum, from the outside, communities formed in exilic realities may be striking because of what they *protest*; however, they may be even more important because of what they help to *foster*. Sadly, these two often get separated, as if they were not mutually interdependent, together shaping our understanding of the life and witness of the community of faith.

What theological resources help to name the way these two, protest and community formation, remain interdependent? Dietrich Bonhoeffer proves helpful in this regard, as he underscores in his *Ethics* the fact that Christ's becoming human involves two moves relative to history: on the one hand, Christ's becoming human inaugurates our true humanity, our "natural" humanness, and, on the other hand, Christ's becoming human casts into question the idols we take as normative for the world, introducing a profound break between God and history.[4] The Plowshares movement suggests the latter when, for example, Father Carl Kabat and others cut through the fences of nuclear weapons sites and then proceeded to hang up banners calling for an end to nuclear weapons, break bread, pray, sing hymns, and then swing hammers to symbolically begin turning our American "swords" (nuclear weapons) into plowshares. Today, after Father Kabat spent some seventeen years in prison, the nation-state labels him, and others like him, a felon and terrorist.[5]

I drove this so-called terrorist and felon to an action outside a nuclear weapons plant in Kansas City, Missouri. As we were going down the freeway, Father Kabat started to rifle through his pockets, muttering irritably to himself, looking for his clerical collar. When he finally found it, he explained its importance: "I don't wear the collar unless I'm going to break the law." Maybe Bonhoeffer would say that Father Kabat wears the collar while "breaking the law" to foreground Christ's crucifixion, dramatizing the *break* between God and history, emphasizing that the One who "breaks the law" of Roman power is, in fact, the One who gives us the true law of God's justice and peace. It is a solemn No, and one that expresses the seriousness of the prophetic opposition to injustice and violence. At the same time, Kabat also reminded us, "Do what you can. And after that, sing and dance, sing and dance." He repeated this several times, and I took it to mean that there is a no within Christian community, something to which we are profoundly obligated, but at least as deep there remains an obligation to "sing and dance" in the freedom and joy of Christ's victory over sin and death.

Someone was listening. During the action itself, I watched as two women who were about to be arrested embraced each other, smiled, waved their hands

---

4. Dietrich Bonhoeffer, *Ethics*, ed. and trans. Isle Tödt, Heinz Eduard Tödt, Ernst Feil, and Clifford J. Green, et al. (Minneapolis: Fortress Press, 2005), 104–7, 173.

5. For firsthand testimonies of the nonviolent peace movement, see Rosalie G. Riegle, *Crossing the Line: Nonviolent Resisters Speak Out for Peace* (Eugene, OR: Wipf and Stock, 2013).

in the air, and danced. It only occurred to me later what they were doing as they adorned their imminent arrest in the natural and joyful dance of the church as it anticipates the resurrection. As Bonhoeffer puts it elsewhere, we may wait for and hope in the last word of grace, but the pilgrimage of faith—the song and dance—moves in the particularity of the *next*-to-the-last word, a natural word open to the coming of Christ. These two, the natural and the Christ, are not separated but joined in a *proleptic*, or anticipatory, sense. Just as the coming of Christ shows the next-to-the-last word, it also opposes the unnatural "as the destruction of the penultimate."[6] Bonhoeffer does not disregard or spiritualize the natural, but instead asserts that the primary sign of the unnatural is a will to destroy the penultimate, to clear the land, so to speak, for a grand project.

When Scripture speaks of this unity, the natural and its openness to God's future, it speaks in a primordial voice, pointing to the creational and natural act of God who clothes the human community amid its actual and spiritual exile. God, who is Spirit, takes from nature the "stuff" that forms human culture, laying hold of it for the narration of God's human story. This act directs the human community toward the otherness of God and liberates the human being to be in fellowship with the other in human community and creation. However, this movement can never be separated from the judgment of the cross, as Bonhoeffer implies when he critiques the false garment of violence: "Nothing betrays the idolization of death more clearly than when an era claims to build for eternity, and yet life in that era is worth nothing, when big words are spoken about a new humanity, a new world, a new society that will be created, and all this newness consists only in the annihilation of existing life."[7] Bonhoeffer wrote these words in the context of Nazi Germany, but the wisdom of his words speak in the North American context where genocidal acts of assimilation were covered with the lie of newness—and, in many cases, remain covered to this day. Hidden beneath the "newness" of the U.S. expansion and assimilation was the wolf of the North American genocide against First Nations peoples. Yet, however devastating and unmaking that power, it remains but one empire, like other empires that have risen and fallen. In the cracks of empire, the weed of the cruciform community grows and prospers.

Scripture abounds with the language of clothing and for good reason: being clothed or getting dressed, or, alternatively, getting undressed, reflects a deep-seated practice in the art of being human and being in community. Michele Saracino speaks of three terms that are used interchangeably to speak of this phenomenon: clothing, dress, and adornment. Clothing, she points

---

6. Bonhoeffer, *Ethics*, 173.

7. Ibid., 91.

out, appears frequently in Scripture and often underscores a symbolic aspect of the biblical story, such as the clothing of John the Baptist. It also appears as a metaphor expressing ethical relationships. Beyond their appearance in Scripture, the verbs *to clothe* and *to dress* are some of the most commonly used in the human language and offer a "succinct way of describing what many of us do daily—put on clothes and accessories in order to participate in the social world." Adornment includes the way dress or clothing introduces "body modification," such as makeup, piercing, and tattooing. In the case of the last, "the borders between our bodies and our dress are becoming increasingly murky."[8] The ethical implications of clothing, thus, run deep, not only in the language of Scripture but also in the way clothing reflects our participation within the human economy.

After the fall, clothing represents God's act of salvage, knitting skins together for Adam and Eve amid their exilic reality. To recall Bonhoeffer's language, we witness in this text the delicate act of being clothed by God for our sojourn in the natural world. Human beings cannot be human without clothing: we are called to "clothe the naked" not because it is charitable but because it humanizes the whole community. If one remains naked while others seem clothed, the nakedness of the one exposes the poverty of the whole—the so-called whole remains profoundly naked. Being clothed presupposes not merely survival but ethical vitality, interdependency, and openness to the other. Maybe this begs the question: What is natural? What does it mean to be a natural human being or a natural church community? It seems like an impossibly subjective term, especially given the way clothing today seems to be focused on self-expression, introducing barriers that often close off rather than open up. If this is the case, how does Scripture express the "natural" clothing of human beings? What wisdom might a Christology of clothing provide for the church as exile, among exiles, and as antidote to exile?

If Scripture does not prescribe what constitutes "natural" clothing, it consistently underscores its dynamism and its variety through what it produces in the creation. Scripture speaks often of clothing and how the earth and its fruits are good together: "The meadows clothe themselves with flocks, the valleys deck themselves with grain, they shout and sing together for joy" (Ps. 65:13). In this image, the earth's clothing not only provides shelter but also exudes and overflows with fruitful gratitude. It gives more than it takes. If there was a flood of judgment that covered the earth, there is within the doctrine of creation a dramatic "flood" of benediction in nature: "You visit the earth and

8. Saracino, *Clothing*, 10–11.

water it, you greatly enrich it; the river of God is full of water; you provide the people with grain, for so you have prepared it" (9).

The psalmist displays the remarkable porousness of God's clothing: "You are clothed with honor and majesty, wrapped in light as with a garment" (104:1b-2a). The psalmist introduces a metaphorical contradiction: light does not close off but illuminates, does not wrap up but rather startles the cover of darkness, pulls it away in one dramatic instant, like the moment when the sun breaks above the horizon, the light dances across the edges of the eastern landscape and skips and casts beams through the atmosphere. To be clothed with light is to open up with contours and colors. According to the psalmist, God wears a garment that acts more like a verb than a noun. Light may be a garment, covering God, but paradoxically it enlivens the other in response to God: the atmosphere swirls and boils, becoming God's messengers, and the creation flashes with the fire of God's messengers; clouds and winds roar and moan with the rushing sound of God's presence. It as if, in the psalmist's mind, the Lord God's garment of light simultaneously covers but also uncovers, catalyzing the creation into thanksgiving and song, its own natural expression of thanksgiving.

Alternatively, the Scripture opposes clothing that closes off or excludes: "You have sown much, and harvested little; you eat, but you never have enough; you drink, but you never have your fill; you clothe yourselves, but no one is warm; and you that earn wages earn wages to put them into a bag with holes" (Hag. 1:6). Similarly in Ezekiel: "You eat the fat, you clothe yourselves with the wool; you slaughter the fatlings; but you do not feed the sheep. You have not strengthened the weak, you have not healed the sick, you have not bound up the injured, you have not brought back the strayed, you have not sought the lost, but with force and harshness you have ruled them" (Ezek. 34:3-4). This kind of clothing does not enliven through offering but kills through exclusion and deprivation. From the perspective of Scripture, it is a form of anticlothing, since it in fact depends on a system of dehumanization rather than on practices that contribute to our collective humanization.

There is a kind of "nakedness" involved in Jesus Christ's becoming human. Clothing that aligns with Christ's self-giving entails a form of transparency, the goodness of fruit and tree together, almost as if the fruit and tree were impossible to imagine except as they are conceived and created together. Paul evokes the nakedness of Jesus Christ in the language of the Christ-hymn of Philippians: "Christ Jesus, who, though he was in the form of God, did not regard equality with God as something to be exploited, but emptied himself, taking the form of a slave, being born in human likeness. And being found in human form, he humbled himself and became obedient to the point of death—even death on a cross" (Phil. 2:5b-8). God becoming human in Jesus Christ inaugurates a double movement, emptying God and filling captive/empty humanity. The naked love of God becomes the garment of the human being. If our light is as darkness compared to God's light, so also our clothing is as destitution compared to God's nakedness in Christ. Being clothed with Christ's naked love we are clothed with a garment that will not perish or be devoured by time. This garment reflects God's own life, poured out and effecting a new outpouring of life in the creation.

In John's Gospel, we get another picture of God's self-emptying as it is metaphorically expressed by Mary, who empties a bottle of costly perfume and "covers" Jesus' feet with her hair—her humanity, as it covers Jesus' feet and body with the aroma of her devotion, foreshadows how Christ covers our own humanity through his death and resurrection (John 12:1-8). This is where we usually go, to the ultimate. But if we linger for a bit with the penultimate, with the broken jar of perfume, with the image of the woman mopping Jesus' feet with the garment of her hair, we see the evocation of the church, Christ's natural covering being this delicate expression of human adoration. She salvages from a broken and fragile life the things that open us and others to the coming of Christ in our world, among its symbols and our physical bodies. She does not set aside her body, but rather her body brings into expression a life toward Christ. John's Gospel supplies a beautiful expression of the penultimate response of thanksgiving, as it is manifested physically.

Colossians announces that Christ "is the image of the invisible God, the firstborn of all creation; for in him all things in heaven and on earth were created, things visible and invisible, whether thrones or dominions or rulers or powers—all things have been created through him and for him" (Col. 1:15-16). Creation, history itself, becomes the garment of Christ. While we may flee history, Christ takes it upon himself because it belongs to Christ. Christ wears it because Christ reconciles it to himself. This means that Christ does not passively wear history, as if it were something apart from him, but forms our history according to himself. Maybe we could say that Christ "adorns" history, introducing the "body modification" of God's intervention in history. Christ makes history his own servant, which means not only is it accountable to judgment but it is also sanctified.

In Bonhoeffer's mind, the church is not so much a space as it is a proclamation toward Christ, a form of Christ's natural witness in community. It is a witness made in order that human beings might become more fully human. Against the church that flees the messiness of the human world, God becomes flesh, becomes human. The world, according to the writer in Colossians, has been clothed with Christ's reconciling image, even apart from the world's knowledge that it is so clothed. The church, as it receives the world's reconciliation in Christ, does so vicariously, for the entire world. But the response of the world belongs to the next-to–the-last word, an utterance that covers for a moment its silence.

A Call Home

"I learned a lot in those years," Rev. Irvin Porter (Pima, T'hono O'dham, Nez Perce) says, as he reflects on his decision to return to his family's church, the First Indian Presbyterian Church in Kamiah (pronounced kam-ee-eye), Idaho. Describing himself as an "urban Indian," he continues, "I'd been to pow-wows, but I didn't really know that much beyond the surface. Going back to Kamiah was an immersion experience." Like many Native peoples, Irvin left the reservation and Native culture, eventually working in the banking industry, which was about as far from Native culture as one could get. However, in 1983, around the time he felt the call to pursue ordained ministry, Irvin made another decision that would change the character and trajectory of his ministry: he chose to return to his people and his home.[9]

Bearing a significance that Irvin did not fully grasp at the time, his decision to pursue ministry was unusual—unusual because, unlike many, he experienced his call, his decision for full-time service to the church, not primarily as a call to "leave" home to "go" to seminary but instead as a call to return to his home—to the very home that the missions of previous centuries had tried to destroy. And perhaps, for this reason, it is not wholly inappropriate that when he talks of going home as an "immersion experience," his story recalls the metaphor of baptism. Indeed, though the historical waters of church missions were often tainted by Babylonian ideologies, God's Spirit was nevertheless working within those waters, as murky and poisonous as they often were and are. And if the story of Moses is any indication, being set adrift on Pharaoh's waters is only part of the story—this is a baptism fraught with pain as well as promise. These complicated, intersecting waters of promise and pain, freedom and oppression, truth and lies, seem to surface as recurring themes within Irvin's pastoral imagination at Indian Fellowship and other area churches, both Indian and non-Indian. The Native baptism is not an easy baptism—it is, instead, a baptism fraught with history, something like Moses' "baptism," a baptism carried along by the historical waters of displacement and

9. Irvin Porter, interview by author, handwritten notes, 9 September 2008.

betrayal. Most prominently, within the Native community baptism recalls a separation, again analogous to the experience of Moses' mother who, believing (not without cause) there was no future for Hebrews, cast him down the river in hopes of his adoption by Egypt. Irvin describes an analogous crisis within Indian Fellowship: "When preaching, I remind the church that our ancestors were eager to become Christian. They had leaders who taught them . . . [and said,] 'Our way of life is changing and we need to change with it.' And that's how they thought. The Chief Joseph people, they said, 'Hang on to what we've got, and we're never going to give in'—a totally different mindset. There's always been animosity between the two."[10] He recalls to the congregation's mind the original construction of Indian Fellowship Church, now 132 years old: "Can you imagine what [Native people on the reservation] thought when they saw these Indians building a White man's church, up on the roof nailing boards together? Can you imagine what they thought, the Nez Perce who *never* had a permanent building and always lived in tipis?" Why does he use such a provocative image? According to Irvin, "[Native] people are shamed around here for being Christian. And what I want people to know is our ancestors experienced it too. It wasn't easy becoming Christian, being called names, being ridiculed. It's the same today." His experience of this shaming is personal: "I've had people tell me that I must not be proud to be an Indian because I am a minister."[11]

For Irvin, preaching has a pastoral responsibility to openly describe what many in the Native pew experience each day and especially on the Lord's Day as they make their way across the reservation to the church, which to some people is still the White man's church. At back of this shame is an ugly polarity that has a long history in Native Christian communities, one that can be traced back to missionary strategies that depicted the Indian "before" Christianization (wild, dark, disheveled) and "after" (dressed in a nice set of European clothes, perhaps with a book).[12] Closely related to the propaganda of the "before" and "after" images of the Native Christian was a modernist bias within missions of this period. That is, missions in the nineteenth and twentieth century were thoroughly modern, bereft of mystery, lacking the wonder (and generosity) of the hymn to Christ in Colossians (1:15-20). Instead, by stripping out mystery, missions created polarities between Native and Christian ways of being, requiring the forfeiture of one in order to have the other. This was

10. Ibid.

11. Ibid.

12. Kim Greenwell, "Picturing 'Civilization': Missionary Narrative and the Margins of Mimicry," *BC Studies: The British Columbia Quarterly* 135 (Autumn 2002): 3–45.

understandably devastating to a people who, for tens of thousands of years, had cultivated a profound spirituality that was inextricably bound up with the physical expression of culture.

Taken together, the combination of shame and propaganda suggests that "Native Christian" is a contradiction in terms. This is a serious problem, especially for Native Christians who nevertheless choose to negotiate their traditional values, symbols, and stories alongside their Christian faith. In the Native context, the act of recovering mystery is one and the same with being Native, seeing God's activity in Christ surfacing in unexpected ways, or at least in ways that are not typically acknowledged as Christian. Irvin's preaching suggests this strategy, which might be dubbed "problematizing the polarities," in a sermon from 1 Pet. 4:1-11, preached at the Talmaks Nez Perce Camp in the summer of 2003. Beginning with the story of an ordained minister, Mitchell White Rabbit (Winnebago), he shares the grandson's testimony about his grandmother: "'Grandma said we should never lock our doors. . . . If someone wanted to get in the house, they must need what is in the house—food, clothing, money—more than we did.'" He layers this radical hospitality with its theological origin: "The Creator gave us plenty, a roof over our heads, enough to eat on most days, warm clothes in the winter." Continuing in the voice of White Rabbit, he brings the ambiguity to a head: "Yes, my grandmother really did teach me about being a Christian. But do you know that she spoke only the Winnebago language? And do you know what else? She never set foot inside a Christian church. She was a follower of the traditional religious way. But she knew Christ's message that we should all be servants and share all that we have."[13]

Another story, this from a sermon delivered on All Saints' Day, recalls the story of James Hayes from the White Bird band of the Nez Perce. The White Bird band was made up of "fierce warriors led by Chief White Bird for whom the band is named." Hayes heard "one of his own Nez Perce elders preaching at a church on the reservation and became curious about this new religion. He went on to become an ordained minister of the Presbyterian Church, carrying the gospel to other Native reservations as far south as the Pima of Southern Arizona."[14] Irvin names others, Narcisse Big Horn (Lakota) and Shirley Johnson (Dakota) among them. He assembles those names with another list of saints, including the apostles, St. Francis of Assisi, Teresa of Avila, and Mother Theresa of Calcutta.

---

13. Irvin Porter, "Talmaks 2003," unpublished document, personal collection, summer 2003.

14. Irvin Porter, "All Saints," unpublished document, personal collection, n.d.

These two sermons create ambiguity on a number of levels. First, Irvin problematizes those interpretations that see Native ways as antithetical to Christian ways. He shows that not only can one can detect within the stories and traditions of Native religions the core of the gospel, but those traditions prove invaluable for Christian faith and life—and perhaps, to use Bonhoeffer's language, natural for Native American Christian life. Second, Irvin suggests that ambiguity retains a place in our conceptions of faithfulness. The very differences between Native ways and the received tradition of Christian life invite us to rest with the mystery, to allow its difference to emerge free from coercion. By creating ambiguity where only polarities existed before, Irvin fosters an active interpretative life, linking Native pre-Christian ancestors to contemporary Native Christians. While not denying the significance of Baptism, he nevertheless creates a point of mixing, where convergences are suggested. These remain penultimate but always oriented toward the coming of Christ. Here the human response is more belief than understanding, more listening than speaking. Third, in the popular historiography of Native history in America, the warrior image of the Native person is hallowed while the Native Christian is often barely acknowledged. By remembering the saints, Irvin recalls to the congregation's imagination their own Christian history, one clothed with the peculiar and prophetic wisdom of their grandparents and ancestors.

In order to build a Native church, he will often use, as he does above, historical narratives that are peopled with ancestors in the faith, ancestors who are "our grandparents, parents, uncles and aunts."[15] It may seem obvious that a preacher would draw on the personal narratives of Native people, but those stories are often hidden in the memories of elders who are quickly passing away, or they are hidden because of shame that those who were baptized had more to do with Babylon than the Creator. While never denying the waters of Babylon, the Native witness is never reducible to Babylon. Raising those stories to the surface of congregational memory permits the Nez Perce people to say that the waters of Babylon have not separated them from their people, that the controlling narrative of the theology of Baptism is that of a covenantal promise, a promise of freedom and not bondage.

While Irvin concentrates his labors among Native peoples, Native pastors and leaders have been historically significant among mostly non-Indian churches. Irvin is no exception and is often invited to participate at regional and national levels of the church. The following sermon, "Many Pathways but One Creator," was originally preached in the summer of 2002 at Queen Anne

15. Ibid.

Presbyterian Church in Seattle, Washington, a mostly White church. Irvin used a revised version of this sermon four years later at a meeting of the Olympia Presbytery. Given that this was a White congregation, he began the sermon by recounting the initial contact between Lewis and Clark and the Nez Perce people in 1805. The explorers left with the promise to send teachers to tell them more about this good news, this gospel that the Creator had sent the Creator's only Son to die for the wrongs of all people.

According to the sermon, the year is now 1831, and no teachers have been sent. The Nez Perce, eager for the "Book of Heaven," decide they must take matters into their own hands. If the book held the power of heaven, they must have it too. Four of their best warriors are chosen. Their names were Speaking Eagle, Black Eagle, Rabbit Skin Leggings, and No Horns on His Head.[16] When they arrive in the cities and towns of White culture, "They are the talk of the city." But, according to Irvin, when the four warriors said why they had come so far, for the Book of Heaven, the churches were not ready and would only promise to send missionaries as teachers. "After a year, disappointed and feeling a sense of failure to their people, they turn west again. Now only two remain as the two older warriors had fallen victim to an unknown disease and died there." Speaking Eagle, Irvin's ancestor, is one of the two who died on the journey.[17] So it was not until 1836 that the Presbyterian Church's Board of Foreign Missions responded to the Nez Perce—when they did, they sent Marcus and Narcissa Whitman and Henry and Elisa Spalding: "Thus began our denomination's work among my mother's people and has resulted in six Nez Perce Presbyterian Churches on the reservation of Idaho. These churches were also responsible for sending out some of the first Native ministers to work among tribes in the northwest and beyond."[18]

Maybe we detect a subtle countertestimony within Irvin's story, since his sermon underscores the Nez Perce yearning for the gospel rather than a particular missionary strategy, whether it was "successful" or not, which is a frequent concern among missions scholars. He locates the initiative among First Nations people, the expression of faith among Native peoples themselves. There may be interdependency within the Native view of spirituality, but it is not dependency. The spirituality of Native peoples preexisted the missionary enterprise of White Christendom. He accentuates the depth and authenticity of Nez Perce spirituality that sought the gospel even before the self-appointed messengers were ready to give it. It is this agency, an agency grounded in the

---

16. Irvin Porter, "Many Pathways, but One Creator," personal collection, 5 May 2002.

17. Ibid.

18. Ibid.

imago dei that allows Irvin to make this more radical affirmation of the rich diversity of Native spirituality and religious practice and its intersection with Christian texts and symbols:

> There are many pathways, but there is only one Creator. He is not brown, white, or black. He is one. The religious life of Native Americans is a rich legacy of many diverse beliefs, ceremonies, and ways of life, little of which is reflected in the history our public schools teach the next generation of Americans. Before the coming of the white man, God had given Native people directions on how to pray, but there was no church building. Their church was the land, the forest, the sky, and the stars, God's own cathedral. As one of our leaders [Chief Joseph Smith] remarked, "The earth and myself are of one mind. We never argue about religion." Religion in Indian society was not something practiced once a week or once a day. It was, and is, a way of life. The rhythms of life are opportunities to be thankful to God. Native American people knew God. They called him by other names like Creator, or Great Spirit, Hinuwat, Wakan Tonka, Josh, Mahalo, and Great One. The pathway was different than the one your ancestors have traveled but we have all arrived at
>
> the same place, the place where the Creator speaks to us.[19]

While there are many pathways, *Deus dixit*, God spoke, is the pivotal act in dignifying ways to God as God's way for the peoples of God.

If God speaks, what can we say of the human answer? The human answer comes through folds of skin and, as language, through layers of culture. In other words, the human response is an artistically laden response. In this regard, recall Irvin's rhetorical question, here paraphrased: Can you imagine what our ancestors thought when they saw Indians building a White man's church? Irvin talks about the church as a structure, but, more profoundly, his testimony finds expression through a consciousness and sensitivity to history often lacking in White testimony. He points to the way that missions intended to reconstruct Native people with "misguided, racist, and cruel acts in the name of God."[20] Among these acts was the demonization and trivialization of Native art, story, and land, and of the body of the voice that testifies to Baptism in the life of the triune God. One of the challenges of Native testimony is cultivating that sanctuary, which, like the sweat house, is a peculiar kind of enclosure,

19. Ibid.
20. Ibid.

intensifying experience by way of architecture, language, and historical narrative. However, like the sweat house, it is provisional space, like breath held for a moment in interiority, yet finally surrendered as utterance shared.

Cultivating such a space was, in fact, one of the first challenges that Irvin faced when, having only just arrived at Indian Fellowship in 2001, he was asked to perform a Baptism. After asking an elder of the church for the community's particular traditions around Baptism, he was shown a faux silver goblet, blistered with rust on one side. For water, he was told, they used the tap. It did not take too long before he began thinking about how the Indian Fellowship could "baptize" their practice in indigenous symbol. After conversation with family and friends of the church, the church as a whole settled on using an abalone shell, which is for the Nez Perce both a food source and raw material for art and jewelry. For water, they had only to look out the window of the church, where the Puyallup River made its way from Mount Rainier to its final destination in the Puget Sound. While people have a choice in how they receive the sacrament, Irvin reports that the community always keeps a gallon of the Puyallup in the pastor's study. When introducing the Baptism, he tells the story of the river, how it has run through that area for thousands of years and that it was this same water that their ancestors canoed and fished. "And now," he says, "we use this water, water of our ancestors, in the celebration of the sacrament of Baptism."[21] Ancient waters, with their own song, the stories of the river, converge with the covenantal promise of God, who can transform mere water into fine wine, and rivers of blood into the river of life.

Dawn Helton-Anishinaabeqwa (Ojibwa) wrote to me about an incident that took place while officiating at a funeral for an Ojibwa/Christian elder. In the course of the service, where prayers were offered in Ojibwa and English, she anointed the body with water from Lake Superior, whose waters have sustained the Ojibwa people for generations. This act provoked a profound as well as haunting response from an Ojibwa elder (non-Christian, Traditionalist): "You take the water of your Baptism which is the water of death and mix it with the water of our lake, the water of life; how does your religion mix the waters of life and death?" While the elder had his own reasons for asking the question the way he did, the question also betrays a profound insight into Christian Baptism, which itself seems to mix the water of promise with the waters of death.

Perhaps this is one of the major features evident in Irvin's preaching, which Joseph Jeter might dub as "re/membering" because his preaching joins together those parts of Native experience and history that have been dis/membered.[22]

---

21. Porter, interview by author, 9 September 2008.

Irvin's preaching re/members Native and Christian witness by collecting from ancient waters the stories that are quickly slipping away from memory, being washed into oblivion by a Babylonian dispensation. In preaching that lives in the dispensation of God's reign of grace, these stories, which seemed to have died, are lifted out of the waters, into the promise of life and benediction announced with the parting of waters. This is not to say there is no death in Christian Baptism. To the contrary, there is a death, but it is not like the death that Babylon announces, that Rome intended to announce, that U.S. ideologies of assimilation imagined for Native peoples—these deaths we call death—but Christ's death is old and new at the same time, particularly since it is connected to Christ's resurrection.

Another parable, this one told by Rev. Walter Soboleff, a Tlingit elder and lifelong Presbyterian pastor with whom I visited during a stay in Juneau, Alaska: A Tlingit man wanted to become a Christian and came to the missionary. At the time, missionaries asked Indians to recite, in English, the Lord's Prayer or the Apostles' Creed as evidence that they knew what being a Christian meant. But, of course, like many Natives at the time, he did not know any English—consequently, he could not recite the creeds or say the prayer. Then, as the missionary was trying to decide what to do, the Tlingit man began to dance and sing. The missionary did not know what this meant. He asked his interpreter to explain it. The interpreter said, "The dance is his death dance."

It strikes me that this is a parable of testimony, a parable intensified through an anticipatory prism, "showing" the promise that we hear, albeit ordinarily more partially and in fragments, in the act of preaching itself. Which is to say, ultimately, what we hear in preaching the word of salvation, preaching that revels in the promise of the Spirit that moves upon waters, is testimony that offers everything and denies nothing, taking abalone shell, salmon, lake, and mountain; taking story and myth and dance and symbol; taking all these, and more, into a dance that is dizzying and almost feverish, dying and dancing blurring together, as dancer and death wait together as nothing for God's speaking, an utterance parting waters, like hands pulling away grave clothes, like heavens torn open with a Word, proclaiming a beloved humanity drawn out of ancient waters.

A Whole Outfit

"My people have been doing this for more than a century," says Audrey Armstrong, an Athabascan who lives in a small village about seven hundred

---

22. See Joseph R. Jeter, *Crisis Preaching: Personal and Public* (Nashville: Abingdon Press, 1998), 28–29.

miles from Anchorage, Alaska, as she talks about making clothing out of fish skin. "I make jewelry, bags and clothing—such as jackets, parkas and boots—out of fish skin. I have made tiny earrings out of halibut and I often use rainbow trout and Dolly Varden, which is like a trout. My favourite is salmon skin, especially king salmon, because of its beautiful colours and its durability—it is so thick and strong." Her art, she says, comes from deep within the historical memory of Athabascan people but it is also distinct: "The quality of my work doesn't compare to the things my ancestors made. No one really does that kind of work now."[23]

While she acknowledges her ancestors and, thus, distinguishes her efforts from modern notions of creativity, she nevertheless believes that the art of making clothing out of salmon skins is more like a vocation than a labor, more a joyful expression of being than a product separate and apart from either herself or the creation: "If I didn't have my art, I don't know what I would do. It gives me such great pleasure and it is an honor knowing that I am bringing back something that in times gone by was made by other Native Athabascans like me." The creation itself remains an important boundary for her work: "You can make many things from fish skin, but first you have to catch your fish. I live in Alaska and in the summer the weather is beautiful, so that is when I fly-fish, standing in the water for between eight or 10 hours everyday. Winters are freezing—I'm stuck at home then, so that is when I sew. I treasure every piece of fish skin because it is so hard to get." There are also threats to this kind of work, some more subtle than others: "I do much of my fishing on the Russian River, where there are a lot of bears. I have had bears coming quite close, but they don't want to bother you—they just want the fish. If you leave the heads around, it will attract them, but I wouldn't do that anyway because I cook them—I love fish-head soup. I don't waste any part except the guts, but I take those with me." Like bears themselves, but more deadly, markets threaten to commodify her work beyond its natural shape: "The attention I have received," she says, "is mind-boggling. It is a bit overwhelming but also wonderful."[24]

Mostly, she does not sell her art to "markets" but to "people who know about me." She does not advertise and does not take orders. Perhaps at some level she suspects such things are to be avoided, like the bears that prowl along the riverbanks, looking for a quick and easy meal. Either way, the natural world, with its limitations, is such an intrinsic part of her art that its rhythms get reflected in it: "I need to have the fish skin first. That can be difficult because of

23. Audrey Armstrong, "First Person: Audrey Armstrong," *Financial Times*, 18 January 2013, http://www.ft.com/intl/cms/s/2/2d55e1da-5f73-11e2-be51-00144feab49a.html#axzz2TTFphrMw.

24. Ibid.

fishing restrictions." While she navigates bears, fishing restrictions, and markets, she also experiments with the medium, mixing different skins that complement each other: "Recently," she says, "I decided to put strips of mink skin around my latest bag, alternating with the fish skin, then put bear skin on the top of it. I like using beads too because we Athabascans are very good at bead work—women around here do a lot of it."[25]

Her way of talking about the art of making clothing out of salmon skin left a lasting impression on me as I thought about this chapter, my experience as a First Nations person, and, especially, the church's return to its natural expression. As the church begins to navigate a return from Christendom, it will be confronted by the loss of its memory. If it imagines that there is a "pristine" return, whether to the early church or to the New Testament churches or to a theologically pure but remote period in its life (e.g., the Reformation or the "world of the text"), it will only replace one false image with another. Native artists, who attempt to bring back to the surface the traditions of their ancestors, understand this more than most theologians and pastors who pine away for a purer expression of church. What will mark the faithful community is not so much its ability to "mimeograph" some other model as its ability to inhabit that tradition in a lively and authentic manner. Inhabiting a tradition suggests that we take the soil of our faith as a real place to grow, the soil of the place we happen to call home as a good place to be. And that we take these two, soil and faith, into a moment of unity. Moreover, those who help congregations navigate a return from their exilic place will need to do so mindful that the return is itself a creative act. Experimentation in the way the community expresses itself, clothing the verbs with natural stories and images of faith life, will continue to be one of the distinguishing marks of the church that offers not only survival but also dignity and historical narrative.

Like the artist, the church's art of being and receiving the clothing of Christ will be, in a manner of speaking, exposed to the seductive powers of the market, markets that, in a sense, promise to deliver a finished product. They sometimes intoxicate the imagination of those who would serve Christ's body. The church will always seek to distinguish between financial system and genuine economy. The market remains a part of the landscape and something the church should acknowledge as part of its own life—however, the church needs to cultivate a healthy sense of its peculiarity. Mostly, today, we are surrounded by a financial system, but what the Native artist practices is something more closely aligned to a local economy. It does not operate as an

25. Ibid.

"economy of scale" or as something that can simply be stenciled " over the skins of other communities, but it can inform those contexts and settings. The church enters a false world, a world that denies the particularity of its natural offering, when it aims to separate the "fruit" from the "tree"—both are good insofar as they are together, united, or, perhaps better, reconciled.

It will also live as a community of anticipation: "Some day it would be great," says Armstrong, "if I could wear a whole outfit made out of fish skin, but I will need to get the fish skin first."[26] The faith of the church, opening toward Christ, longs to be clothed with him, to be known by him even as we are fully known: "For in this tent we groan, longing to be clothed with our heavenly dwelling—if indeed, when we have taken it off we will not be found naked. For while we are still in this tent, we groan under our burden, because we wish not to be unclothed but to be further clothed, so that what is mortal may be swallowed up by life" (2 Cor. 5:2-4). So we pray, so we wait together for a perfection to be given rather than a completeness to be seized by our own hand: "All these, though they were commended for their faith, did not receive what was promised, since God had provided something better so that they would not, apart from us, be made perfect" (Heb. 11:39-40). In the meantime, it should not surprise anyone if the church sings and dances in this place, the next-to-the-last word of grace.

26. Ibid.

7

Conclusion

Setting Waters on Fire

*"We confess as we depart and return,
that you are the God of all our comings
and goings, you are the one who watches
our going out and our coming in."*

–Walter Brueggemann[1]

Over the course of writing this book, the questions people asked me about my work have changed. When I started, they wanted to know what sorts of communities I would be visiting. As the project progressed, the questions shifted: "Well, what have you learned? What is the church in these places and among these communities?" And, finally, as I shared an early draft of this work with a group of seasoned pastors, the question morphed into something like a yearning: "We hope you will help us, those of us in 'typical' settings, to benefit from your work." Don't leave us out, they seemed to be saying. We too feel like exiles, but maybe not so obviously. What they named was a desire, I think, to see the church as an actual body, formed where, by the criteria of the world, it ought not to be formed: as the found among the lost, as the living among the dead, as the free among the captives. A hope not at all uncommon among those who walk in the way of the crucified and risen Lord. So a deep relation exists between the communities represented in this book and more "typical" congregational settings.

1. Walter Brueggemann, *Prayers for a Privileged People* (Nashville: Abingdon Press, 2008), 94.

Yet the communities formed as a direct and theologically intentional response to exile did yield something in a sense uncommon—namely, the clarity with which they grappled with exile as both a concrete reality and a spiritual phenomenon. Many congregations may talk about exile, but the act of spiritualizing exilic language anesthetizes the church to its sociopolitical and ethical difference. Crucially, such spiritualizing distances communities from the Christ who took such concrete realities as basic to the good news he proclaimed. Perhaps it is a form of good news that today's congregations and pastors feel displacement with greater sharpness than they did in the past. If God sends the church into exile, so that exile is a "natural" expression of the church, maybe the question becomes this: instead of fleeing from that sense of displacement, or fighting it, how might congregations come to embrace it?

In this concluding chapter, I raise some questions for pastors and congregations to ask themselves as they seek to bring into articulated shape what it means to be a church as exile, among exiles, and as antidote to exile. One of my hopes is that readers will find within these questions a migration already underway.

QUESTIONS

Over the course of the book, three metaphors for the life and witness of the church emerged as focal points of reflection: the shrine, the labyrinth, and finally the dress or skin of Christ's body the church. Worship, of course, remains a central feature of each metaphorical expression, but the place of witness animates the life of worship, sustaining it as a gesture of love for the world and offering to God. Worship and witness seem to be mutually informative, interdependent in ways that deepen and extend the faith community's vocation. Interestingly, because these communities understood their exile as an intentional rather than accidental feature of their community life, they claimed that space and condition even as they witnessed to One who surpassed and subverted it. The questions introduced below attempt to draw out the implications of those metaphors for the church as it continues into its life in the twenty-first century.

The first set of questions addresses issues of space: How does the church inhabit twenty-first-century socio-political and economic space? Would the congregation or perhaps onlookers say that the community is more a noun or a verb? And if it is a verb, what does it enliven? What verbs convey this community's life in the place it calls home? How does it interact with the political and economic soil around it? To what human end do these verbs speak?

At a critical level, these questions go to the sense that many congregations have become captives to nouns: a people, a place, or a thing only. Obviously, there is something to being a noun. The church is called to be God's people, called to be a city on a hill, to use Matthew's language. "On this rock," Jesus declares, "I will build my church" (16:18). On the other hand, even the rocks and the creation groan with thanksgiving at God's coming in Christ. In other words, the coming of Christ inaugurates a movement where no movement seemed possible. The rock the builders rejected has become the cornerstone. The rock that sealed the tomb has been rolled away. In each evocation of the church in the preceding chapters, one detects the "movement" of the community as it gathered what it called "out" of the world to name as its life before God, whether it was a shrine on a migrant trail or a sweat house and its relationship to North America's historical narrative relative to First Nations peoples. It was not enough for these communities to sport a monogrammed identity borrowed from a national entity, but rather it was necessary to sanctify and transform our migration into a holy journey, gathering contradictions into a reconciling figuration of the body of Christ.

As I experienced time and again, there should be a sense in which every community of faith throws the world slightly off balance. Driving through the desert, John Fife reflected that Christ was a profoundly asymmetrical person. According to Fife, Christ wasn't the "center" so much as an Other who probed and undermined our assumed centers. One of the most common "centers" of a congregation might be its membership roll. A membership-driven congregation may not see itself as moving waters, as a stream set aflame with something like a holy migration. Instead, the journey ends up being a cul-de-sac of membership and perhaps "volunteering" in one ministry or another. It does not create tension or ambiguity, except perhaps in the most personal way, at the level of private religious experience. A community of this kind remains eminently predictable rather than being a lively expression of the Spirit. It may speak of a larger and more radical vision within its walls, but beyond those walls, the community mostly resembles what it has actually become: a noun without a dynamic or uneasy relationship to the history, place, or consumerist system around it.

The communities that sought to live authentically and theologically amid exilic realities had to confront their own complicity in systems of exile, to actually encourage heterogeneity as a matter of faithful response even as they cultivated the particular expression of faithful discipleship in the way of Jesus Christ. This confrontation was destabilizing in the way that the resurrection destabilized the assumption of death; in the way that the Gospels showing a soldier "recognizing" Jesus as the Son of God leads to us to question just who it is that has "eyes to see and ears to hear"; in the way that Acts underscores the wisdom and perception of an Ethiopian eunuch, the ultimate outsider, who declares, "What is to prevent me from being baptized?" (Acts 8:36b). A sense of moving toward the fullness of Christ tilts the congregational space in a way that leads the community to follow the Magi, early astrologers, who after their encounter with the infant Christ, returned home but by another route (Matt. 2:12).

Perhaps the most profound manifestation of the worldly heterogeneity represented by these communities was that they expressly rejected any criterion of success for their actions. Success would mean in many contexts "winning" a new member, or a new disciple, or a few more beds at the shelter, or an expansion of the institutional plant—all these criteria tend toward measureable outcomes rather than faithful practice. Faithful practice enacted and reflected upon was characteristic of each community. While they tried to make a little difference in their work for justice, in their liturgical performances, in their hospitality, they were wary of making any criterion of success—for example, moving people out of poverty, or making people into believers—definitive for their actions. They strove instead to be faithful, to give shape to their understanding of gospel obedience. It is too easy for the church to substitute a cheap success in place of a more costly and ultimately more mysterious faith in God's sovereignty.

Another set of questions examines the way the communities understand visibility: When and how does the church become visible? What kinds of activities or "garments" name the church as an agent of transformation or prophetic body within a given community? Each of these communities suggested just how foundational liturgy was in "garbing" the life of the church in exile. While the communities joyfully worked with others for justice, the expression of liturgy was born of their own lives, their own determination to live as followers of Jesus Christ. While the canopy of justice was wide and generous, these communities did not so much "translate" justice as a universal concern of all people but instead, using the natural idiom of Christian worship, performed that language as the church's public liturgy.

Indeed, while each of the communities was more ecumenical in practice than most congregations, in other ways each was more confessional in its public witness than most congregations are even on Sunday. These communities suggested the consistency of their confession, that what was "proclaimed" on the Lord's Day found resonance or expression in myriad contexts, both through publicly performed liturgies and through the practices and decisions made in the name of that proclamation. That proclamation was exposed in the same way Christ is "exposed" in the life of the church, full of the confidence of his promise. Benjamin M. Stewart, professor of worship, says it this way: "When liturgy steps vulnerably into the world, when the stability or strength provided by the church walls is stripped away, the band of pilgrims may themselves become a sign of the strange, other world within this one, where the promises of scripture are being fulfilled."[2] Our liturgies may have fire in them, but many churches have kept these fiery words and their catalytic potentiality beneath the canopy of the church ceiling—and we have almost, but not quite, extinguished them by leaving them there. The communities that took exilic reality seriously understood that keeping the Lord's Day liturgy under wraps was false not only to God's love for the world but also for the church.

As it deliberately wed itself to the condition of poverty, Cherith Brook joined its body to the body of the poor in something resembling a public declaration of marriage. It took upon itself the proclamation that God dwells among the downcast and the brokenhearted and that it, as a community, would find that Christ had gone there ahead of it. It found Christ as the poor, through the wisdom of the poor, and in ordinary fellowship with those trapped in conditions of precarity; at the same time, it sought to contribute to an economy of home through acts of hospitality and table fellowship, figuring as a community the world's life toward Christ even as the community celebrated the gift of Christ for the world.

Each of the communities subjected borders, both real and symbolic or ideological, to regular "crossings"—part of the task, then, for a community that desires to catalyze an antidote to exclusivist borders is to acknowledge borders that exist within the community already. What kinds of borders contribute to a sense of congregational stability? How do we not only inherit those borders but also reinforce them? What borders do we cultivate? I am always intrigued to see a congregation describe itself as a community of "educated professionals"—just how porous is that sort of border? Is that any way to "name" the life of a congregation that seeks to follow Jesus Christ? Are there no other forms of identity in such a community? Where are the stigmata in the church, the marks of discipleship by which it bears witness to Christ? When communities of faith cultivate borders, they should exercise care that they can be traced to a Christological pattern. In addition to superimposing alien sorts of borders, boundaries between church and society can be overdrawn to the point that the church community and the "world out there" are opposed. Over time, the

2. Benjamin M. Stewart, "Worship without Walls," *Christian Century* 129, no. 20 (3 October 2012): 25.

liturgy, shorn of its political and socioeconomic edge, loses its relevance to the political and economic body, to say nothing of its relevance to the reign of God announced in Jesus Christ..

What would it mean, for instance, for a White suburban congregation to corporately declare sins of systemic racism in the ghetto? I suspect, first of all, the congregation would be concerned because the liturgy would be exceedingly close, skin-on-skin close. I also suspect it would entail more than a White church; it would require a larger community of faith, including African American communities. It would entail more than a liturgical "flash"; rather, it would require a long, slow burn, with conversation, education, and an attempt to journey together. There would be a sense of exquisite vulnerability in both the White and African American communities as they journeyed down a common road and committed to making the journey together. The point here is not to tell White churches to run to the ghetto to say their corporate confessions (although that may not be a bad idea) but rather to underline the proximity between our societal skin and our liturgical practices.

Some congregations may have sympathy for the situation of the exile but believe there is a great distance between their congregational life and the actual exile. Perhaps there is also a sense of fear on the part of the pastoral leadership. As one pastor reflected, "The congregation I serve seems far removed from the exilic communities addressed in *By the Rivers*. How can I help the congregation get physically close enough to such borders to actually challenge them? How would I assist the congregation to cross such borders with me?" Perhaps one way to think about the challenges of these communities is not to begin with an action as such (literally crossing borders) but rather with a reflection on actions we take as routine, repeated behaviors and assumptions that, unexamined, simply reinforce borders as normative. The routine character of many borders—which we reinforce through secular liturgies of consumerist behavior—can render them mostly invisible.

A congregation that does not see itself as living among displaced peoples or near "borders," could begin through a form of critical reflection, broadly conceived as "Who cleans the toilets?" In other words, where and when do members of the church interact with displaced people, people who take "3D jobs" (dirty, dangerous, and disdained) and "SALEP jobs" (shunned by all the citizens except the poor)? What is the nature of that interaction between the "typical member of the church" and the laborer? Around the table of fellowship? At the Wal-Mart? As we calculate the tip for the meal? Who are we in that interaction? A professional or a kindred soul? A companion or a consumer? Both? If so, how? What are the markers of a consumer? What are the markers of companions? Where are the tensions? Do we imagine ourselves as free or captive in this economy? Who are we or who do we imagine ourselves to be when we do business with companies that pay employees less than a living wage? Who are you to the displaced? How much of any of this carries over into the witness and community of the church on the Lord's Day? Significantly, however, those questions need to undergo a transformation from what is routine to what is transformative by asking how might these currently "segregated" communities be moved closer to the character and spirit of table fellowship?

Of course, at some point, congregations will have to act in order to reflect. Unfortunately, churches may imagine talk about missions is as good as missions or, alternatively, that mission is straightforward rather than complex. For example, often the act of service is seen as an end in itself: the church volunteer dropped off the clothes at the shelter; the volunteers served the meals from behind the counter; the church "did" mission. The following Sunday, the pastor reports how many people were fed, how many bags of food were delivered to the food pantry, how much mission weighed in an empirical sense. Often when missions look like this it is because the fellowship between the "helper" and the "helped" are defined by a transaction rather than a more complex relationship. Pastors and congregations should exercise care that in settings of missional activity there are opportunities to share table fellowship in actual community, embodying Christ's reconciling activity with humility and with as few agendas as possible. Let bread and table fellowship be the agenda—and let God be present throughout. Afterward, the participants should be given an opportunity to reflect on the experience, thinking out loud about what happened, what did not happen, what resistances they experienced, what they hoped would happen, what surprises and what invitations may be arising in the midst of those encounters.

For those communities that like to manage risk the temptation will be to study the prospect of mission without ever actually risking mission. Obviously, one wants to supply adequate understanding of the context, expectations, and character of missions, but the church has to remember that it does not finally act out of its understanding but out of a faithful response to the God who first loved us. There was always a sense of unknown in every attempt to be faithful in the communities represented in this book: people were learning to be strangers in a strange land, and as such, they did not speak fluently. They made mistakes. But those mistakes were not cause for shame; instead, they rejoiced in those mistakes, as a gift because those mistakes are symptomatic of a people bumping up against the mystery of the other, of our mutual interdependence, and need for one another.

At the heart of these questions is an attempt to recover theological metaphors for the witness and worship of the church. Eric Garbison of the Cherith Brook Catholic Worker House believes that most new church developments proceed without testing the assumptions of the financial system. The question of faithful practice, namely, reconciliation, peacemaking, justice, and liberating the captive—in other words, the church Christ gives us—these are reserved for Sunday morning eloquence rather than supplying the substance or the heart of the church we put into practice. Instead, all too often, plans for new churches are predicated on the presence of middle-class families, which, in turn, presupposes a financial system skewed to represent middle-class economic interests. Even before the groundbreaking ceremonies, the church enacted is not so much a gift of the holy imagination as it is a production of the financial system.

Bill Bishop, author of *The Big Sort: Why the Clustering of Like-Minded America is Tearing Us Apart*, believes that while educated Americans may imagine themselves to be diverse, open-minded, cosmopolitan, and so on, the fact remains that a "higher education" does not necessarily make us more open or more diverse: "The more educated Americans become—and the richer—the less likely they are to discuss politics with those who have different points of view." Ironically, those who are poor, according to Bishop, are "more likely than those who are rich and white to be exposed to political disagreement." The most homogenous groups are formed among those who have gone through graduate school while the most heterogeneous groups are formed among people who have not graduated from high school.[3] Cherith Brook supplies anecdotal evidence for this kind of diversity. Seminaries, by contrast, often lack diversity or, if they are diverse, manage to self-segregate into ideological camps, thus having the appearance of diversity but holding tightly to the life of homogeneity. This reality makes it all the more imperative for congregations to be open to the other, not through acts of charity but through the formation of authentic solidarity.

When the ethical dynamism of reconciliation and solidarity form the "habit" of Christian community, the art of living together becomes more holistic, subjecting all of life to the pattern of Christ's body. Learning to love one another in our differences as well as our shared identities takes a spirit of humility. The Church of the Indian Fellowship enshrined a process of learning

---

3. Bill Bishop, *The Big Sort: Why the Clustering of Like-Minded America Is Tearing Us Apart* (Boston: Houghton Mifflin, 2008), 286–87.

as well as being open to the fact that mistakes would be made. This was also true among the people at Cherith Brook and Frontera de Cristo. They embarked on a journey sufficiently large and complex to challenge themselves with the call to be willing to make mistakes and to revisit their practice so as to continue learning. Perhaps one of the marks of this kind of community is its ability not only to name its "successes" but, even more importantly, to name how it continues to learn to live together.

Each community exhibited a personal quality, where participant narratives prompted reflection and action in response to the call to discipleship. There is a sense in which there is too much personal experience in the popular imagination already. However, the cost of a theology bereft of the personal is too high: there is no theology and no church without the personal narrative that is prompted by Christ. When Jesus says to the paralytic, "Stand up, take your mat and walk," he prompts a story, one that continues. While serving in a First Nations church in Alaska, I was often moved at how open the prayers of the community could be: a member of the church, she was drinking again, it was announced. Or another was suffering through a season of depression. The prayers were real, as were the stories that went with them. They weren't offered as voyeuristic tours of the self, but rather as ordinary expressions in the life of the community living hopefully and prayerfully amid adversity.

How might the church cultivate a different way of being personal? In other words, how could our stories of community be personal in the way of Christ, where the narrative informs and is deepened through communal sharing? It would be impossible for me to write about these communities without naming how they interacted with my own narrative. Theology is not a professional science but a deeply personal one. At first, as I was writing, I struggled to name this part of the narrative, feeling as if it were intrusive. But as I continued writing, my own sense of the life of this work took on a much more personal dimension than I had imagined or intended. It is not that my personal narrative is sufficient as explanation for these communities any more than a testimony actually and adequately exegetes a text. But these communities, all of them, awakened within their shared life a deeper and heightened sense of my personal return. Perhaps that was because they were similarly engaged in a critical but loving examination of their life together. The tradition of the Catholic Worker inspired by Dorothy Day reflected this kind of personal dimension to faith. It was always messy, it was always difficult, but the benediction from that messiness was profound and lasting, as the continuing vitality of the Catholic Worker testifies.

Testimony is a practice enjoying a resurgence in mainline denominations, although it is usually not called "testimony"—during the season of Easter, the church where we worship includes laypeople from the congregation as they share how they have "encountered" Christ in their personal lives. This remains an immensely popular part of the worship service for a lot of good reasons. However, this approach, as it singles out the individual's "encounter" with Christ, almost always reflects a particular genre of the personal narrative—namely, a struggle with illness, psychological or physical, or some personal hardship in which individuals found Christ in a deeply intimate way. It strikes me as a more Johannine take on the way we experience Christ, with the fourth Gospel's emphasis on the personal connection between Jesus Christ and the one who believes in him. This represents a powerful tradition in Christian witness and preaching. However, Matthew's Gospel, as it emphasizes meeting Christ in the other (the naked, the prisoner, and the destitute), does not appear as often. What would it look like for a congregation to include a Sunday "testimony" involving "Encountering Christ, the Undocumented" or "Encountering Christ in the Closet" (LGBTQ), or "Encountering Christ in the Conscientious Objector"? Any of these encounters would cultivate in the congregation's imagination the voice of the other as Christ's testimony to the church. Most importantly, the church would begin to explore the political and economic ramifications of being a reconciling community in a sociopolitical context of alienation and secrecy.

Setting Waters on Fire

When I was a boy we would sometimes visit the streams in order to watch as the salmon returned to spawn. There was a particular stream I looked forward to visiting, near Eyak Lake in Cordova. Maybe I loved it because of its familiarity. I suspect my parents took us there because it was easy and, for us, inexpensive entertainment. An added bonus: while we were at this creek, we would sometimes see bears. One afternoon we watched a year-old cub, a black bear, from the safety of our Chevy Blazer. He was swatting at the salmon, but ineffectually. There were so many it must have been frustrating for him to see one after another escape. I felt frustrated for him, or, more likely, I just wanted to see him catch a fish. However, unlike the impatience I felt, the cub seemed patient with its hunger. Perhaps the cub understood the odds were with him: the water literally rippled with the red skins of the salmon, their nearly black backs riding up out of the stream, brushing with the skins of other salmon, resembling the skin of the water itself, their bodies ripe from their immersion in freshwater, their snouts turned into aggressive-looking snaggletoothed beaks, their bodies no longer glistening and fat but ragged with the battle to return to the waters of their birth. Perhaps, in a way, the bear was part of their return, just as the salmon were connected to the life cycle of the bear.

After the spawning season was over, the beaches and streams would be littered with the remains of dead salmon. Some died after spawning and drifted back downstream; some were left as carcasses, gutted and abandoned by bears greedy for nothing but roe; most of their eye sockets were empty, the delectably soft bits gobbled up by eagles or other scavengers. While the death of the salmon was evident, upstream, hidden in the spawning beds, the salmon fry were just beginning their freshwater life cycle, nourished in part by the decaying bodies of their mothers and fathers. They were just beginning a life that would eventually culminate by setting this very same stream, the stream of their ancestors, on fire with yet another act of returning, a returning that would deliberately set into motion the cycle of death and life.

This memory speaks to me now as I reflect on the communities of this book, each forged amid exilic realities. As an analogy for the church, it suggests that the church lives at home both abroad and in the soil of its beginning, because both belong to God and our beginning is in God. Our alienation and our return and everything in between belong to God's economy of salvation. Of course, like all analogies, this one breaks down if pushed too far, since it seems to suggest a never-ending cyclical process, a process that does not align with a theology of history and revelation. For one, theological history, at least the one I subscribe to, does not repeat endlessly, but culminates in the new creation. Moreover, the natural cycles of migration and reproduction do not convey the revelatory nature of Christ's own appearing, an event that, in the biblical imagination, introduces transfiguration as a stunning, even annihilating expression of God's manifestation to human beings, an appearance that creatures cannot receive on their own without perishing. The analogy also becomes strained if it turns into an allegory, in which the ocean signifies "exile" and freshwater streams represent "home"—for the salmon, at least, these waters represent natural habitats at different points in their life cycle.

On the other hand, as metaphor this memory does convey something that the church claims to be true about its current condition: the church belongs to God whether it is in the far country of exile or in the community it calls home. As metaphor, it echoes the biblical theology of creation that God's mercy and hospitality extend to all, whether just or unjust. There is everywhere the appearing of God's steadfast love and mercy. And perhaps the metaphor works another way as well: as the salmon enter different stages in their life cycle, they mature only by undergoing a transformation of their physiology, first as they prepare to enter the salt waters of the ocean and then as they return to the freshwater streams of their birth, a return that entails a decision to die. Likewise, the community only knows its home through transformation, by becoming what it is not, following the same pattern of Christ: "For our sake[God] made [Christ] to be sin who knew no sin, so that in him we might become the righteousness of God" (2 Cor. 5:21). In Christ the "old has passed away; see, everything has become new!" (5:17b). The fullness of God is revealed in Christ, a fullness that elects cross and tomb, epicenters of annihilation and shame, to inaugurate the new creation. The church finds its home not by purifying its membership rolls or its dogmas, but by radicalizing its faith. In and through practices of return, the church appears to be scattered by powers even as it is awakened through the activity of the Spirit to the new creation taking shape already.

The activity of the church may, in some sense, seem like searching, but even more it is emboldened by the faith of God's promise that the lost will be found and the exiles will return, no matter how outrageous that may seem. Often, the members of the communities I visited confessed to not knowing just how to proceed but, in the face of the deep contradictions of exilic reality, attempted to act in a faithful way. There was no clear indication of where to go or what to do except insofar that the communities practiced a form of salvage, whether that meant gathering up the discarded symbols of the migrant trail as a shrine to God's shalom or, on the First Nations reservation in Washington, that meant the recovery of the sacredness of the creation, laying hold of the land as God's gift to generations of Native people. The words of Isaiah come to mind: "Though the Lord may give you the bread of adversity and the water of affliction, yet your Teacher will not hide himself any more, but your eyes shall see your Teacher. And when you turn to the right or when you turn to the left, your ears shall hear a word behind you, saying, 'This is the way; walk in it'" (Isa. 30:21). A secular and utilitarian geography of colonization became the "house" or "theater" of biblical and theological liturgies, scattering liturgies of colonization with the liturgies of sanctification.

Each of these communities was engaged in an attempt to return to the radical expression of faithfulness and community. Each seemed as if it was pulled along by something deeper than simple social and human need, though these clearly were at least part of the reason their lives came together as a community, and specifically as something resembling the passion of the church at worship. The houses they lived in seemed like shrines built along the paths of history as a response to God's historical faithfulness rather than like institutions designed to reproduce their own identities and commitments indefinitely.

Often, it seemed that members of these communities, as well as guests, were engaged in a pilgrimage, at once new and ancient. It was not a path that any one person could make alone, nor was it a path that the communities themselves cut through the wilderness of exile. The Lord God makes a way through the desert and the sea, through profoundly "wild" or "hostile" spaces; God creates a path. The sense of God creating a movement amid deeply hostile conditions points to the "new creation" promised by God in Christ and the resurrection. And perhaps this faith bequeathed to these communities knowledge that they were, indeed, new creations already. Not that they dismissed the reality of the tensions and conflicts of living today, but that their formation as a community betrayed sensitivity to the new creation awakening amid the catacombs of hostility and defeat.

May it be so for all of us.

Bibliography

Adams, Mark S. Interview by author, written notes, Douglas, AZ, 18 February 2013.

———. Interview by author, handwritten notes, Douglas, AZ, 18 February 2013.

Adams, Mark S., Danielle Alvarado, Rickey Cheney, Hannah Hafter, Phil Kennedy, Vicki Kline, Molly Little, et al. *A Culture of Cruelty: Abuse and Impunity in Short-Term U.S. Border Patrol Custody.* N.p.: No More Deaths, 2011.

Adams, Mark S., and Tommy Bassett III. *Just Coffee: Caffeine with a Conscience.* Douglas, AZ: Just Trade Center, 2009.

Alexander, Michelle. *The New Jim Crow: Mass Incarceration in the Age of Colorblindness.* New York: New Press, 2010.

Armfield, Josh, Garbison, Eric, and Rutschman, Elisabeth. Interview by author, audio recording, Kansas City, MO, 24 January 2012.

Armstrong, Audrey. "First Person: Audrey Armstrong." *Financial Times*, 18 January 2013. http://www.ft.com/intl/cms/s/2/2d55e1da-5f73-11e2-be51-00144feab49a.html#axzz2TTFphrMw.

Artress, Lauren. *Walking a Sacred Path: Rediscovering the Labyrinth as a Spiritual Practice.* Revised edition. New York: Riverhead Books, 2006.

Bass, Diana Butler. *The Practicing Congregation: Imagining a New Old Church.* Herndon, VA: Alban Institute, 2004.

Bass, Diana Butler, and Joseph Stewart-Sticking, eds. *From Nomads to Pilgrims: Stories from Practicing Congregations.* Herndon, VA: Alban Institute, 2006.

Bassett, Tommy A., III. Interview by author, audio recording, Douglas, AZ, 19 July 2011.

Batten, Alicia. "Reading the Bible in Occupied France: André Trocmé and Le Chambon." *Harvard Theological Review* 103, no. 3 (July 2010): 309–28.

Beck, Robert R. *Banished Messiah: Violence and Nonviolence in Matthew's Story of Jesus.* Eugene, OR: Wipf and Stock, 2010.

Bishop, Bill. *The Big Sort: Why the Clustering of Like-Minded America Is Tearing Us Apart.* Boston: Houghton Mifflin, 2008.

Bledsoe, Greg, and R. Stickney. "US Border Patrol Reports 70 Percent Spike in Assaults on Agents." *NBCNews.com*, 14 March 2013.

http://usnews.nbcnews.com/_news/2013/03/14/17315534-us-border-patrol-reports-70-percent-spike-in-assaults-on-agents#.

Bonhoeffer, Dietrich. *The Collected Sermons of Dietrich Bonhoeffer.* Edited by Isabel Best. Translated by Isabel Best, Douglas W. Stott, Anne Schmidt-Lange, et al. Minneapolis: Fortress Press, 2012.

———. *Ethics.* Edited and translated by Isle Tödt, Heinz Eduard Tödt, Ernst Feil, Clifford J. Green, et al. Minneapolis: Fortress Press, 2005.

Brown, Raymond. *The Churches the Apostles Left Behind.* Ramsey, NJ: Paulist Press, 1984.

Brueggemann, Walter. *Cadences of Home: Preaching among Exiles.* Louisville: Westminster John Knox Press, 1997.

———. *Prayers for a Privileged People.* Nashville: Abingdon Press, 2008.

Carter, Warren. *Matthew and Empire: Initial Explorations.* Harrisburg, PA: Trinity Press International, 2001.

Cavanaugh, William. *Migrations of the Holy: God, State, and the Political Meaning of the Church.* Grand Rapids, MI: William B. Eerdmans, 2011.

Cherith Brook Catholic Worker. "Report on Nuclear Weapons Plant in KC." Cherith Brook Catholic Worker, 12 May 2011. http://cherithbrookcw.blogspot.com/2011/05/report-on-witness-against-nuclear.html.

Cruz, Gemma Tulud. "Between Identity and Security: Theological Implications of Migration in the Context of Globalization." *Theological Studies* 69, no. 2 (2008): 357–75.

———. "Expanding the Boundaries: Turning Borders into Spaces." In *Mission after Christendom: Emergent Themes in Contemporary Mission*, ed. Ogbu U. Kalu, Peter Vethanayagamony, and Edmund Kee-Fook Chia. Louisville, KY: Westminster John Knox Press, 2010.

Davis, Ellen F., author, and Margaret Parker Adams, illustrator. *Who Are You, My Daughter: Reading Ruth through Image and Text.* Louisville, KY: Westminster John Knox Press, 2003.

Day, Dorothy. *Dorothy Day: Selected Writings.* Edited by Robert Ellsberg. Maryknoll, NY: Orbis Books, 1983.

———. *Loaves and Fishes.* Maryknoll, NY: Orbis Books, 1963.

———. *The Long Loneliness.* New York: Harper & Row, 1952.

de Genova, Nicholas, and Nathalie Peutz, eds. *The Deportation Regime: Sovereignty, Space, and the Freedom of Movement.* Durham, NC: Duke University Press, 2010.

Drash, Wayne. "Priest: 'Nobody Can Tell Me to Shut Up.'" *CNN.com/US*, 15 October 2008. http://articles.cnn.com/2008-10-15/us/postville.priest_1_meatpacking-plant-illegal-immigrants-postville?_s=PM:US.

Duara, Nigel, William Petroski, and Grant Schulte. "Claims of Fraud Lead to Largest Raid in State History." *Des Moines Register*, 12 May 2008. http://www.desmoinesregister.com/print/article/20080512/NEWS/80512012/Claims-ID-fraud-lead-largest-raid-state-history.

Dulles, Avery Cardinal. "Mary's Yes and Our Response to God," *Living Pulpit*, October-December 2001, 30–31.Eberle, Gary. *The Geography of Nowhere: Finding One's Self in the Postmodern World*. Kansas City, MO: Sheed and Ward, 1994.

Fewell, Danna Nolan, and David Gunn Miller. *Compromising Redemption: Relating Characters in the Book of Ruth*. Louisville, KY: Westminster John Knox Press, 1990.

Forest, Jim. *All Is Grace: A Biography of Dorothy Day*. Maryknoll, NY: Orbis Books, 2011.

———. "The Catholic Worker Movement." In *The Encyclopedia of American Catholic History*, edited by Michael Glazier and Thomas J. Shelley. Collegeville: Liturgical Press, 1997.

Garbison, Eric. "Being Placed: More on Stability." *Cherith Brook Catholic Worker*, 14 July 2012, 1, 10.

———. Interview by author, audiovisual recording, Kansas City, MO, 25 January 2012.

Garbison, Jodi. Interview by author, audiovisual recording, Kansas City, MO, 27 January 2012.

Gaventa, Beverly Roberts. *Our Mother Saint Paul*. Louisville, KY: Westminster John Knox Press, 2007.

Goodwin, Liz. "Years after Immigration Raid, Iowa Town Feels Poorer and Less Stable." *The Lookout, Yahoo! News*, 7 December 2011. http://news.yahoo.com/blogs/lookout/years-immigration-raid-iowa-town-feels-poorer-less-133035414.html.

Greenwell, Kim. "'Picturing 'Civilization': Missionary Narrative and the Margins of Mimicry." *BC Studies: The British Columbia Quarterly*, no. 135 (Autumn 2002): 3–45.

Hall, Douglas John. *Cross in Our Context*. Minneapolis: Fortress Press, 2003.

Hallie, Philip Paul. *Lest Innocent Blood Be Shed: The Story of the Village of Le Chambon and How Goodness Happened There.* New York: Harper & Row, 1979.

Hare, Douglas R. A. *Interpretation: Matthew.* Louisville, KY: John Knox Press, 1993.

Hoch, Robert. "Season of Epiphany." In *New Proclamation (Year A 2011): Advent through Holy Week,* edited by David Lott. Minneapolis: Fortress Press, 2011.

———. "Theologizing from the Sweat House: Re-Membering Kinship, Spirituality, Liturgy, Land, and Voice." Paper presented at the annual meeting of the Academy of Homiletics, Boston, MA, December 2008.

Homaiak, Chris Brennan. "Seeds of Beauty." *Cherith Brook Catholic Worker,* Lent 2012: 4.

Hsu, Spencer S. "Immigration Raid Jars a Small Town." *Washington Post,* 18 May 2008. http://www.washingtonpost.com/wp-dyn/content/article/2008/05/17/AR2008051702474.html.

Jeter, Joseph R. *Crisis Preaching: Personal and Public.* Nashville: Abingdon Press, 1998.

"Joshua." Interview by author, audio recording, Douglas, AZ, 17 July 2011.

Lopez, Davina C. *Apostle to the Conquered: Reimagining Paul's Mission.* Minneapolis: Fortress Press, 2008.

Lopez, Pedro Maldonado. Interview by author, translated by Mark Adams, audio recording, Agua Prieta, Mexico, 20 July 2011.

"Lucia." Interview by author, audiovisual recording, trans. by Gabriela Vega, Tucson, AZ, 5 August 2011.

Luti, J. Mary. "Enlarging Hospitality: Where are the Children." In *From Nomads to Pilgrims: Stories from Practicing Congregations.* Edited by Diana Butler Bass and Joseph Stewart-Sticking. Herndon, VA: Alban Institute, 2006.

McCarthy, Allison L. "The May 12, 2008 Postville, Iowa Immigration Raid: A Human Rights Perspective," *Transnational Law and Contemporary Problems* 19 (Winter 2010): 293–315. http://www.uiowa.edu/~tlcp/TLCP%20Articles/19-1/mccarthy.finalfinal.mlb.022710.pdf.

McKanan, Dan. *The Catholic Worker after Day: Practicing the Works of Mercy in a New Generation.* Collegeville, MN: Liturgical Press, 2008.

New, Jeffrey. Interview by author, audiovisual recording, Kansas City, MO, 23 January 2012.

Newman, Paul. Interview by author, audiovisual recording, Kansas City, MO, 24 January 2012.

Pickrell, Nick. Interview by author, audio recording, Kansas City, MO, 25 January 2012.

———. "Transformation not Annhilation." Youtube video posted 2 May 2011. http://www.youtube.com/watch?v=T-s329ZW97k.

Porter, Irvin. "All Saints." Unpublished document, personal collection, n.d.

———. Interview by author, handwritten notes, Puyallup, WA, 9 September 2008.

———. "Many Pathways, but One Creator." Unpublished document, personal collection, 5 May 2002.

———. "Talmaks 2003." Unpublished document, personal collection, Summer 2003.

Preston, Julia. "Life Sentence Is Debated for Meat Plant Ex-Chief." *New York Times*, 28 April 2010. http://www.nytimes.com/2010/04/29/us/29postville.html?_r=0.

Riegle, Rosalie G. *Crossing the Line: Nonviolent Resisters Speak Out for Peace.* Eugene, OR: Wipf and Stock, 2013.

Roberts, Bryan, Gordon Hanson, Derekh Cornwell, and Scott Borger. "An Analysis of Migrant Smuggling Costs along the Southwest Border." Working Paper, Department of Homeland Security, Office of Immigration Statistics, November 2010. http://www.dhs.gov/xlibrary/assets/statistics/publications/ois-smuggling-wp.pdf.

Rozga, Allison. Interview by author, audiovisual recording, Kansas City, MO, 24 January 2012.

Saracino, Michele. *Clothing.* Minneapolis: Fortress Press, 2012.

Scarry, Elaine. *The Body in Pain.* New York: Oxford University Press, 1985.

Smith-Christopher, Daniel. *A Biblical Theology of Exile.* Minneapolis: Fortress Press, 2002.

Smith, James K. A. *Desiring the Kingdom: Worship, Worldview, and Cultural Formation.* Grand Rapids, MI: Baker Academic, 2009.

Steiner, George. *Real Presences.* Chicago: The University of Chicago Press, 1989.

Stetzer, Ed. "The World as God Intends." *Sojourners* 42, no. 9 (September–October 2013): 30-33.

Stewart, Benjamin M. "Worship without Walls." *Christian Century* 129, no. 20 (3 October 2012): 22–25.

Trible, Phyllis. *God and the Rhetoric of Sexuality.* Philadelphia: Fortress Press, 1978.

UNICEF. "Global Estimates of Migrant Children and Adolescents." http://www.unicef.org/socialpolicy/files/ Handout_Children_Adolescents_and_Migration_Nov_2010.pdf.

U.S. Department of State. *Trafficking in Persons Report 2012*. Washington, DC: U.S. Department of State, 2012.

USA Today. "Border Patrol under Scrutiny for Deadly Force." 14 November 2012. http://www.usatoday.com/story/news/nation/2012/11/14/border-patrol-probe/1705737/.

Vanier, Jean. "Reflections on Christian Community." *Sojourners* 6 (1 December 1977): 10–12.

Vendel, Christine. "Homeless Man Is Found Dead behind Gas Station." *Kansas City Star*, June 13, 2013. http://www.kansascity.com/2013/06/13/4290639/body-found-behind-gas-station.html.

Weinstein, Adam. "A Privately Owned Nuclear Weapons Plan." *Mother Jones*, 29 August 2011. http://www.motherjones.com/politics/2011/08/nuclear-weapons-plant-kansas-city.

Wilner, Eleanor. "Emigration." In *Vital Signs: Contemporary American Poetry from the University Presses*, edited by Ronald Wallace. Madison: University of Wisconsin Press, 1989.

Wittner, Lawrence. "Kansas City Here It Comes: A New Nuclear Weapons Plant!" *Huffington Post*, 14 September 2011. http://www.huffingtonpost.com/lawrence-wittner/kansas-city-here-it-comes_b_949165.html.

Index

CPSIA information can be obtained at www.ICGtesting.com
Printed in the USA
BVOW02s2258130114

341378BV00006B/14/P